Learning Language Arts Through Literature

THE TAN
TEACHER BOOK
3rd Edition

By

Diane Welch

and

Susan Simpson

Common Sense Press
Simple to teach. Easy to learn.

The *Learning Language Arts Through Literature* series:

The Blue Book - 1st Grade Skills
The Red Book - 2nd Grade Skills
The Yellow Book - 3rd Grade Skills
The Orange Book - 4th Grade Skills
The Purple Book - 5th Grade Skills
The Tan Book - 6th Grade Skills
The Green Book - 7th Grade Skills
The Gray Book - 8th Grade Skills
The Gold Book - *World Literature* - High School Skills
The Gold Book - *American Literature* - High School Skills
The Gold Book - *British Literature* - High School Skills

Our thanks to Debbie Ward for her work on the 3rd edition of this book.

Common Sense Press of Melbourne LLC
3121 Skyway Circle, Suite A
Melbourne, FL 32935
www.commonsensepress.com

Cover Design: Kate White, 2017
Cover art: grandfailure/Bigstock.com

Printed in the United States of America.

Rev. 9/17
Printed 11/17

ISBN 978-1-929683-43-7

Introduction

As parents we watched and marveled at the way our little ones learned to talk. By listening and responding to English spoken well, they were able to communicate quite clearly. The process was so gradual that they were not even aware it was taking place.

It is the belief of the publisher and authors of the *Learning Language Arts Through Literature* series that written language can best be learned in the same manner. By reading fine literature and working with good models of writing, children will receive a quality education in language arts. If you desire to teach using this integrated approach to language, this curriculum is for you.

In her books, Dr. Ruth Beechick has confirmed that this method of teaching is an appropriate and successful way to introduce our young students to the joys of reading, writing, and thinking. Our own experiences using these lessons have encouraged us to share them with you. Their enjoyment and enthusiasm for reading and writing is an unmatched recommendation for this method of teaching.

The **integrated language approach** has the benefits of all teaching methods. By working with pieces of literature, you focus on grammar, vocabulary, writing, reading, spelling, penmanship, and thinking skills. Your student has the best advantage for learning skills in this effective and lasting manner.

Grammar is taught in conjunction with writing, not as an isolated subject. Your student's **vocabulary** will be enhanced by reading the literature selections which have been carefully chosen for this grade level. We realize that every student functions at a different reading level. For the more hesitant reader, we recommend you, the teacher, read aloud with your student. Grade appropriate **reading skills** are included. Helpful **Spelling Tips** are included to help your student develop spelling skills. **Penmanship** skills may be developed as your student writes dictation or any other writing assignment. **Thinking skills** are developed throughout the activities in this manual. Anytime a student is asked to respond to the literature with discussion, writing, drawing, or completing an activity, your student is developing higher order thinking skills.

How to Use this Book

This book provides materials, activities, and suggestions that will encourage and benefit you as you create a learning environment for your student. Since everyone is different, we suggest that you try our ideas and then freely experiment until you find patterns that work for you.

Let us first introduce *Learning Language Arts Through Literature.*

Dictation Lessons

Each lesson found in this section contains a passage of literature and learning activities. These activities are designed to help your student learn language skills in their context while developing writing and thinking skills. An emphasis is placed on grammar skills appropriate for sixth grade.

Dictation is a very powerful learning activity which trains a student to look for details, strive for accuracy, and learn to write. After the student has made his first copy, ask him to check it with the model (also found in the *Student Activity Book*) and make any necessary corrections. When dictation is used in the lesson, the passage will need to be read clearly, sentence by sentence. It is also important to use your voice to stress pauses and indicate punctuation marks.

Since this method may be new for you, here are a few suggestions:

1. Before dictation, read the entire passage to your student.
2. Begin the dictation by reading one sentence at a time. If necessary, repeat the sentence, reading it one phrase at a time.
3. Instruct your student to leave a blank space between each line so that corrections are easy to make.
4. After dictation, allow your student to use the passage to edit the work. At first have the student check his work one line or phrase at a time. Asking the student to correct the work all at once may prove to be frustrating.

After taking dictation, any words that were misspelled should be added to a *Spelling List* to be studied throughout the week along with any words your student has misspelled in writing done in other subjects. To this spelling list can be added words studied with the *Spelling Tips* in some lessons and the vocabulary words introduced in the *Book Studies.*

Optional Book Studies

In addition to the 36 weekly lessons, your student will have the opportunity to read four novels throughout the year. These books can be read as your schedule allows. You will find a suggested schedule in the Table of Contents. Each study provides a summary of the book for the teacher. As the book is read, the student will review vocabulary words and learn to interpret word meaning from understanding its context. You may also choose from a variety of suggested activities that will expand his understanding of what has been read. Discussion questions have been provided to aid in building reading comprehension. Do not make this a tedious task, but rather use the questions as a springboard for your student to tell you about the story.

Review Activities

Review Activities are found directly after each lesson. New skills taught in each lesson are included in the *Review Activities*. It is not necessary to do each activity. Choose the skills your student needs.

Assessments

Four assessments are provided throughout the program. Easy to use and administer, these tools help you assess the progress of your student. The goal of the assessments is to obtain information about your student's progress in order to determine how you, the teacher, can better assist your student.

An I C.A.N. Assessment has been created for each *Book Study*. At this grade level, you can expect your student to complete his work neatly with a good attitude. You may use these assessments to grade your student accordingly.

Appendix

In the back of this book you will find the *Appendix* which includes: *Enrichment Answers*, *Skills Index*, lists of *Prefixes* and *Suffixes*, and a *Bibliography*.

Enrichment Answers

In each lesson you will find optional enrichment activities which are located in the Student Activity Book (SAB). Answers to these actitivities are found in the back of this manual. While optional, these acitivities develop thinking and reasoning skills necessary for higher level learning.

Skills Index

You can easily locate lessons that will address specific skills using the Skills Index.

Bibliography

This page includes information to locate books your student needs to complete the Book Study lessons as well as the books used in the Dictation Lessons. You may purchase them or find them in the library.

☆ ☆ ☆ ☆

Materials to Use

You may use a *Student Activity Book* or a loose leaf notebook for your student's work.

Previous lessons are sometimes used again, so keep all the student's work until the entire program is completed.

Reference materials such as a dictionary, thesaurus, or Internet sources will be used. Availability of these materials in either the home or library is required.

For the optional *Book Studies* you will need the following books which can be found in the library or purchased:

Carry On, Mr. Bowditch by Jean Lee Latham
The Bronze Bow by Elizabeth George Spear
Big Red by Jim Kjelgaard
The Horse and His Boy by C. S. Lewis

Student Activity Books

Student Activity Books are available for your students. Daily exercises corresponding to each lesson are included for easy use. *Enrichment Activities* are also included.

The Tan Student Activity Book is not a duplicate of *The Tan Teacher Book,* therefore does not contain all the information found in the *Teacher Book. The Student Activity Book* is **not** intended for use without its companion *Teacher Book.*

Table of Contents

	Page
Lesson 1 *"The Taming of the Shrew"*	1
Lesson 2 *Carry On, Mr. Bowditch*	7
Lesson 3 *Bambi*	12
Lesson 4 "The Eagle"	20
Book Study A *Carry On, Mr. Bowditch*	29
Lesson 5 *Little House in the Big Woods*	44
Lesson 6 *The Story of a Bad Boy*	54
Lesson 7 *Prince Caspian*	63
Lesson 8 *Ivanhoe*	72
Lesson 9 *King of the Wind*	80
Assessment 1 (Lessons 1-9)	88
Lesson 10 *The Wheel on the School*	90
Lesson 11 *The Wheel on the School*	97
Lesson 12 How to Conduct Personal Research	105
Lesson 13 How to Conduct Personal Research	108
Book Study B *The Bronze Bow*	111
Lesson 14 "Jest 'Fore Christmas"	118
Lesson 15 *Swiss Family Robinson*	127
Lesson 16 Research Essay	135
Lesson 17 Research Essay	146
Lesson 18 Research Essay	151
Assessment 2 (Lessons 10-18)	156
Lesson 19 *Swallows and Amazons*	158

Lesson 20 *Kidnapped* 169
Lesson 21 *Robinson Crusoe* 176
Lesson 22 *Wind in the Willows* 182
Book Study C *Big Red* 189
Lesson 23 *Caddie Woodlawn* 196
Lesson 24 The Gettysburg Address 204
Lesson 25 The Gettysburg Address 208
Lesson 26 *Where the Red Fern Grows* 210
Lesson 27 *Where the Red Fern Grows* 214
Assessment 3 (Lessons 19-27) 228
Lesson 28 *The Railway Children* 228
Lesson 29 *The House at Pooh Corner* 235
Lesson 30 *Big Red* 240
Lesson 31 *Anne of Green Gables* 249
Book Study D *The Horse and His Boy* 255
Lesson 32 "The Crow and the Pitcher" 263
Lesson 33 *Little Women* 269
Lesson 34 *Little Women* 276
Lesson 35 *Invincible Louisa* 281
Lesson 36 "The Undecided Man" 287
Assessment 4 (Lessons 28-36) 293
Appendix
- Enrichment Answers 296
- Skills Index 301
- Prefixes 305
- Suffixes 307

Bibliography 309

Hence comes it that your kindred
  shuns your house,
As beaten hence by your strange lunacy.
O noble lord, bethink thee of thy birth,
Call home thy ancient
thoughts from banishment
And banish hence these abject lowly
  dreams.
Look how thy servants do attend on thee,
Each in his office ready at thy beck.
Wilt thou have music?

The Taming of the Shrew, Prologue, Scene 2

Teacher's Note: As your student completes each lesson, choose skills from the Review Activities that he needs. The Review Activities follow most lessons.

Day 1

a. Listen as your teacher reads the literature passage. This passage was taken from *The Taming of the Shrew*, a play written by William Shakespeare believed to have been written between 1590 and 1594. Notice that some of the words sound differently from the way we speak today. Circle these words. The reason we no longer use these words is because English is a **living language**. A living language is a language that is spoken and used in daily communication. The language changes as new words are added, words are changed, and certain words are no longer used. For example, fifty years ago words such as video, modem, and Internet were not a part of our language. They are words that have been added. Can you think of any new words that have been added to our language in the last fifty years?

Day 1
a. hence, bethink, thee, thy, wilt, thou

b. Copy the literature passage. Compare your copy to the passage and check for mistakes.

Make your own spelling list from any misspelled words in dictation or use the following list of suggested words:

kindred	lunacy	banishment	abject
strange	music		

c. A **prefix** is a letter or group of letters which comes before the main part, or root of the word. **Pre-** is a prefix which means *before*. Knowing the meaning of a prefix will help you understand the meaning of a word, as in *preview* which means *to view* or *show before.*

Day 1
d. bethink; to recall or remember

d. A prefix in the literature passage is **be-.** Underline the word in the literature passage that has this prefix. The prefix **be-** as used in this word means *to make* or *cause to seem*. Knowing the meaning of this prefix, how would you define the word *belittle*?

e. Look at the Commonly Used Prefixes list in the *Appendix*. Find the prefix chart in the *Student Activity Book* and follow the instructions. If you are not using the *Student Activity Book* set up a sheet of notebook papers like this example:

Prefix	Meaning	Word Examples
pre-	before	preview, precede

Write the prefixes **pre-** and **be-** in the spaces provided under the prefix heading. Add a definition and think of two word examples for each prefix. Refer to your dictionary if you need help. Keep this list available for easy reference as you will add to this list throughout the program.

Day 2

a. The type of English used during the period Shakespeare wrote is called Middle English. Middle English was in use from the time of the Norman Conquest of 1066 to the introduction of printing in England in 1476. Many words of French origin became part of the English language at this time. Old English is the name given to the earliest English which was mostly Germanic in content. Modern English is the name given to the language from the time period extending from 1476 to present day.

b. The origin of a word is referred to as its **etymology**. Most dictionaries give the etymology of a word, as in the sample below:

kindred (kin/drid) n. [M.E.]
a body of persons related to another or a family, tribe, or race.

Notice the abbreviations that appear in the brackets, [M.E.]. The abbreviation stands for Middle English and tells us the origin of this word into the English language. Use your dictionary to look up the suggested spelling words:

lunacy banishment abject

See if you can find the etymology for each word. (The meanings of the abbreviations used are usually found in the front section of the dictionary.)

c. Some of the words in the literature passage are expressed differently today. For example the word *thee* would be *you*. Circle all the words that are no longer used and translate into Modern English.

d. Review your spelling words.

Day 3

a. Write the list of suggested spelling words from the literature passage. Using a thesaurus, write a synonym for each word. **Synonyms** are words which have the same or similar meaning. Be sure the word you choose can be substituted for the original word in the passage without changing the meaning.

b. Sometimes the best way to picture the order in which events happened is by creating a timeline. Using the information from the following page about British literature, make a timeline. The timeline should have earliest work listed starting at the far left-hand side of the timeline with dates and names continuing in correct sequence up to the most current work, which would appear at the far right-hand side. Only the information in bold print should be written on the timeline, with the dates at the top of the line.

Teacher's Note: Not all dictionaries have etymologies.

Day 2

b. lunacy (loo-nuh-see) n. [from L, luna, the moon] a type of insanity supposed to be influence by the moon; madness in general

banishment (ban-ish-muhnt) n. [M.E.] the act of a government compelling a citizen to leave the country; the act of driving away

abject (ab-jekt) adj. [L. abjectus] sunk to a low condition; worthless, mean

c. hence - therefore
bethink - think
thee - you
thy - your
wilt - will
thou - you

Day 3

a. kindred
ex: relatives, family
lunacy
ex: madness, insanity
banishment
ex: exile, explusion

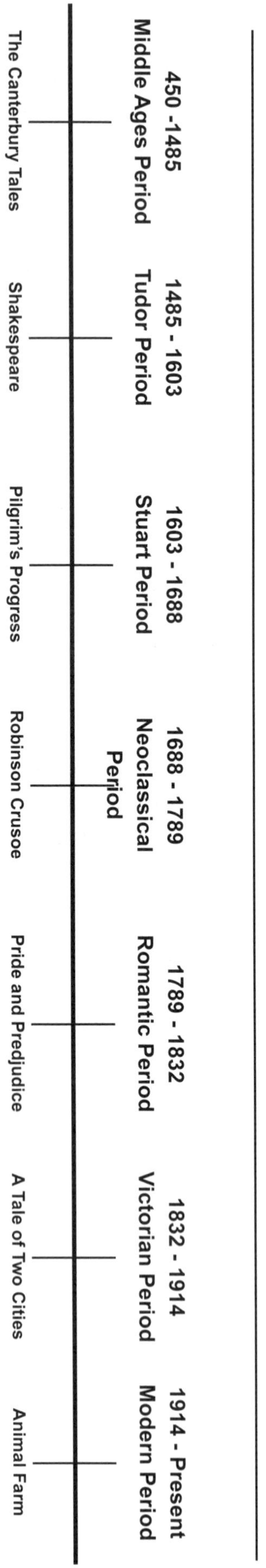

Ex:

450-1485
Middle Ages Period

The Canterbury Tales

The Middle Ages Period, **450-1485** **The Canterbury Tales**

The Tudor Period, **1485-1603** **Shakespeare**

The Stuart Period, **1603-1688** **Pilgrim's Progress**

The Neoclassical Period, **1688-1789** **Robinson Crusoe**

The Romantic Period, **1789-1832** **Pride and Prejudice**

The Victorian Period, **1832-1914** **A Tale of Two Cities**

The Modern Period, **1914-Present** **Animal Farm**

c. Optional: Enrichment (SAB)

Day 4

a. Read the passage again. Rewrite it as we might say it today. Use some of the synonyms you listed in **3a**.

b. Take a pretest of your spelling words. Review any words you found difficult to spell.

c. Optional: Enrichment (SAB)

Day 5

a. Take the following passage from *The Taming of the Shrew* from dictation:

Why, how now, dame! whence grows this insolence?
Bianca, stand aside. Poor girl! she weeps.
Go ply thy needle; meddle not with her.
For shame, thou hilding of a devilish spirit,
Why dost thou wrong her that did ne'er wrong thee?
When did she cross thee with a bitter word?
Act 2, Scene 1

b. Rewrite the above passage in Modern English.

c. Take a written or oral spelling test.

d. Choose skills from the *Review Activities*.

Day 4

a. This is why your relatives don't come to your house. They are scared away because of your weird craziness. O Great One, think about your heritage. Remember the way things used to be and forget your evil desires. See how your servants wait on you, eager to do what you ask? Do you want to hear some music? Listen to what's playing.

Day 5

b. What is going on here? Girl, you are way out of line! Bianca, go do some sewing and stay away from your sister. Katherine, you little demon, you should be ashamed of yourself! Why would you want to hurt someone who has never hurt you? When has she ever been mean to you?

Review Activities

Choose skills your student needs to review.

1. *Prefixes*
   Add the prefix that fits the definition in parentheses.

   a. The _____liminary (*before*) practice test will help you review for the final test.
   b. The whole school _____moaned (*to make* or *cause to seem*) the loss of the state tournament.

1.
a. pre
b. be

2. *Etymology*
   Use your dictionary and find the etymology of the following words.

   a. dominant
   b. health

2.
a. Latin
b. Middle English and Old English

3. *Synonyms*
   Use a thesaurus to find two synonyms for each of the following words.

   a. run
   b. talk
   c. walk
   d. think

3.
Possible answers:
a. sprint, scurry, race
b. discuss, confer, chat
c. stroll, pace, hike
d. believe, consider, imagine

4. *Timeline*
   Write down important events that have occurred in your life and the year these events occurred. List the events in chronological order on a timeline. Remember to keep each entry as concise as possible.

Nat shrugged and turned back to his bookkeeping. Even while he was still thinking of Sammy, his glance flicked down a column of figures and his fingers jotted the answer. He realized his mind was wandering. He jerked his thoughts back in line, and added the figures again. He'd been right the first time. For almost nine years now, he'd been right about figures. What would he do with the next nine years? Go on adding columns and columns of figures?

Carry On, Mr. Bowditch, by Jean Lee Latham

Day 1

a. Write the literature passage from dictation. Proofread and correct any errors.

b. Make a spelling list from any misspelled words in the dictation or use the following list of suggested spelling words:

bookkeeping column thoughts realized

c. Find the two words in the suggested spelling list that have the /**k**/ sound. Note that one spells the /**k**/ sound with the letter **k** and the other with the letter **c**.

Spelling Tip

To spell a word with a */k/* sound, remember that *k* usually comes before *e* or *i*; *c* usually comes before *a*, *o*, or *u*.

Teacher's Note: As your student completes each lesson, choose skills from the Review Activities that he needs. The Review Activities follow most lessons.

Teacher's Note: Personalize your student's spelling lists by adding misspelled words from writing done in this class or in other areas. Also, add words that reinforce the Spelling Tips.

Day 1
d. 1) caught
2) kitten
3) kindle
4) correspond
5) kettle
6) cubic
7) keyboard
8) carmel
9) commission
10) kitchen

Day 2
c. Common:
1) bookkeeping
2) glance
3) column (used 3 times)
4) figures (used 3 times)
5) fingers
6) answer
7) mind
8) thoughts
9) time
10) years

Proper:
1) Nat
2) Sammy

d. Using this *Spelling Tip*, add the correct letter to the following words.

Ex: k̲ite; c̲ake

1) ______aught	6) ______ubic
2) ______itten	7) ______eyboard
3) ______indle	8) ______amel
4) ______orrespond	9) ______ommission
5) ______ettle	10) ______itchen

Day 2

a. In the English language we identify words by placing them in one of eight different groups. These eight groups are called the **parts of speech.** The eight different parts of speech are nouns, pronouns, verbs, adjectives, adverbs, prepositions, conjunctions, and interjections. It is important to know the part each of these groups plays in a sentence and to know how to identify each of them.

b. A **noun** is a word that names a person, place, thing, or idea. If the word names a *general* person, place, thing, or idea then it is a **common noun** and is not capitalized. If a noun names a *specific* person, place, or thing, then it is a **proper noun** and the word begins with a capital letter.

Ex: Proper nouns: Jake, Mt. Rushmore, Florida, etc.
Common nouns: father, mountain, state, hope, etc.

c. Look over the literature passage and circle all the nouns you find. Above each noun write a **C** if it is a common noun and a **P** if it is a proper noun.

d. Review your spelling words.

Day 3

a. **Verbs** are words that show action or a state of being. They can also link a word to the subject or help another verb.

Ex: Jim *ran* all the way to the field. (action verb)
We *are* here with the Brown family. (state of being verb)
She *was thinking* about the answer. (helping verb)
Jim *looks* handsome in his suit. (linking verb)

b. Often helping verbs and the main verb make up a **verb phrase**. Sometimes other words divide a verb phrase.

Ex: Many different songs *were used* in the event. (undivided verb phrase)

The children *were* often *divided* into groups. *Could* he *have* accomplished his goals with more determination? (divided verb phrases)

Look at the list of common helping verbs.

Common Helping Verbs				
have	do	shall	would	must
has	does	will	may	can
had	did	should	might	could

All forms of the verb *be* may also be used as helping verbs.

Being Verbs			
is	are	was	were
am	been	being	

c. Underline the verbs in the literature passage. Be sure to underline both parts of a verb phrase.

d. Examine the following sentences. Identify and underline the verb phrases and circle the helping verb.

Ex: The otter (could) not slide down the riverbank.

1) Would you run in the race on Saturday?
2) The computer has replaced the typewriter in the business office.
3) She has almost perfected that piece of music on the piano.
4) Goats were often used to graze areas of rough terrain.
5) Could you have avoided the accident?

Day 3

c. shrugged, turned, was thinking, flicked, jotted, realized, was wandering, jerked, added, had been, had been, would do, go, adding

d. 1) (would) run
2) (has) replaced
3) (has) perfected
4) (were) used
5) (could have) avoided

Day 3

e. He was not really bragging; he had a realistic view of his skills.

e. Nat knew what he could do well. Was he bragging? What are some things you can do well? Ask your teacher or friends what they think you do well. Are they the same things?

f. Review your spelling words.

Day 4

a. A **biography** is a true story of a person's life. *Carry On, Mr. Bowditch* is a biography about Nathaniel Bowditch. Find out more about him. Look online or research his name at the library.

b. A **summary** is a brief description covering the main points of a certain topic. Write a short summary, about one page, of Nathaniel Bowditch's life. Make sure you include when he was born, when he died, and what he did in his life that is important to history.

c. Take an oral or written spelling pretest. Review any words you found difficult to spell.

d. Optional: Enrichment. (SAB)

Day 5

a. Write the literature passage from dictation. Compare your copy to the model and correct any mistakes you may have made.

b. Nat wonders what he will be doing in the future. What do you think you will be doing next year? Write a few paragraphs explaining what you feel you might be doing and give reasons for your predictions.

c. Take an oral or written spelling test.

d. Choose skills from the *Review Activities*.

Review Activities

Choose skills your student needs to review.

1. *Parts of Speech*
   List the eight parts of speech. Give a definition for a noun and a verb.

2. *Nouns and Verbs*
   Circle the nouns and underline the verbs in the following sentences. Write a **C** above the common nouns and a **P** above the proper nouns. Be sure to underline all parts of a verb phrase.

   a. The monkeys swing from branch to branch.
   b. Ships will often sail through the Straits of Magellan.
   c. Children should learn to enjoy good literature.
   d. Mary teaches Spanish to the children in her neighborhood.
   e. The car swerved on the slippery road.

3. *Literary Terms*
   Define a biography.

4. *Prefixes*
   Add the correct prefix to the following words. Use the definition in the parentheses and your list of prefixes to help you choose the correct prefix.

   a. In science I am going to study _____logy. (living)
   b. The movie was so long we had an _______mission. (between)
   c. We went to a _______-serve (by ones self) ice cream shop.
   d. The restaurant was _______ground. (beneath)

5. *Synonyms*
   Find two synonyms for each of the following words.

   a. understand
   b. love
   c. watch
   d. make

1.
noun, pronoun, verb, adjective, adverb, conjunction, interjection, preposition.
A noun names a person, place, thing, or idea. A verb shows action or state of being.

2.
a. The (monkeys)[C] swing from (branch)[C] to (branch)[C].
b. (Ships)[C] will often sail through the (Straits of Magellan)[P].
c. (Children)[C] should learn to enjoy good (literature)[C].
d. (Mary)[P] teaches (Spanish)[P] to the (children)[C] in her (neighborhood)[C].
e. The (car)[C] swerved on the slippery (road)[C].

3.
A true story about a person's life.

4.
a. bio
b. inter
c. self
d. under

5.
a. comprehend, appreciate, recognize
b. like, adore, worship
c. observe, inspect, examine
d. create, generate, build

Bambi walked under the great oak on the meadow. It sparkled with dew. It smelled of grass and flowers and moist earth, and whispered of a thousand living things. Friend Hare was there and seemed to be thinking over something important. A haughty pheasant strutted slowly by, nibbling at the grass seeds and peering cautiously in all directions. The dark, metallic blue of his neck gleamed in the sun.

Bambi by Felix Salten.
Used by permission, Simon and Schuster, Inc.

Day 1

a. Just as an artist uses color to paint a picture, an author uses words to "paint" a word picture. Listen to the word picture the author "paints" as your teacher reads the literature passage aloud.

b. Write the literature passage from dictation. Proofread your copy for any mistakes. Make a spelling list from any misspelled words or use the following suggested list:

sparkled	whispered	gleamed
nibbling	peering	strutted

c. The prefix **im-** has two meanings. It can mean *not*, as in *impatient* (not patient). The prefix **im-** can also mean *into*, as in *implant*. Find the word in the literature passage with this prefix and underline it. Add this prefix to your list of prefixes you started in Lesson 1. List the prefix, its meaning, and two examples of words that contain the prefix.

Day 1
c. important

im-; into; Possible examples: important, imprison

d. A **suffix** is a letter or group of letters which comes at the end of the **base** or **root** of the word. While prefixes give you an understanding of the meaning of a word, suffixes can often help in determining the part of speech of a word, whether it is a verb, adjective, etc. Notice that all the words from your suggested spelling list end in **-ing** or **-ed**. These endings do not have specific meanings, but a word ending with these suffixes is usually a verb, a word that expresses action in the sentence. All the words in your spelling list are used as verbs in the literature passage.

e. Locate the *Commonly Used Suffixes* at the back of this book. Referring to this list, write the suffix **-ed** in the space provided under the suffix heading. Write "no meaning" under *Meaning*, write "usually a verb" under *Part of Speech*, and write example words from the spelling list under *Word Examples*. Do the same for **-ing**. If you are not using a *Student Activity Book*, set up a blank sheet of notebook paper as follows:

Suffix	Meaning	Part of Speech	Word Examples
-ed		usually a verb	sparkled, gleamed

You will be using this list throughout the program.

Day 2

a. Writers often use figurative language to express thoughts. Sometimes it helps to produce a picture in your mind by using a comparison. When a comparison of two unrelated things is made using the words *as* or *like*, it is called a **simile**.

Ex: smooth *as* silk — *like* a raging bull
warm *as* toast — *like* the quiet after a storm
sweet *as* honey — *like* a newborn babe

b. Finish the following expressions with words that create similes.

1) as quiet as ____________________
2) as light as ____________________
3) as hungry as a ____________________
4) sticky like ____________________
5) sparkled like ____________________

c. Create two of your own similes. Remember to use the words *as* or *like* when you make your comparison.

Day 1
e. ed - usually a verb
- sparkled, whispered, gleamed, strutted

ing - usually a verb - nibbling, peering

Day 2
b. Possible answers:
1) as quiet as a mouse
2) as light as a feather
3) as hungry as a bear
4) sticky like honey
5) sparkled like diamonds

d. Review your spelling words.

e. Optional: Enrichment (SAB)

Day 3

a. Look at your spelling list from **1b**. One way to learn how to spell a word correctly is to divide the word into syllables. A **syllable** is a division of a word that contains a vowel sound. You can usually hear each syllable as you say the word slowly. It will help to clap each time your hear a syllable division in a word. The number of times you clap is the number of syllables the word contains.

For example, the word *thinking* is divided into two syllables, *think* and *-ing* because it has two vowel sounds. The word *walked* is only one syllable because it only contains one vowel sound; the suffix **-ed** has a **/t/** sound. Write the words from your spelling list, dividing the words into syllables. If you are unsure how a word should be divided, check your dictionary.

Ex: thou - sand

b. **Personification** is a form of figurative language which gives human characteristics to an idea, object, or animal. Look at the third sentence of the literature passage. How did the meadow behave like a person?

c. Read the following sentence:

I heard the wind muttering through the trees.

The wind does not literally mutter, but by giving the wind human qualities, it becomes vivid and alive. What else might the wind do like a person?

d. Create a sentence using personification for each of the following phrases. Be sure to use your imagination!

1) peeked through the clouds
2) stubbornly refused to move
3) danced among the flowers
4) swallowed him up

Day 3

a. spar-kled
whis-pered
gleamed
nib-bling
peer-ing
strut-ted

b. (The meadow) whispered

c. The wind might howl, laugh, bite, etc.

d. Possible Answers:
1) The (sun/plane) peeked through the clouds.
2) The (donkey/stump) stubbornly refused to move.
3) The (butterfly/bee) danced among the flowers.
4) The (hole, ocean) swallowed him up.

e. Review your spelling words.

Day 4

a. A good author desires to keep the attention of the reader, their audience. Using colorful words will capture a mood or setting, allowing the reader to feel he is experiencing the scene. Often this is done through the use of adjectives. **Adjectives** are words that describe nouns, the words which name persons, places, things, or ideas. Adjectives answer the following questions: Which one? What kind? How many? How much? Whose?

b. Look at the first sentence of the literature passage. In this sentence the adjective *great* describes the noun *oak*. Locate the other adjectives used in the literature passage and circle them. Now read the passage without these words. Did you notice how it is more difficult for you to picture the scene without these words?

c. Find a picture in a book or magazine of mountains, trees, clouds, animals, or anything you might want to describe using figurative language. Write a few sentences to describe the picture using similes and/or personification. Be sure to use adjectives to help you with your description. When you are finished, read your sentences aloud. Do they "paint" a good word picture of the scene you are describing?

d. Take an oral or written spelling pretest. Remember, sounding out the syllables as you write them will help you spell them correctly.

e. Optional: Enrichment (SAB)

Day 5

a. Write the literature passage from dictation.

b. Choose a poem that offers a good descriptive image and read it to your teacher. After you have finished reading the poem, point out to the teacher any examples where the author used a simile or personification.

Day 4

b. great, moist, thousand, living, haughty, all, dark, metallic

Day 5

c. Possible answer: Bambi walked cautiously under the great oak tree at the edge of the meadow. Shadows danced across the grasses outlining strange shapes, and the wind whispered of a thousand living things. Suddenly Friend Hare and a haughty pheasant appeared out of the tall, green grasses, startling Bambi.

c. How does the literature passage make you feel? Does it sound like a place you would like to be? Rewrite the literature passage and change the mood by describing the scene differently.

d. Take an oral or written spelling test.

e. Choose from the *Review Activities*.

Review Activities

Choose skills your student needs to review.

1. *Syllables*
   Divide the following words into syllables.

   a. important
   b. pheasant
   c. direction
   d. meadow
   e. metallic

1.
a. im-por-tant
b. pheas-ant
c. di-rec-tion
d. mead-ow
e. me-tal-lic

2. *Prefixes*
   Add the correct prefix to the following words. Use the definition in the parentheses and your list of prefixes to help you choose the correct prefix.

   a. The company wants to _____port (*into*) raw material for making the product.
   b. It would be ____thinkable (*not*) to be absent from the wedding.
   c. You are listening to the _____lude (*before*) of the musical symphony.

2.
a. import
b. unthinkable
c. prelude

3. *Suffixes*
   Find the verbs in the following paragraph and circle them. Look for the suffixes **-ed** and **-ing** to help you identify the verbs. If there is a verb phrase, be sure to circle the full phrase.

   Mary loved to visit her cousins at the farm. The car ride seemed to take forever, but they finally arrived. "All the children are swimming in the lake," her aunt announced. "The horses are also waiting in the barn for you to see."

3.
loved
seemed
arrived
are swimming
announced
are waiting

4. *Similes*
   Write two similes. Be sure to use the words *like* or *as*.

4.
Examples:
The mosquitoes attacked us like little torpedoes.
The wind was as sharp as a knife.

5.
Example:
The waves teased the shore.

6.
- **a. The <u>quiet</u>, <u>smooth</u> (water) sparkled with <u>cheerful</u> (sunlight).**
- **b. <u>Soft</u> <u>brown</u> (eyes) peeked out from under the <u>long</u>, <u>silky</u> (hair).**
- **c. The <u>sleek</u>, <u>shiny</u> (car) sped down the <u>busy</u> (street).**
- **d. A <u>gentle</u> (breeze) swept through the <u>tall</u> (trees).**
- **e. The <u>bright</u> <u>red</u> (apple) crunched as the <u>little</u> (girl) bit into it.**

5. *Personification*
   Write a sentence using personification.

6. *Adjectives*
   Underline the adjectives in the following sentences and circle the noun each adjective describes.

   a. The quiet, smooth water sparkled with cheerful sunlight.
   b. Soft brown eyes peeked out from under the long, silky hair.
   c. The sleek, shiny car sped down the busy street.
   d. A gentle breeze swept through the tall trees.
   e. The bright red apple crunched as the little girl bit into it.

Notes

The Eagle

He clasps the crag with crooked hands;
Close to the sun in lonely lands,
Ringed with the azure world, he stands.

The wrinkled sea beneath him crawls;
He watches from his mountain walls,
And like a thunderbolt he falls.

Alfred , Lord Tennyson

Day 1

a. Poems are divided into groups of lines called **stanzas.** This poem is written in two three-line stanzas called **triplets.** Close your eyes and imagine the eagle as your teacher reads the poem aloud. What kind of picture did you get as you listened? Now you read it aloud.

Day 1
b. of a sky blue color

b. Write the poem from dictation. Look at the last line of the first stanza. What do you think *azure* means? Often if you do not know the meaning of a word, you can guess at its meaning by using context clues. **Context clues** are the other words that appear in the line or sentence that can help you to figure out the meaning of a difficult word. Read the first stanza of the poem again. Using context clues, decide what you think the meaning of *azure* might be. Look up the word in the dictionary to check its meaning.

c. beneath
be-; on, away;
Possible examples:
beneath, bestow

c. In Lesson 1 we learned that the prefix **be-** sometimes means *to make or cause to seem.* Look at the first line of the second stanza. Locate the word with the prefix **be-**. Here the prefix **be-** means *on* or *away.* Find your prefix list and add this meaning and example words.

d. Make a spelling list from any words you misspelled in the dictation or use the following suggested spelling list:

clasps	crawls	crooked
wrinkled	ringed	watches

Look at the word *wrinkled.* The root of this word is *wrinkle.* Notice that the silent **e** was dropped before the suffix **-ed** was added.

Spelling Tip
Words that end in a silent e usually drop the silent e before adding a suffix beginning with a vowel.

e. Add the suffixes **-ed** and **-ing** to the following words. If the word ends in a silent **e**, be sure to drop the **e** before adding the suffix beginning with a vowel. The first one is done for you.

		-ed	**-ing**
Ex:	practice	practiced	practicing
1)	guide		
2)	escape		
3)	dictate		
4)	create		
5)	behave		
6)	believe		

Day 2

a. In line 3 of the second stanza, what two things are said to be alike? These really aren't alike in most ways, but the poet shows us one way they are similar. The speed of the eagle falling is like the thunderbolt striking the earth. As we discussed in Lesson 3, when the words *like* or *as* are used to make a comparison, the writer is using a powerful writer's technique called *simile.*

b. The author also makes use of personification in this poem. Read the poem again, circling any words that give human qualities to animals and objects. In what ways are the eagle, lands, and sea given human qualities?

c. As well as the figurative language techniques of simile and personification, the author also makes use of adjectives to help create a picture in the reader's mind. Underline any adjectives you can identify in the poem.

Day 1

e. 1) guide, guided, guiding
2) escape, escaped, escaping
3) dictate, dictated, dictating
4) create, created, creating
5) bohave, behaved, behaving
6) believe, believed, believing

Day 2

a. the eagle falling and a thunderbolt

b. crooked hands - the eagle's talons are compared to hands

lonely lands - the lands are given the quality loneliness

wrinkled sea crawls - the sea's movement is compared to crawling

c. crooked, lonely, azure, wrinkled, mountain

Day 3
a. rest, best

d. Choose an animal and write a few sentences to describe it. Be sure to use adjectives and the technique of simile or personification.

e. Review your spelling words.

Day 3

a. In "The Eagle" the last word of each line rhymes with the other words in the stanza. Words that rhyme have similar sounds in the last syllable. For example, the words *hands, lands,* and *stands* from the first stanza all rhyme because they all end with the same *ands* sound. The rhyming of words at the end of the line is called **end rhyme.** Complete the lines of the following stanza using end rhyme.

Nestled in her elaborate nest
The swallow laid her head to ________________.
She knows she did her very ________________.

b. The best way to write a poem with end rhyme is to write the first line of the poem about your subject and then write a list of words that rhyme with the end word that could be used in your poem. Make sure you do not choose a difficult word for your end word that would be hard to rhyme with. For example, if the first line of a poem is "He stalks the skink with spiteful eyes," then a list of words should be made that rhyme with eyes. It could include: spies, lies, cries.

c. Using "The Eagle" as a model, try writing a poem about the animal you chose in **2d**. Write two **triplets** (three-line stanzas) ending with rhyming words. Read "The Cat" as an example.

The Cat

He stalks the skink with spiteful eyes,
Close to the grass and dirt he lies,
And like a wraith, he sneaks and spies.

At night he curls by fire bright,
And in his eyes there gleams a light
Of pride's self-satisfied delight.

d. Practice writing your suggested spelling words, dividing them into syllables.

e. Optional: Enrichment (SAB)

Day 4

a. **Prose** is ordinary writing; the type of writing you would use in a report or story. If you were to rewrite the first stanza of "The Cat" from **3c** in prose form, it could read as follows:

The cat, with a spiteful look in his eyes, stalks the skink through the grass and dirt. Like a wraith he sneaks around and spies on everything.

b. Notice the meaning of the poem has not changed by rewriting it, just the form. Read over the poem, "The Eagle." Write this poem in prose form. After you have completed rewriting the poem, read both the original version and the prose version. Which do you prefer?

c. This poem is talking about an eagle, but notice that aside from the title of the poem, the noun *eagle* is never used. Instead pronouns have been used to identify the subject. **Pronouns** are words that take the place of nouns.

PERSONAL PRONOUNS

Singular

Subjective	Possessive	Objective
I	my, mine	me
you	your, yours	you
he, she, it	his, her, hers, its	it, him, her

Plural

Subjective	Possessive	Objective
we	our, ours	us
you	your, yours	you
they	their, theirs	them

Day 3

d. clasps, crawls, crook-ed, wrin-kled, ringed, watch-es

Day 4

b. ex: He holds onto the steep, rugged rock with his claws; beneath is the blazing sun in a barren land amidst the blue sky. The waves below beckon him as he watches from the cliff, and with the speed of lightning he falls.

Day 4

e. He, he, him, He, his, he

Without pronouns the poem sounds repetitive and is tiresome to read. It would be difficult to write without using pronouns.

d. The noun which the pronoun takes the place of is called the **antecedent**. A pronoun must agree with the antecedent in number and gender.

Ex: *Mary, Lois, and Ginger* went to the mall where *they* shopped for new shoes. (Number - Since the antecedent is plural, the pronoun must be plural.)

John will need to take the tent, and *he* will also need *his* fishing pole. (Gender - Since the antecedent is masculine, the pronouns also need to be masculine.)

e. In the poem, "The Eagle," the antecedent is the *eagle*. Underline the pronouns that appear in the poem. (The poet chose to give the eagle a masculine pronoun.) Try reading the poem using "the eagle" wherever a pronoun appears. How does this change the effect of the poem? Do you think it would be difficult to write without pronouns? Why or why not?

f. Take an oral or written spelling pretest. Review any words you found difficult to spell.

Day 5

a. Write the poem from dictation once more.

b. A poem can create a world and bring an idea to life. Other forms of art can produce the same effect in a different way. Create a picture or clay sculpture to illustrate the poem, "The Eagle."

c. Take time to enjoy reading selections of poetry aloud. Look for examples of similes and personification in the poems you read. Have your teacher (or another student) read several poems aloud without reading the titles. Try to give them new titles and compare them to the original ones.

Suggested sources for selections:

A Child's Garden of Verses by Robert Louis Stevenson
When We Were Young, Now We Are Six by A. A. Milne
Oxford Book of Poetry for Children by Edward Blishen
Favorite Poems Old and New by Helen Ferris

d. Take an oral or written spelling test.

e. Choose skills from the *Review Activities*.

Review Activities

Choose skills your student needs to review.

1. *Definitions*
   Refer to your lesson for the information to write the correct answer in the blank provided in the following sentences.

   a. Poetry written in ordinary language that does not rhyme is called ____________.
   b. Words that take the place of nouns are called __________.
   c. The noun the pronoun takes the place of is called the ____________.
   d. Poems are divided into groups of lines called _________.
   e. Poems written in groupings of three lines are called ____________.
   f. Words that appear in a sentence that help you figure out the meaning of a word you do not know are called _____ __________________.
   g. The rhyming of words at the end of a line is called ____________.

2. *Poetry*
   Write a poem in triplet form with end rhyme. Write the same poem in a prose form.

3. *Context Clues*
   Determine from the context clues the meaning of the underlined word in the following sentences.

   a. In order to avoid the traffic on the main highway, we decided to take a <u>byroad</u>.
   b. He was so impressed with his successful boss that he <u>emulated</u> his qualities.
   c. We are not sure, but he is <u>reputed</u> to be the leader of the neighborhood gang.

1.
a. prose
b. pronouns
c. antecedent
d. stanzas
e. triplets
f. context clues
g. end rhyme

2.
Examples:
The children play along the shore
Imagination was their door
To land where they had never been before.

The children play on the shoreline pretending to go to native lands they had not visited before.

3.
a. a road that is not the main road
b. to copy
c. to regard or consider

4. *Prefixes*
Add the prefix **be-** to the following root words. Determine the definition of each word you create.

a. _____neath
b. _____side
c. _____siege

5. *Suffixes*
Add the suffixes **-ed** and **-ing** to the following words.

Ex: love loved loving
a. skate ____________ ____________
b. smile ____________ ____________
c. chase ____________ ____________

6. *Figurative Language*
Read the sentences below. If the sentence contains an example of personification, write **P** in the space provided. If the sentence contains an example of a simile, write **S** in the space provided.

a. ______The birds chatted back and forth throughout the forest.
b. ______The eagle soared like a plane through the sky.
c. ______The picture was as refreshing as a garden on a spring day.
d. ______The brook laughed for joy as it cascaded over the rocks.
e. ______He ran as swiftly as a cheetah when he neared the finish of the race.

7. *Pronouns and Antecedents*
Underline the pronouns and draw a line to its antecedent in the following sentences.

Ex: The fledglings were ready to leave their nest.

a. Jim was very proud of his new car.
b. Kelly went to the swimming pool this morning, and she was going to her friend's house this afternoon.
c. The bicycle damaged its wheel on the rough terrain.
d. The Wilsons are having their house painted.

4.
a. beneath - underneath
b. beside - at the side
c. besiege - to close in on

5.
a. skated, skating
b. smiled, smiling
c. chased, chasing

6.
a. P
b. S
c. S
d. P
e. S

7.
a. Jim was very proud of his new car.

b. Kelly went to the swimming pool this morning, and she was going to her friend's house this afternoon.

c. The bicycle damaged its wheel on the rough terrain.

d. The Wilsons are having their house painted.

Notes

BOOK STUDY A

Carry On, Mr. Bowditch

Carry On, Mr. Bowditch
by Jean Latham
Published by Houghton Mifflin

Readability level:
5th grade

Teacher's note:
This summary is intended for the teacher's use.

Introducing
Carry On, Mr. Bowditch

Have you ever been tempted to give up because a task was difficult or seemed just impossible to do? Instead of getting frustrated, think about the life of Nathaniel Bowditch, a famous nineteenth century mathematician and navigator. When he met an obstacle in his life, he learned to "sail by an ash breeze," a shipping term that referred to using the oars for power when there was no wind to move the ship. For Nathaniel Bowditch this meant not allowing obstacles to keep him from pursuing his dreams.

Summary

Nathaniel Bowditch grew up in the shipping town of Salem, Massachusetts, in the late 1700s. Even at a young age he had an extraordinary understanding of mathematics and dreamed of one day attending Harvard College. Good fortune, however, seemed to elude the Bowditch family. After the deaths of his mother and grandmother, his father had trouble providing for the family and rather than being able to continue his education, Nathaniel was indentured at the age of twelve as bookkeeper at a ship chandlery for nine years.

Instead of giving up on his dream of getting an education, Nathaniel turned every situation into a learning opportunity, writing down everything he learned in notebooks. He first inquired and learned all he could about shipping, the items sold in the chandlery, how sails were made, and how chaulking on a ship was done. Soon his curiosity extended to surveying, navigation, algebra, astronomy, Latin, and French.

Eventually his time of indenture was finished, and he was free to pursue his dreams. After a brief time working as a surveyor, Nathaniel decided to go to sea, working as a ship's clerk and second mate. The ship was traveling to the Isle of Bourbon, also known as Reunion, off the east coast of Africa. Aboard ship he put his navigational knowledge to practical use and was soon teaching these skills to the other seamen. Often when he found an explanation that helped a man understand a skill, he would write it down in one of his notebooks so he would remember it. His mathematical calculations were so accurate that he found mistakes in the tables of Moore's *Practical Navigator*, considered to be the most accurate book of navigation available at that time.

Nathaniel's second voyage took him to Lisbon, Portugal, and on to Manila Harbor. Again, he taught navigation skills to the seamen, and to one man in particular, Lem Harvey, who became a lifelong friend. Nathaniel found that when the men realized they could learn, they had more pride in themselves and were a more cooperative crew.

Upon his return, Nathaniel married Elizabeth Boardman, a longtime friend. He was not married long before he took a voyage to Cadiz, Spain, and into the Mediterranean, to Alicante. However, before he returned, word came that his wife had died of consumption. Nathaniel found that keeping busy helped him deal with his grief, and he signed on for the position of supercargo with a ship headed for Batavia (now known as Djakarta, Indonesia) to buy coffee. When the ship arrived at Batavia, they found no coffee available to buy and traveled to Manila Harbor in the middle of monsoon season, an amazing feat of navigation. However, upon Nathaniel's return to Salem, he found that Lem Harvey's ship had sunk due to an error in Moore's navigation tables. Lem was believed drowned, however, he was later found to be alive. Then word came to him that his brothers, William and Hab, had died when their ships sunk, also due to errors in the navigation tables.

Nathaniel decided an accurate book on navigation and sailing needed to be written, and he was determined to write it. The book would contain three things: (1) correct navigation tables, (2) every sea term and maneuver would be explained in words that able seaman could understand, (3) mathematical tables that would allow any seaman to solve problems in navigation. He worked on his book day and night. The only interruptions he would tolerate were visits from Polly, Elizabeth's cousin, whom he eventually married. Finally, his book, *New American Practical Navigator*, was finished. The book was immediately accepted in the United States and even in England.

Finally, Nathaniel Bowditch felt that in order for his book to be accepted by common seamen everywhere, he must command his own ship on a voyage. He sailed to Sumatra, Indonesia, loaded a cargo of pepper, and returned home safely.

Nathaniel's philosophy of "sailing by an ash breeze" helped him to accomplish writing an accurate book of navigation to make sailing safer for all seamen. To honor his achievements, Harvard College awarded him the degree of Master of Arts, and he was elected a Fellow of the American Academy of Arts and Sciences.

1. 

sextant - an instrument used by navigators for measuring the distance of the sun or a star from the horizon in order to fix the position of the ship

2. 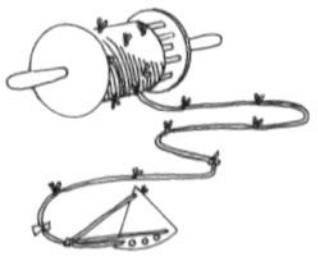

ship log or chip log - an instrument used for measuring the speed of a vessel. It consists of a triangular piece of wood to which a line is attached that has knots that divide the line into lengths

3. 

compass - an instrument with a rotating magnetized needle used for determining direction

4. 

chronometer - a timepiece used in determining longitude at sea

5. 

spyglass - a small telescope used to observe objects far away

Vocabulary

As you read the book, use the sentences before and after each word to determine its meaning. Then use your reference materials to locate a definition for the word.

1. sextant - (Chapter 6)

2. ship log or chip log - (Chapter 6)

3. compass - (Chapter 12)

4. chronometer - (Chapter 12)

5. spyglass - (Chapter 15)

Use the definitions of your vocabulary words to help you match each word with the correct picture.

____

____

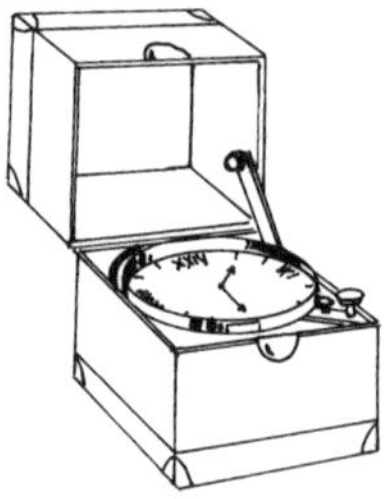

____

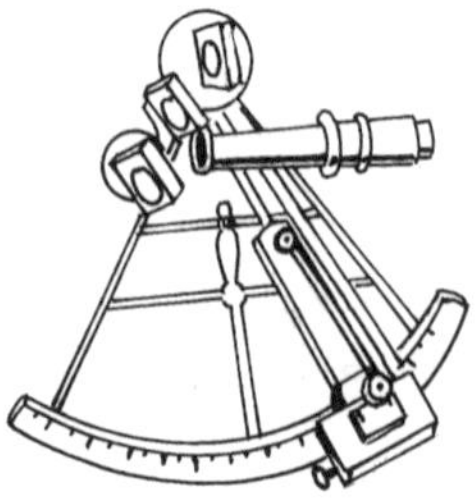

____

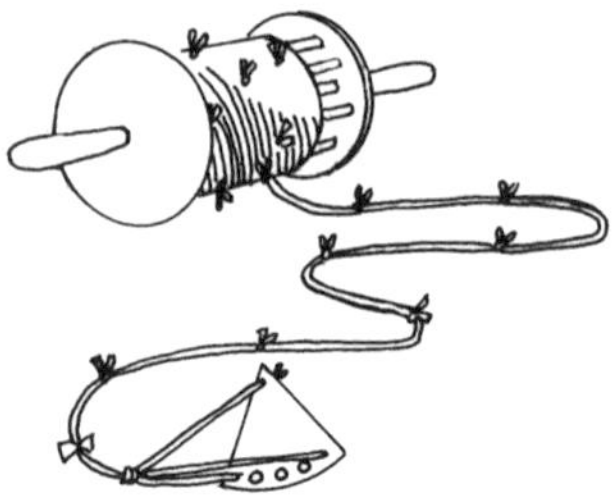

____

Optional: Enrichment (SAB)

Discussion Questions

Find sections of the book that tell you the answers to these discussion questions. Be prepared to read some of them aloud in the discussion.

Chapters 1 - 2
1. Why did Nat use the shilling he found to buy an expectation?

Chapters 3 - 4
2. Why was Nat unable to continue going to school?

Chapters 5 - 6
3. What did Nat mean when he said that he was sailing by "an ash breeze?"

Chapters 7 - 8
4. Why did Nat decide to teach himself Latin?

Chapters 9 - 10
5. Why did Nat feel he was collecting his expectation from the *Pilgrim* when he was invited to join The Salem Philosophical Library?

Chapters 11 - 12
6. How did Nat apply Elizabeth Boardman's expression about "stumbling on people's dumbness" to teaching the seamen navigation?

---

1. **Nat's family was poor and in financial trouble. His father told him that if he had a lot of money he would buy an expectation, so that is what Nat did with his shilling.**

2. **His father was unable to pay for him to go to school. Also, his older brother, Hab, had gone to sea, and he was needed in the cooperage to help his father.**

3. **He decided that he would not get discouraged even though he was indentured for nine years. He was determined to continue to learn even though he could not continue going to school.**

4. **Nat wanted to be able to read Isaac Newton's *Principia* so he could learn more about astronomy. However, since the book was written in Latin, he had to learn Latin in order to read it. Also, he was offered a tutoring position that would allow him to go to Harvard if he was released from his indenture; and he wanted to know Latin so he would be prepared if the chance came.**

5. **Many of the books in the library were cargo that was taken by the *Pilgrim*, the ship on which he had purchased an expectation when he was a young boy. He was now able to read those books.**

6. **Every time he would get impatient when it took the men so long to understand something he was teaching them, he would remember what she said and be more patient.**

Chapters 13 - 14

7. Why was Nat so upset when he found a mistake in Moore's *Navigator*?

Chapters 15 - 16

8. How did Nat handle the troublemaker, Lem Harvey, aboard the *Astrea*?

Chapters 17 - 18

9. Who did Nat marry and why was it only for a short time?

Chapters 19 - 20

10. What three things did Nat decide his book of navigation would contain?

Chapters 21 - 22

11. What honor was awarded to Nat by Harvard College and why was it so important to him?

Chapters 23 - 24

12. Why was it so important to Nat to command a ship on a voyage?

---

7. First of all he felt that mathematics must be accurate if it was to be worth anything. Second, men's lives depended upon those tables being accurate. Mistakes could cause ships to sail off course and into danger.

8. He convinced him that he could learn navigational skills along with the other men if he could learn to control his temper and not get frustrated when it was hard for him. Soon Lem was so busy learning that he was no longer causing any problems.

9. Nat married Elizabeth Boardman, a longtime friend. However, their marriage did not last long because Elizabeth died of consumption while Nat was away on a voyage.

10. 1) correct navigation tables
2) every sea term and maneuver a seaman needs to know in words any seaman can understand
3) mathematical tables that would allow any seaman to solve problems in navigation

11. A Master of Arts degree was awarded to Nat by Harvard College. He had always wanted to attend Harvard College, so it was the fulfillment of a lifelong dream.

12. He felt his navigation book would never be accepted by the common seaman if he had never commanded a vessel. He felt he must prove that "book sailing" worked.

Activities

To help you continue your enjoyment of *Carry On, Mr. Bowditch*, complete the following activities.

1. Journal Writing
2. Parts of a Ship
3. Mapping Skills

Journal Writing

After completing Activity 3, *Mapping Skills*, use one of the journeys to create a journal as if you were Nat writing in one of his notebooks. Tell about the sights you would have seen on that journey. Refer to your book for the information you need.

1. rigging - tackle, chains, and ropes used to support and control sails, masts and yards of a sailing vessel
2. mast - the long upright pole of wood or metal supporting sails and the rigging
3. quarterdeck - after part of the upper deck (usually reserved for officers)
4. capstan - vertical cylinder rotated to wind in the anchor cable. In the past, sailors hoisted the anchor or raised the heavy sails by turning the capstan
5. yard - long pole slung to mast to support head of sail
6. halyard - rope used to raise or lower sail or flag
7. poopdeck - deck at the stern (above ordinary deck); often forms the roof
8. stern - rear part of ship
9. bow - front section of ship
10. keel - strong beam (wood or metal) running along center line of a vessel from end to end
11. hull - framework or body
12. prow - forward part of a ship's hull; the bow
13. boom - long pole extending from the mast of a ship to secure or stretch out the bottom of a sail
14. bowsprit - long pole extending from front of ship to which lines are attached for securing sails
15. forecastle - section of the ship's upper deck; forward of the foremast

Parts of a Ship

Look up the following words in a dictionary to find the part of the ship it identifies. Write the correct word in the space provided on the illustration of the ship on the following page.

1. rigging
2. mast
3. quarterdeck
4. capstan
5. yard
6. halyard
7. poopdeck
8. stern
9. bow
10. keel
11. hull
12. prow
13. boom
14. bowsprit
15. forecastle (also called fo'c'sle)

#5
#2
#1
#6
#7
#15
#13
#14
#3
#9
#4
#12
#11
#10
#8

Mapping Skills

Nathaniel Bowditch took a series of five voyages listed below. On the following map, draw the paths that the ship took using different colored pencils. Use a world atlas to help you locate the various seaports.

1. **Voyage 1** - (red pencil) Left Salem and sailed across the Atlantic Ocean and around Africa to the Isle of Bourbon also known as Reunion, a French-owned island off the east coast of Africa

2. **Voyage 2** - (blue pencil) Left Salem and across the Atlantic Ocean, sailed to Lisbon, Portugal, then stopped over in Funchal in the Madeira Islands (off the northwest coast of Africa), sailed around Africa and through the Indian Ocean to Manila Harbor in what is now the Philippines

3. **Voyage 3** - (green pencil) Left Salem and sailed across the Atlantic Ocean to Cadiz, Spain (a seaport in southwest Spain) and into the Mediterranean Sea to Alicante, Spain (a seaport in southeast Spain)

4. **Voyage 4** - (purple pencil) Left Boston and sailed across the Atlantic Ocean around Africa, through the Indian Ocean to Batavia (now known as Djakarta, a seaport of Indonesia on the northwest coast of Java) then sailed to Manila Harbor located in what is now the Philippines

5. **Voyage 5** - (yellow pencil) Left Salem and sailed across the Atlantic Ocean, around Africa, across the Indian Ocean to Sumatra, a western island of Indonesia

Voyage 1

Voyage 2

Voyage 3

Voyage 4

Voyage 5

This page may be photocopied for student's use.

Answers

Voyage 1

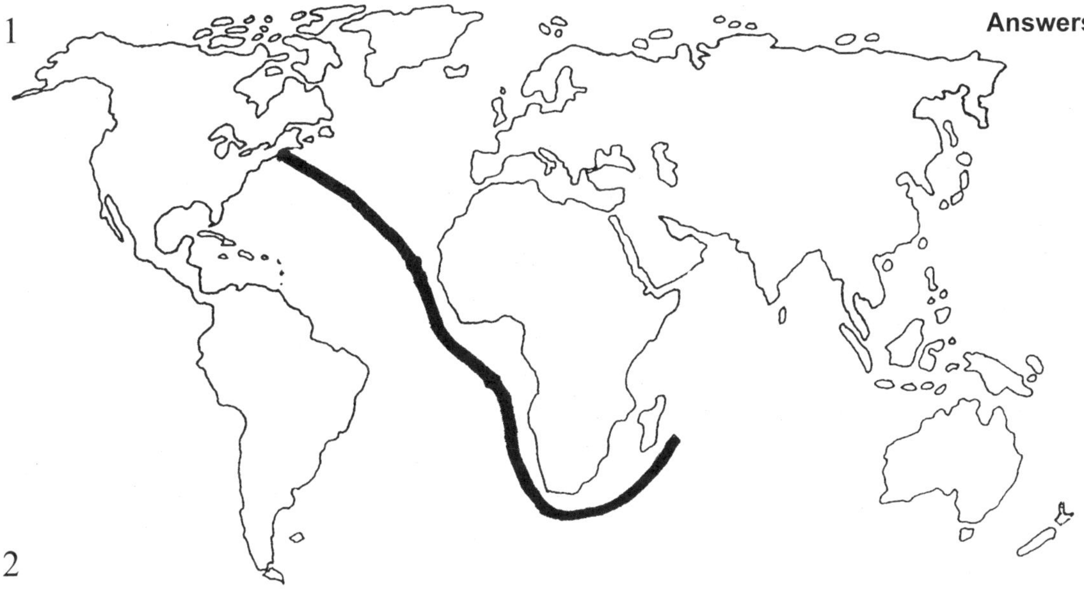

Voyage 2

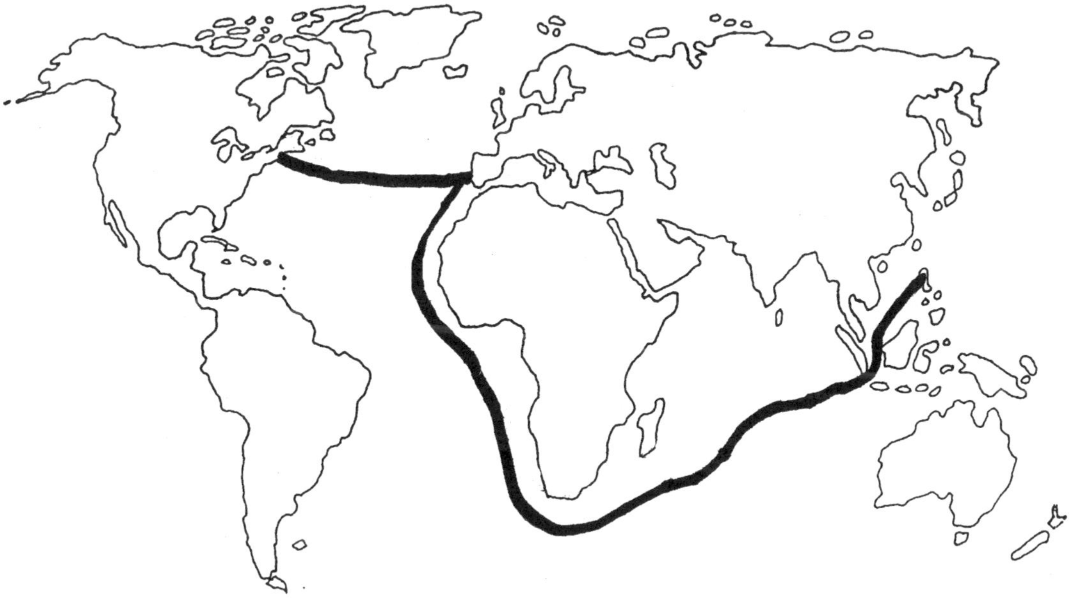

Voyage 3

Answers

Voyage 4

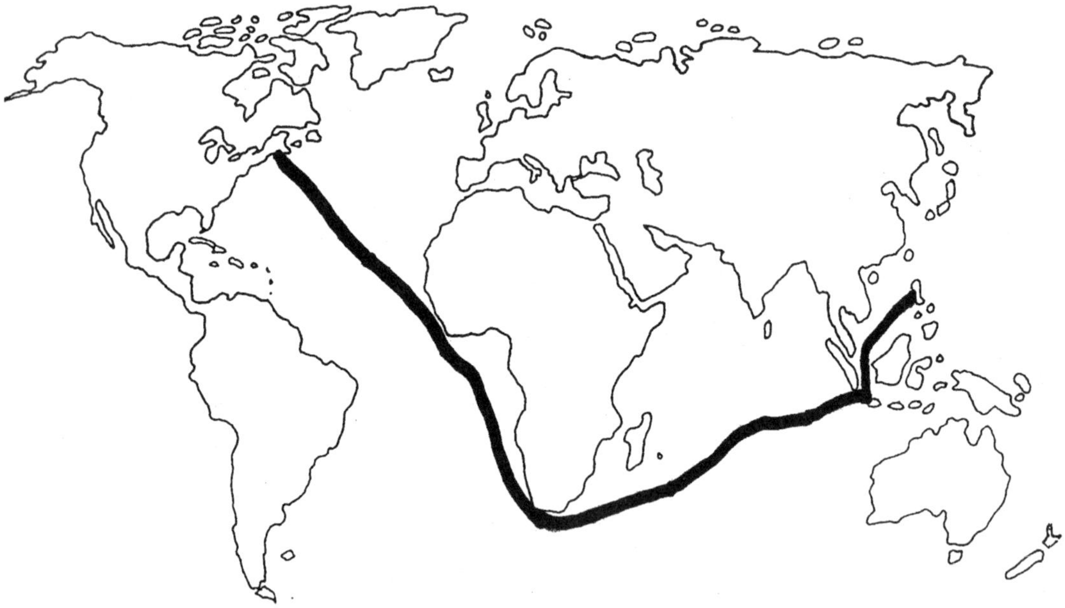

Voyage 5

I **C.A.N.** Assessment
Carry On, Mr. Bowditch Book Study A

After the *Carry On, Mr. Bowditch* Book Study is completed check off each I **C.A.N**. objective with your teacher.

_____	**C**	I can **complete** my work.
_____		I can be **creative**.
_____	**A**	I can be **accurate**.
_____		I can do my work with a good **attitude**.
_____	**N**	I can do my work **neatly**.

For breakfast there were pancakes, and Ma made a pancake man for each one of the children. Ma called each one in turn to bring her plate, and each could stand by the stove and watch, while with the spoonful of batter Ma put on the arms and the legs and the head. It was exciting to watch her turn the whole little man over, quickly and carefully, on a hot griddle. When it was done, she put it smoking hot on the plate.

Little House in the Big Woods by Laura Ingalls Wilder. Used by permission, Harper and Row.

Day 1

a. Write the passage from dictation. Compare your copy with the model, correcting the spelling and punctuation.

b. Using the description in the literature passage, draw a picture on a seperate sheet of paper of the pancake man. Compare it to the description given. Do you feel you have drawn an accurate representation? With supervision, try cooking a pancake man.

c. The prefix **ex-** also appears in the literature passage. It means *forth* or *out*. Locate the word in the literature passage that has the prefix **ex-** . Add this prefix to your list along with the definition and word examples.

d. Make your own spelling list from any misspelled words in the dictation, or use the following list of suggested words:

breakfast	pancake	exciting
griddle	smoking	children

Notice that the words *breakfast* and *pancake* are nouns that are made up of two separate complete words. These are called **compound words**.

Day 1
c. exciting
ex-; forth or out;
Possible examples:
exclaim, expel

Spelling Tip

It will be easier to remember how compound words are spelled if you recognize the two separate words it contains. For example, breakfast is made up of the words *break* and *fast*. Remembering the spelling of the two separate words is less difficult than trying to remember the spelling of the whole word.

e. Divide the following compound words into separate complete words.

1) smokehouse
2) peanuts
3) pancake
4) gingerbread
5) blackboard

Day 1
e. 1) smoke - house
2) pea - nuts
3) pan - cake
4) ginger - bread
5) black - board

Day 2

a. Underline the two words in the literature passage that have the suffix **-ly**. The suffix **-ly** usually means *like* or *manner of* and often changes words into adverbs. Add this suffix to your list. Write "usually an adverb" under the part of speech, then fill in the definition and word examples.

b. **Adverbs** are words that describe a verb, an adjective, or another adverb.

Ex: He ran *swiftly*. - The adverb *swiftly* describes the verb *ran*.
The garden was *very* colorful. - The adverb *very* describes the adjective *colorful*.
She drives *too* slowly. - The adverb *too* describes the adverb *slowly*.

Adverbs answer the following questions:

How? When? Where? To what extent? How often?

Find the two adverbs you underlined. What do they describe? What question do they answer? Read the sentence from the literature passage without the adverbs. Notice how the adverbs help you to picture the action that is happening.

Day 2
a. quickly, carefully

-ly - like, manner of
Possible examples: neatly, slowly

b. how the pancake was turned

c. The best way to locate adverbs is to first find the verb in the sentence and then find any words that answer the adverb questions.

Ex: The team screamed excitedly after they won.

The verb in this sentence is *screamed.* If you then ask *how did they scream*, you will find the word *excitedly* answers that question. It is an adverb describing how the team screamed.

d. Circle the verb in each of the following sentences. Then find and underline the adverb that describes that verb. Remember, the suffix **-ly** often indicates the word is an adverb. What question does the adverb answer?

Ex: The horse (pranced) nervously. how

1) We went to the park yesterday. ___________
2) They are leaving quickly. _______________
3) The cats seldom fight.____________________
4) The children play outside during recess. ________
5) The play is almost finished. ________________

e. Add adverbs to the following sentences in order to better describe the action that is taking place. The word in parentheses following each sentence will tell you what question the adverb should answer.

Ex: The kitten purred softly. (How?)

1) The diamond sparkled _______________. (How?)
2) We will go to the concert _______________. (When?)
3) We _____________ miss a meeting. (How often?)
4) A school of fish swam ___________. (Where?)
5) She was _____concerned about her grade. (To what extent?)

f. Review your spelling words.

Day 3

a. A group of sentences about one main idea is divided into paragraphs. A **paragraph** is a grouping of sentences about one specific part of the topic. The paragraph will include a sentence that expresses the main idea of the paragraph and sentences that support that main idea.

Day 2

d. 1) We (went) to the park yesterday. When?
2) They (are leaving) quickly. How?
3) The cats seldom (fight). How often?
4) The children (play) outside during recess.Where?
5) The play (is) almost finished. To what extent?

e. Possible answers
1) brightly, brilliantly
2) tomorrow, tonight
3) often, seldom
4) nearby, away
5) very, scarcely, not

b. Read over the literature passage. Using your own words, explain what this paragraph is describing. Which sentence do you feel best expresses the main idea of the paragraph? This sentence is called the **topic sentence**. It is the sentence that tells what the paragraph is about. The first sentence of the paragraph is usually the topic sentence.

c. The rest of the sentences in the paragraph support or give more information about the topic. These are called **supporting sentences**. Supporting sentences make up the body of the paragraph. If a sentence in the paragraph does not support the main idea, it is not a supporting sentence and should not be in the paragraph.

Which sentences in the literature passage are supporting sentences?

d. Each paragraph should end with a **closing sentence** that summarizes or comments on the topic of the paragraph. Identify the closing sentence in the literature passage.

e. The literature passage paragraph explains how Ma made pancake men. Choose something you know how to do and write a topic sentence for a paragraph explaining how it is done. Keep your subject simple, such as how to wash the family car, set the table, or bake a cake.

f. Think about the activity you chose and the steps you take to complete it. You might want to act it out and write the steps in order as you go. For example, to bake a cake you might write:

How to Bake a Cake

1) Preheat oven to 325°
2) Grease and flour two round cake pans.
3) Mix boxed cake mix with eggs, oil, and water according to the directions on the box.
4) Pour the mixture into cake pans, place in oven, and bake for 30 minutes.
5) Take the pans out of the oven and allow them to cool.
6) Remove cakes from pans and frost.

Day 3

b. For breakfast there were pancakes, and Ma made a pancake man for each one of the children.

c. Except for the topic sentence, all the other sentences are supportive sentences. They all tell about Ma making pancakes.

d. When it was done, she put it smoking hot on the plate.

Be sure to write your steps in the correct sequence. Don't put the batter in the cake pan before you have given instructions to grease and flour the pans.

g. Review your spelling words. Remember to sound them out by syllables as you spell them. If a word is a compound word, be sure to break the word into separate words as you spell it.

Day 4

a. Read the sample paragraphs below. Notice the step-by-step instructions for planting a garden.

> Planting a vegetable garden is a fun project that anyone can do with a little hard work and instruction. The first step to planting a garden is to choose a site for your garden. It should be a sunny location with good, rich soil, and a source of water nearby. Then you test your soil to determine what fertilizer you need to apply. Next, plan what types of vegetables you want to plant and draw out a diagram of how you want to arrange your garden.
>
> Be sure to run your rows north and south so more sunlight will reach the plants. Then prepare the soil by breaking up any sod and turning the soil. Also remove all woody weeds and trash from the garden plot. Rake and smooth out your planting surface. Next, it is time to plant your seeds.
>
> Use a string with stakes at each end to help you to plant a straight row. Consult your seed package for information on planting depth and spacing and follow the instruction. Attach your seed package or other identification to the stake so you will know what you have planted in that row.
>
> Finally, keep your garden well watered, free from weeds, and apply the proper fertilizers. Now that you have learned how to plant a vegetable garden, enjoy the harvest!

b. The topic sentence tells what the paragraphs are about. The topic sentence is often the first sentence. Underline the topic sentence. All the other sentences must support the main idea.
Transitional words help tie thoughts together. They can show time or order throughout the paragraphs. Some transitional words are *first*, *then*, *next*, and *finally*. Underline the transitional words.

c. Now using the steps you listed in **3f** write sentences to form your paragraphs. Begin with your topic sentence. All the other sentences must support the main idea. Use transitional words that show time or order throughout the paragraph such as *first*, *then*, *next*, and *finally*, but do not begin all your sentences with the same word.

d. Read your paragraph. Does the topic sentence tell what the paragraph is about? Are the steps in the explanation written in order? Does each sentence support the topic? Does the closing sentence summarize or comment on the topic of the paragraph?

e. Give your paragraph to someone and ask him to follow the directions. Can he understand them? Do any changes need to be made to make the directions easier to follow? Make any corrections and complete your final copy.

f. Take an oral or written spelling pretest. Review any words you found difficult to spell.

g. Optional: Enrichment (SAB)

Day 5

a. Write your literature passage from dictation, paying special attention to spelling.

Day 4

b. Topic Sentence:
Planting a vegetable garden is a fun project that anyone can do with a little hard work and instruction.

Transitional words:
The first step
Then
Next
Then
Next
Finally

b. Ma took the extra time to make the pancake men because she knew it was special for the children. Think of someone in your life who takes time to do special things for you. Write a letter thanking him or her. A friendly letter should include a **date**, **salutation**, **body**, **closing**, and **your signature**. Follow the format on the following page for your letter. (The words in parentheses identify the parts of the letter and are not to be written as part of the letter.)

> *(Date)*
> June 30, 2014
>
> *(Salutation or Greeting - remember the comma)*
> Dear Jordan,
>
> *Indent*________*(Body)*____________________________
> ____
>
> *(Closing - comma)*
> Your friend,
> *(Signature - no period)*
> Emma

c. Take an oral or written spelling test.

d. Choose skills from the *Review Activities*.

Review Activities

Choose skills your student needs to review.

1. *Prefixes and Suffixes*
Use your prefix and suffix list to fill in the correct prefix or suffix to complete the word. The definition of the prefix or suffix is in parenthesis. Check to see how many you get correct. Using context clues and prefix or suffix definitions, see if you can accurately guess the meanings of the words.

   a. I believe I ____cede you in line. (*before*)
   b. The boy grinned sly___ at his friend with a water balloon hidden behind his back. (*like*, *manner of*)
   c. Mary was mirth______ when she discovered the joke had been played on her. (*full of*)
   d. His warnings went ____heeded by the sailors. (*not*)
   e. He _____pounded upon the reasons for his belief. (*forth*, *from*, *out*)

1.
a. pre(cede)
b. (sly)ly
c. (mirth)ful
d. un(heeded)
e. ex(pounded)

2. *Compound Words*
Create five compound words from the following words.

wood	rain	foot	pecker	room
son	bow	grand	ball	class

2.
woodpecker, rainbow, football, classroom, grandson

3. *Adverbs*
Underline the adverbs in the following sentences. What question does the adverb answer?

   Ex: We walked <u>quickly</u> to the class. How?

   a. I will write you a letter soon.
   b. I could hardly see the road through the fog.
   c. I have always completed the assignment.
   d. I searched everywhere for the perfect gift.
   e. We must be sure to leave quietly for the early morning trip.

3.
a. <u>soon</u> When?
b. <u>hardly</u> To what extent?
c. <u>always</u> How often?
d. <u>everywhere</u> Where?
e. <u>quietly</u> How?

4.
Topic sentence: Many animals have unique techniques for escaping from their enemies.

Cross Out: The armadillo feeds at night on insects, birds' eggs, roots, and fruit.

5.
June 19, 2015

Dear Emily,

Your friend,

4. *Paragraphs*
Read the following paragraph and underline the topic sentence. There is one sentence in the paragraph that does not support the topic sentence. Cross out that sentence.

Many animals have unique techniques for escaping from their enemies. The opossum fools its enemies by rolling over, lying very still, and pretending to be dead. The armadillo protects itself from attack by rolling itself into a tight ball with only its bony plates exposed. The armadillo feeds at night on insects, birds' eggs, roots, and fruit. When a skunk is attacked it squirts a terrible-smelling liquid from under its tail at its enemy. Many attackers are defeated by these escape techniques and move on to find easier prey.

5. *Letters*
Add the correct punctuation to the following letter.

June 19 2015

Dear Emily

I really miss you, and I wish you were here with us on our family vacation. The mountains are beautiful. We have enjoyed fishing, hiking, and sightseeing. Our vacation ends next week, so I should be home soon.

Your friend

Logan

Notes

There was very little hard study done in the Temple Grammar School the week preceding the Fourth of July. For my part, my heart and brain were so full of fire-crackers, Roman-candles, rockets, pin-wheels, squibs, and gunpowder in various seductive forms, that I wonder I didn't explode under Mr. Grimshaw's very nose. I couldn't do a sum to save me. I couldn't tell, for love or money, whether Tallahassee was the capital of Tennessee or of Florida. The present and the pluperfect tenses were inextricably mixed in my memory, and I didn't know a verb from an adjective when I met one.

The Story of a Bad Boy by Thomas Bailey Aldrich

Day 1

a. Write the passage from dictation. Carefully proofread and correct any errors. Pay close attention to the words which are capitalized.

b. Is Tallahassee the capital of Tennessee or Florida? If you don't know, look in an atlas or on a map to find out.

Day 1
b. Tallahassee, Florida

c. Locate the word *inextricably* in the literature passage. The prefix **in-** means *not* or *into*. Try to guess the meaning of inextricably using prefix meaning and context clues. Check your definition with the dictionary. Add the prefix **in-** to your prefix list, along with its definition and word examples.

c. in-; not or into
Possible examples: incorrect, inside

d. Some compound words are joined together by a hyphen. Find the compound words in the literature passage that have hyphens. Locate the one compound word in the passage that is not joined together by a hyphen. What two words make up that compound? It is hard to know whether a compound word is joined together with or without a hyphen. If you are unsure of the correct way to write a compound word, check with a dictionary.

d. fire-crackers, Roman-candles, pin-wheels

gunpowder

e. Make your own spelling list from any words you misspelled in the dictation or use the following suggested list:

preceding	gunpowder	whether
memory	couldn't	didn't

Two of the suggested spelling words are contractions. **Contractions** are words formed by joining two words and leaving out one or more letters. An **apostrophe** (') shows where the letter(s) have been left out.

Spelling Tip

It will help in the spelling of contractions to remember that the apostrophe is always placed at the exact point where letters are omitted.

f. Underline the four contractions used in the paragraph. What two words does each represent? Some contractions are formed by joining a verb to the word *not*, while others are formed by joining a pronoun and verb. Write the following words as contractions. Be sure to place the apostrophe in the correct position.

Ex: could not - couldn't

1) did not
2) have not
3) she will
4) let us
5) we have

Day 1

f. didn't - did not (used twice)
couldn't - could not (used twice)

1) didn't
2) haven't
3) she'll
4) let's
5) we've

Day 2
a. Mr. Grimshaw's

b. 1) kitten's - kittens'
2) teacher's - teachers'
3) mouse's - mice's
4) girl's - girls'
5) goose's - geese's

c. very (little)
so (full)
(did)n't
(could)n't
(could)n't
inextricably (mixed)
(did)n't

Day 2

a. In **1f**, we used the apostrophe in contractions to show where letter(s) had been omitted. An apostrophe can also be used to show possession. The possessive form of a singular noun is made when an apostrophe **s** (**'s**) is added to the noun. This is called a **singular possessive noun**.

Ex: the horse belonging to Joanna - Joanna's horse

Locate an example of a singular possessive noun in the literature passage.

b. The plural possessive form of a noun is formed by placing the apostrophe after the ending **s**. If a plural noun is irregular and does not end in **s**, then an apostrophe **s** (**'s**) is used to form the possessive. This is called a **plural possessive noun**.

Ex: the room belonging to the girls - girls' room
the cars belonging to the men - men's cars

Write each of the following nouns as a singular and plural possessive. Remember, if the plural of the noun is irregular, then an apostrophe **s** (**'s**) is used to form the plural possessive.

Noun	Singular Possessive	Plural Possessive
Ex: dog	dog's	dogs'

1) kitten
2) teacher
3) mouse
4) girl
5) goose

c. Read the literature passage once more. Locate the adverbs used in the literature passage and circle them. Remember, adverbs answer the questions: Where? When? How? How often? To what extent? Since adverbs describe verbs most of the time, first find the verb, then ask the questions adverbs answer. The word **not** is a frequently used adverb. It is often in the contraction form, **n't**. Notice how the author's use of adverbs helps to convey a mood of excitement.

d. Have you ever been so excited over an upcoming event you couldn't concentrate on anything? Share about the event with your teacher or other students.

e. Review your spelling words.

Day 3

a. Reread the literature passage paying special attention to the capitalization. Capitalization is used in two main ways:

1) to indicate the beginning of a sentence
2) to help the reader quickly identify proper names and titles

Although there are many specific capitalization rules, most rules fall under one of the two main categories listed above. The one rule that does not fall under one of these categories is the capitalization of the letter **i** when it is used as a word. The letter **i** is always capitalized when it is used as the pronoun *I*.

b. Circle all the words in the paragraph that begin with a capital letter. Write each of the words under the correct capitalization rule would fall under. The first one is done for you as an example.

Beginning of Sentence	Proper Name	Title
There		

c. Pretend you are this boy's friend. Briefly write a few sentences explaining to him the difference between a verb and an adjective. Refer to the definitions for a verb and an adjective in Lessons 2 and 3 if you need help.

d. Review your spelling words.

e. Optional: Enrichment (SAB)

Day 3

b. Beginning of Sentence: There, For, The

Proper Name: Temple Grammar School, Fourth of July, Roman-candles, Grimshaw's, Tallahassee, Tennessee, Florida

Title: Mr.

c. Verbs show action or state of being. Adjectives describe nouns.

Day 4

a. The boy in the literature passage describes his excitement concerning a holiday. What is your favorite holiday? Today you are going to write a paragraph describing your favorite holiday.

b. Before you begin writing your paragraph, it is a good idea to think about what you want to write and organize your thoughts. One of the best methods for doing this is to use a "circle word picture." Find the circle word picture in Lesson 6 of the *Student Activity Book* or draw the following diagram on a sheet of paper.

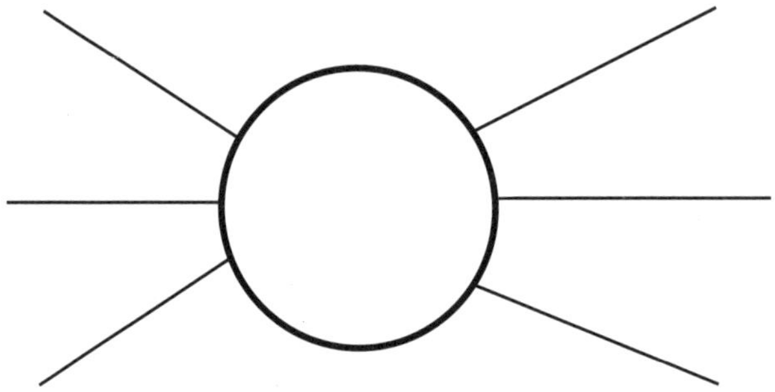

c. Look at the following circle word picture about the Fourth of July as it was described in the literature passage. After you have reviewed the example, choose your favorite holiday and write it in the center circle of the diagram. Now brainstorm. Why do you like the holiday? What special things happen? What makes it special? Put your ideas on the lines extending from the center circle.

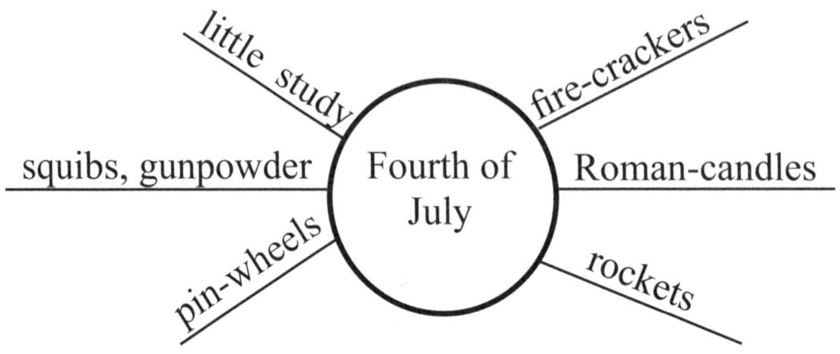

d. Look over your completed diagram. Begin writing your paragraph by starting with a good topic sentence. All the other sentences you write should tell about and support the topic sentence. Then end your paragraph with a closing sentence. Be sure to use adjectives and adverbs to help convey your excitement about the holiday.

e. Look over your paragraph for any mistakes in punctuation, spelling, and capitalization. Once you are satisfied, write the paragraph neatly for your teacher to review.

f. Take an oral or written spelling pretest. Remember, sounding out the syllables as you write them will help you spell them correctly.

g. Optional: Enrichment (SAB)

Day 5

a. Write the literature passage from dictation.

b. A caricature is a cartoon type drawing used to stretch the imagination. Can you envision this boy with his heart and brain full of firecrackers, Roman-candles, etc. right under his teacher's nose? Close your eyes and think how this would look. Draw a caricature of this scene. You don't have to be an artist to draw a caricature. There's no right or wrong way. Draw it the way you "see" it. Have fun!

c. Take a written or oral spelling test.

d. Choose skills from the *Review Activities*.

1.
Answers will vary:
in - means not or into

2.
a. shouldn't
b. she'll
c. aren't
d. they've
e. we'd

3.
a. forty-five
b. brother-in-law
c. hand-me-downs
d. runner-up

4.
a. dogs' tails
b. trees' leaves
c. deer's prints
d. ladies' cars
e. Larry's motorcycle

Review Activities

Choose skills your student needs to review.

1. *Prefixes*
   Look in your dictionary and find three words with the prefix **in-**. How does the prefix **in-** change the meaning of the root word?

2. *Contractions*
   Write the contractions for the following words.

   a. should not
   b. she will
   c. are not
   d. they have
   e. we would

3. *Hyphens in Compound Nouns and Number Words*
   Identify the compound words in the following sentences and add hyphens.

   a. I have saved forty five dollars.
   b. Jim is his brother in law and good friend.
   c. Being the youngest, she always wore hand me downs.
   d. She was the runner up in the contest.

4. *Possessives*
   Write each of the following expressions as a possessive.

   Ex: the earrings of the girl - the girl's earrings

   a. the tails of the dogs
   b. leaves of the trees
   c. prints of the deer
   d. the cars belonging to the ladies
   e. the motorcycle belonging to Larry

5. *Capitalization*
The following paragraph is written without capitalization. Circle the words that need to be capitalized and explain why.

our trip to washington, d.c. was so exciting. there was so much there to see and do. the first stop on our tour was the lincoln memorial. made out of white colorado-yule marble, the memorial is similar in shape to the greek parthenon. it took over six years to complete and was dedicated on memorial day, may 30, 1922. abraham lincoln's statue is located in the center of the memorial and the gettysburg address is etched in marble on the south wall.

6. *Writing Skills*
Choose a writing topic of your choice. Draw a circle word picture and brainstorm, writing down your ideas on the lines extending from the main circle. Write a paragraph about your topic using the ideas you have written down.

5.
Beginning of a sentence: Our, There, The, Made, It

Proper Name or Title: Washington, D.C., Lincoln Memorial, Colorado, Greek Parthenon, Memorial Day, May, Abraham Lincoln's, Gettysburg Address

Notes

After that they went on till they came among tall beech trees and Trufflehunter called out, "Pattertwig! Pattertwig! Pattertwig! Pattertwig!" and almost at once, bounding down from branch to branch till he was just above their heads, came the most magnificent red squirrel that Caspian had ever seen. It was far bigger than the ordinary dumb squirrels which he had sometimes seen in the castle gardens. Indeed it was nearly the size of a terrier and the moment you looked in its face you saw that it could talk. Indeed the difficulty was to get it to stop talking for, like all squirrels, it was a chatterer.

Prince Caspian by C.S. Lewis.
Used by permission, Wm Collins & Sons, Inc.

Day 1

a. Write the literature passage from dictation. Proofread and correct any errors.

b. Find the word *indeed* in the literature passage. What prefix does this word contain? You know from Lesson 6 that the prefix **in-** means *not* or *into*. The root word is *deed*. The root or base of a word can be free or bound. A root word that is **free** is a word that can stand by itself, such as deed. If the root is not a word by itself, then the root is said to be **bound**. For example, the root in the word *presume* is *sume*. Since there is no such word in the English language, the root is considered bound.

c. Find the word *almost* in the literature passage. This word has the prefix **al-** which means *to* or *towards*. Look at the root or base part of the word. Is it free or bound? Add the prefix **al-** to your list and be sure to write the definition and word examples.

Day 1
b. the prefix in-

c. free
al-; to or towards
Possible examples:
almost, always

d. Unlike the prefix, the suffix is always added to an existing word. The suffix **-er** means *one who* or *that which*. The suffix **-er** usually changes the word into a noun or adjective. Find the word *chatterer* in the literature passage. Identify whether the word is an adjective or noun from the way it is used in the sentence. Add the suffix **-er** to your list of suffixes and write the definition along with word examples. Under the part of speech section include the information, noun or adjective.

Now find the word *bigger* in the literature passage. The suffix **-er** in this word is used to compare two things.

e. Make your own spelling list from any misspelled words in the dictation you misspelled or use the following list of suggested words:

bigger	chatterer	ordinary
sometimes	difficulty	magnificent

Look over the suggested spelling list. The word *bigger* has the suffix **-er**. The root of this word is *big*. When a one-syllable word ends with a short vowel and a consonant, double the last consonant before adding a suffix beginning with a vowel. Therefore, when the suffix **-er** is added to the word big, the **g** is doubled, forming the word *bigger*.

Spelling Tip

When a one-syllable word ends with a short vowel and a consonant, the final consonant must be doubled before adding a suffix beginning with a vowel.

f. Add suffixes to the following words. The first one is done for you as an example:

Root Word	Add Suffix	New Word
Ex: swim	**-ing**	swimming
1) mop	**-ed**	
2) bat	**-er**	
3) get	**-ing**	
4) run	**-er**	
5) dig	**-ing**	

Day 1
f. 1) mopped
2) batter
3) getting
4) runner
5) digging

Day 2

a. Adjectives are words that describe nouns. Adjectives often show how one person or thing compares to another. There are three degrees of comparison in adjectives: *positive, comparative*, and *superlative*.

b. Circle the word in the first sentence of the literature passage that describes the beech trees. This is an adjective in the **positive form**. It only describes the noun; it does not compare the noun to anything else.

Ex: Joan is tall. (positive form)

Day 2
b. tall

c. Find the phrases that describe Pattertwig. Underline the word that compares the size of the squirrel with other squirrels. When comparing two objects or people, the suffix **-er** is added to most one-syllable adjectives and many two-syllable adjectives. Use the word *more* with adjectives of three or more syllables. This is the **comparative form** of an adjective.

Ex: Joan is taller than Mary.
The berries are more plentiful on this bush.
(comparative form)

c. bigger

Day 2
d. the most magnificent red squirrel

f. 1) wiser, wisest
2) more dangerous, most dangerous
3) worse, worst
4) faster, fastest
5) better, best

d. When three or more objects or people are being compared, the suffix **-est** is added to most one-syllable adjectives and many two-syllable adjectives. Use the word *most* with adjectives of three or more syllables. This is the **superlative form** of the adjective.

Ex: Joan is the tallest of all the girls. (superlative form)
She is the most cooperative student in class. (superlative form)

Find the example in the literature passage where a superlative form is used to describe Pattertwig.

e. The comparative and superlative forms of some adjectives are formed irregularly. The most commonly used forms of irregular comparisons are listed below:

Positive	Comparative	Superlative
good, well	better	best
much, many	more	most
bad, ill	worse	worst
far	farther, further	farthest, furthest

f. Fill in the following chart with the comparative and superlative forms of each of the positive forms of adjectives listed below. The first one is done for you as an example. Watch for irregular forms.

Positive	Comparative	Superlative
Ex: small	smaller	smallest
1) wise		
2) dangerous		
3) bad		
4) fast		
5) good		

g. Read the literature passage once more. Draw a sketch or describe what you think Pattertwig looks like.

h. Review your spelling words, sounding them out by syllables.

Day 3

a. In this story the animals talk and have very distinct personalities. Mr. Lewis describes the squirrels as "chatterers." Think about other stories you have read in which animals have personalities. As we learned in Lesson 3, anytime an animal or object is given human qualities, the writing technique of personification is being used.

b. Choose four of the animals listed below and decide what personality traits would best suit them. List words beside each name that you feel would describe that animal.

bear	deer	lion	dog	mouse
tiger	cat	eagle	horse	dolphin
an animal of your choice				

Ex: horse: stubborn, intelligent

c. Next choose two of the animals you wrote personality traits for and write one or two sentences about each animal describing the animal in a way that gives him at least one of the personality traits you chose.

Ex: horse - Lucky shook his head angrily at Vanessa when he found no treat in her pocket. Then, like a spoiled child, he refused to cooperate.

d. Review your spelling words.

e. Optional: Enrichment (SAB)

Day 4

a. Stories often contain parts in which the characters are speaking to one another. This is called **dialogue**. Dialogue is used to help the story seem more real and alive. Whenever dialogue is used, the actual words spoken by the characters in the story are called **direct quotations**. Direct quotations are surrounded by **quotation marks** (**" "**) to set them apart. Examine the literature passage and underline the direct quotation. Note that a comma precedes the direct quotation in the literature passage.

Day 4

a. "Patterwig! Patterwig! Patterwig!"

Quotation Rules

Direct Quotations

1. Be sure to capitalize the first word of a direct quotation.

2. When the speech tag comes before the direct quotation, place a comma before the direct quotation.

   Ex: Jim asked, "Can you come with us tonight?"

3. When the speech tag comes after the direct quotations, place the punctuation after the direct quotation inside the closing quotation marks.

   Ex: "We will go to the movies together," announced Sarah.
   "When does the movie start?" asked Tim.
   "You went without me!" gasped Luke.

4. Whenever punctuation is a part of the direct quotation, it appears inside the quotation marks. Punctuation goes outside the closing quotation mark if it applies to the whole sentence instead of just the direct quotation.

   Ex: The team exclaimed, "We will win this game!" (punctuation is part of the direct quotation)

   Who said, "Give me liberty or give me death"? (punctuation applies to the whole sentence)

5. When writing dialogue be sure to indent and start a new paragraph each time the speaker changes.

6. When direct quotation is more than one sentence and is not divided, then quotation marks should be used at the beginning of the quote and the end of the quote. Quotation marks should not enclose each sentence separately.

7. In a split quotation, the second part of the direct quotation does *not* begin with a capital letter.

   Ex: "Yesterday," said Amy, "we went to the beach."

b. Look over the quotation rules listed in this lesson. Add correct punctuation to the following sentences. Be sure to enclose all direct quotations with quotation marks and capitalize the first word of a direct quotation. Note the use of the comma.

Ex: Jean said we cannot all fit in the car
Jean said, "We cannot all fit in the car."

1) The ringmaster cried welcome to the circus
2) There are many formulas used in solving this equation the teacher announced
3) Is there only one doughnut left asked Sue
4) Touchdown yelled the announcer
5) Did Mrs. Scott say "Matthew cannot go"

c. Write a short conversation between the two animals you described in **3b** and **3c**. The conversation should reflect the personality traits you have assigned to each animal. Be sure to set off each speaker's words with quotation marks, and follow the rules for direct quotations. When writing your conversation, indent and begin a new paragraph each time the speaker changes.

d. Take an oral or written spelling pretest. Review any words you found difficult to spell.

Day 5

a. Take the literature passage from dictation paying careful attention to spelling and punctuation.

b. Examine your work from **4c** and make any edits. Use your thesaurus to improve your writing by substituting synonyms that add more description. For example, instead of saying *the dog said*, substitute a more descriptive word such as exclaimed, growled, or questioned. When you have done your best and are pleased with your work, make a neat copy to give to your teacher.

c. Take a written or oral spelling test.

d. Choose skills from the *Review Activities*.

Day 4

b. 1) The ringmaster cried, "Welcome to the circus!"

2) "There are many formulas used in solving this equation," the teacher announced.

3) "Is there only one doughnut left?" asked Sue.

4) "Touchdown!" yelled the announcer.

5) Did Mrs. Scott say, "Matthew cannot go"?

Review Activities

Choose skills your student needs to review.

1. *Suffixes*
   Add the suffix to each of the following words. Be sure to double the last consonant if it is necessary.

   Ex: sit + er = sitter

   a. clap + ing
   b. trot + ed
   c. train + er
   d. sad + est
   e. lean + ing

1.
a. clapping
b. trotted
c. trainer
d. saddest
e. leaning

2. *Prefixes and Suffixes*
   Using your list of prefixes and suffixes, add the prefix or suffix that is indicated by the definition in parentheses.

   Ex: _in_stead (*not* or *into*) free

   a. _____caution (*before*)
   b. _____cove (*to, towards*)
   c. _____definite (*not*)
   d. paint _____ (*one who, that which*)
   e. rest _____ (*full of*)

2.
a. precaution, free
b. alcove, free
c. indefinite, free
d. painter, free
e. restful, free

3. *Adjectives*
   Underline the correct adjective in the following sentences.

   Ex: Mary can finish her math problems (quicker, quickest) than Samantha.

   a. Of the two athletes, Mary is (*faster*, *fastest*).
   b. In our family Matthew is the (*taller*, *tallest*).
   c. Why is this dress (*more expensive*, *expensiver*) than the other one?
   d. This butterfly is the (*most beautiful*, *beautifullest*) of them all.
   e. This storm is (*badder*, *worse*) than the one we had earlier.

3.
a. faster
b. tallest
c. more expensive
d. most beautiful
e. worse

4. *Personification*
   Write two sentences describing a tree using personification.

5. *Punctuation (quotation marks, commas, period, question marks, exclamation mark)*
   Add the correct punctuation mark in the following sentences.

   a. How long does it take a caterpillar to become a butterfly Jim asked
   b. His teacher replied Once the caterpillar forms a pupa it takes about two weeks for the transformation to be complete
   c. That's amazing declared Olivia
   d. Dan commented I once saw a butterfly emerge from its pupa. It looked rather wet and crumpled at first
   c. Blood pumping from the abdomen into the veins causes the wings to unfold, and when they are dry, the butterfly is able to fly away remarked his teacher

4.
Examples:
The weeping willow sighed in the dusk.

I could see the palm trees dancing in the breeze.

5.
a. "How long does it take a caterpillar to become a butterfly?" Jim asked.

b. His teacher replied, "Once the caterpillar forms a pupa it takes about two weeks for the transformation to be complete."

c. "That's amazing!" declared Olivia.

d. Dan commented, "I once saw a butterfly emerge from its pupa. It looked rather wet and crumpled at first."

e. "Blood pumping from the abdomen into the veins causes the wings to unfold, and when they are dry, the butterfly is able to fly away," remarked his teacher.

While these measures were taken in behalf of Cedric and his companions, the armed men by whom the latter had been seized hurried their captives along towards the place of security where they intended to imprison them. But darkness came on fast, and the paths of the wood seemed but imperfectly known to the marauders. *They were compelled to make several long halts, and once or twice to return on their road to resume the direction which they wished to pursue. The summer morn had dawned upon them ere they could travel in full assurance that they held the right path. But confidence returned with light, and the cavalcade now moved rapidly forward.*

Ivanhoe by Sir Walter Scott

Day 1

a. Ivanhoe is set in twelfth century England.

c. The root of return is free. The root of resume is bound.

Day 1

a. Read the literature passage. *Ivanhoe* is an example of **historical fiction**. Historical fiction is a story that is set in a period of history, and, along with the author's characters and events, can also contain real people and/or real events. In what time is *Ivanhoe* set?

b. Write the bold print in the literature passage from dictation.

c. Look at the words *return* and *resume* in the literature passage. The prefix **re-** means back or again. Is the root of these words bound or free? Add this prefix to your list. Be sure to write the definition and word examples.

d. Make your own spelling list from any misspelled words in the dictation, or use the following list of suggested words:

companions	seized	marauders
assurance	confidence	cavalcade

Spelling Tip

It is easy to confuse the *ie* with the *ei* letter combination. *ie* is used in most words; *ei* is used after the letter *c* and in words that make the long /*a*/ sound. The following rhyme will help you to remember which to use: *ie* or *ei*.
/ before *e* except after *c*, and in words that say /*a*/ as in neighbor and weigh.

e. Write **ie** or **ei** in the following words.

1) sl___gh	6) fr___nd
2) rec___ve	7) ch___f
3) sh___ld	8) y___ld
4) fr___ght	9) v___n
5) bel___ve	10) conc___ve

Day 2

a. A **complete sentence** expresses a complete thought and has two parts. The part which tells who or what the sentence is about is called the **complete subject**. The other part of the sentence tells what the subject is or does and is called the **complete predicate**. Most sentences can be divided between the complete subject and the complete predicate.

Ex: The family / enjoys the amusement park.
Mary Anne / is my friend.

b. Very often the subject comes at the beginning of the sentence, but not always. The subject always has a noun as its focal point. The predicate always has a verb as its focal point telling what the subject is or what action the subject is doing. It is usually easier to locate the predicate of the sentence first. Read the following sentence:

The runner raced across the finish line.

Now ask yourself the following questions to help locate the subject and the predicate of the sentence.

Teacher's Note:
Read the words aloud to the student so he can fill in the letters.

Day 1
e. 1) sleigh
2) receive
3) shield
4) freight
5) believe
6) friend
7) chief
8) yield
9) vein
10) conceive

Day 2
b. 1) raced
2) runner

1) What action is taking place?
2) Who or what is doing the action?

The answer to the first question is the predicate of the sentence, and the answer to the second is the subject.

c. It is a little harder to find the subject in a sentence which asks a question. Try putting the question in statement form.

Ex: What had the man meant?
Make it into a statement: The man had meant what.
By doing this you put the subject in front of the verb, making it easier to find.

d. The armed men / hurried their captives along towards the place of security.

They / were compelled to make several long halts.

The summer morn / had dawned upon them.

The cavalcade / now moved rapidly forward.

d. Draw a line dividing the complete subject from the complete predicate as in **2a** in the following simplified sentences taken from the literature passage.

The armed men hurried their captives along towards the place of security.
They were compelled to make several long halts.
The summer morn had dawned upon them.
The cavalcade now moved rapidly forward.

e. Every sentence has to have a subject and predicate to be complete. A sentence that does not contain both parts does not express a complete thought is called a **fragment**. A writer should always be careful to only use complete sentences in his writing.

Ex. Going to the store (fragment – subject missing)
Mary is going to the store. (complete sentence)

My brother and his friend. (fragment – predicate missing)
My brother and his friend went with us. (complete sentence)

While we were at the beach. (fragment – incomplete thought)
While we were at the beach we found a starfish. (complete thought)

f. Read the following sentences. If the sentence is a complete sentence, write **C** in front of the sentence. If it is a fragment, write **F** in front of it and rewrite the sentence to add whatever is necessary to make it a complete sentence.

_____1) Going to the mall.
_____2) The butterfly flew from flower to flower.
_____3) The sixth grade class at school.
_____4) As we were climbing up the mountain.
_____5) When he realized his error.

g. Review your spelling words, sounding them out by syllables.

Day 3

a. There are four types of sentences, each expressing a different purpose.

Sentence Types

1) A **declarative** sentence makes a statement and ends with a period.
Ex: Chickens are a type of bird found on most farms.

2) An **interrogative** sentence asks a question and ends with a question mark.
Ex: Who is coming skating with us?

3) An **imperative** sentence gives a command or makes a request. They often contain the understood subject *you*. An imperative sentence ends with a period or exclamation mark.
Ex: Come over here now!
Please put the books back on the shelf.

4) An **exclamatory** sentence expresses strong emotion or surprise and ends with an exclamation point.
Ex: What a noise those dogs make!
You scared me!

Day 2

f. 1) F ex: We are going to the mall.
2) C
3) F ex: Mary was in the sixth grade class at school.
4) F ex: It began to rain as we were climbing up the mountain.
5) F ex: He quickly corrected the problem when he realized his error.

b. Notice that in imperative sentences the subject is often said to be understood. This means that although the subject is not stated, the sentence is understood to have the subject *you.* Read the following paragraph from *Ivanhoe.*

"Shame on ye all!" cried De Bracy to the soldiers around him. "Do you call yourselves cross-bowmen, and let these two dogs keep their station under the walls of the castle? Heave over the coping stones from the battlement, an better may not be. Get pickaxe and levers, and down with that huge pinnacle!"

Day 3

c. The soldiers around De Bracy

c. Who is directed to heave over the coping stones? Who is directed to get pickaxe and levers? The understood subject *you* is being directed to do both.

d. declarative

d. What type of sentence are all of the sentences in the dictation passage?

e. declarative: Things will be but as they were when we commenced our enterprise.

interrogative: No - a prison were better; and whether in Britain or Austria, what matters it?
or
"Who spoke of harming him?" said Prince John, with a hardened laugh.

exclamatory: The knave will say next that I meant he should slay him!

e. Find an example of a declarative sentence, an interrogative sentence and an exclamatory sentence in the following excerpt from *Ivanhoe.*

"Who spoke of harming him?" said Prince John, with a hardened laugh. "The knave will say next that I meant he should slay him! No – a prison were better; and whether in Britain or Austria, what matters it? Things will be but as they were when we commenced our enterprise."

f. Practice writing your spelling words, sounding them out by syllables. Remember to apply your spelling rule to help you in writing **ie** in the correct order.

g. Optional: Enrichment (SAB)

Day 4

a. In **3a** you learned there are four types of sentences: declarative, interrogative, imperative, and exclamatory. Read each of the following sentences and decide if they are declarative **(D)**, interrogative **(I)**, imperative **(Imp)**, or exclamatory **(E)**. Fill in the blanks and add the correct punctuation at the end of each sentence.

Ex: __I__ Where are you going?

_____1) Be sure to wash the dishes
_____2) How beautiful the stars are
_____3) There is a great variety of life in a rainforest
_____4) Where will you be going this evening
_____5) The races will begin this evening at dusk
_____6) Who will be cooking dinner tonight
_____7) Go to your room right now
_____8) What a surprise to see you
_____9) What is the agenda for tonight's meeting
___10) Northern Lights are a beautiful sight to see

b. Review the Quotation Rules found in **Lesson 7, 4a**. Write the passage in **3e** from dictation.

c. Read the literature passage again. Write a paragraph telling what might happen next.

d. Take an oral or written spelling pretest. Review any words you found difficult to spell.

e. Optional: Enrichment (SAB)

Day 5

a. Write the literature passage from dictation paying special attention to spelling and punctuation.

b. Choose skills from the *Review Activities*.

c. Take a written or oral spelling test.

Day 4

a.

1) D - (.)
2) E - (!)
3) D - (.)
4) I - (?)
5) D - (.)
6) I - (?)
7) Imp. - (!)
8) E - (!)
9) I - (?)
10) D - (.)

Review Activities

Choose skills your student needs to review.

1. *Prefixes*
   Add the prefix **re-** to the following words. How does the prefix change the meaning of the root word?

   a. ____turn
   b. ____form
   c. ____ examine

2. Complete the following examples of similes.

   a. as fancy as ________________
   b. fluffy like ________________

3. *Complete Subject and Complete Predicate*
   Draw a vertical line between the complete subject and the complete predicate.

   Ex: Birds/are the only animals that have feathers.

   a. The ostrich is the largest bird in the world.
   b. Down feathers keep birds warm in cold weather.
   c. Penguins use their wings as flippers to help them swim faster.
   d. Birds build many different types of nests.
   e. Baby birds are always hungry.

4. *Fragments*
   Read the following sentences. If it is a complete sentence, write **C** in the space provided. If it is a fragment, write **F**.

   a. _____ When I travel on the bus.
   b. _____ This road has some dangerous curves.
   c. _____ Going to the beach this afternoon.
   d. _____ Since you will not be able to come with us.
   e. _____ The beautiful green forest.

1.
a. return
b. reform
c. reexamine

2.
a. peacock's tail
b. newly washed poodle

3.
a. The ostrich / is the largest bird in the world.
b. Down feathers / keep birds warm in cold weather.
c. Penguins / use their wings as flippers to help them swim faster.
d. Birds / build many different types of nests.
e. Baby birds/ are always hungry.

4.
a. F
b. C
c. F
d. F
e. F

5. *Types of Sentences*
Identify each of the following types of sentences. On the line next to each sentence write **D** for declarative, **I** for interrogative, **Imp** for imperative, or **E** for exclamatory, and fill in the correct punctuation at the end of the sentence.

a. ______ Watch out for that bee
b. ______ Why do bees fly from flower to flower
c. ______ Bees collect nectar from the flowers
d. ______ What hard workers they are

6. *Compound Words*
Make as many compound words as you can with the ones listed below. You may use a word more than once.

ball body time where foot any base soft basket

7. *Synonyms*
Rewrite the paragraph below, replacing the underlined words with synonyms.

Lucy walked to the store yesterday. She understands the importance of fresh vegetables in her diet. She loves tomatoes and cucumbers soaked in vinegar. She also likes to make fresh salads for her family. She learns new things by watching cooking shows.

5.
a. Imp (. or !)
b. I (?)
c. D (.)
d. E (!)

6.
football, baseball, basketball, softball, anybody, anywhere, anytime

7.
Possible answer:
Lucy strolled to the store yesterday. She appreciates the importance of fresh vegetables in her diet. She adores tomatoes and cucumbers soaked in vinegar. She also likes to create fresh salads for her family. She learns new things by observing cooking shows.

Icicles were forming on Sham's feelers, yet his body was wet with sweat. He backed up. He lowered his head, and as the whip struck him, he made a snatching pull. The load moved, and as if by some supernatural power Sham kept on going up the incline. When almost at the top, however, his forefeet began slipping. He clawed with them. The whip snarled and cracked. It cut deep into his hide. Groaning, he tried again, and again. His veins swelled to bursting.

Day 1

a. Read the literature passage. Copy the passage from dictation and compare your copy to the model. Correct any errors.

Day 1
b. fore-; before in time
Possible examples: forerunner, forefeet

b. Look at the fifth sentence of the literature passage and find the prefix **fore-**. This prefix means *before in time*. Does knowing the meaning of this prefix help you to understand the meaning of the word *forefeet*? Add this prefix to your prefix list along with its definition and some word examples.

c. Look over the first sentence of the literature passage. Why is an apostrophe used in *Sham's feelers*? Review the rules for use of apostrophes in Lesson 6 if you are not sure.

d. Make your: own spelling list from any misspelled words in the dictation, or use the following list of suggested words:

snatching	snarled	cracked
groaning	tried	slipped

e. *Snatching* is used as an adjective to describe *pull*.

e. Note that each of the spelling words has the suffix **-ed** or **-ing**. Usually words with these suffixes are verbs; however, one of these words is used as an adjective. Read each of the words in the context of the sentence in the literature passage. Can you identify the word that is used as an adjective?

f. In Lessons 4 and 7, you learned *Spelling Tips* for adding suffixes to words. Two of the tips are as follows:

Drop the silent e from a word before adding a suffix that begins with a vowel.

When a one-syllable word ends with a short vowel followed by a consonant, then the last consonant is doubled before adding a suffix beginning with a vowel.

Find the word in the suggested spelling list that follows one of these *Spelling Tips* and tell your teacher which rule it follows.

g. Find the word *tried* in the suggested spelling list. The **y** in the root word *try* has been changed to an **i** before the suffix **-ed** was added.

Spelling Tip

When a word ending in *y* is preceded by a consonant, the *y* is changed to *i* before adding a suffix, except for a suffix beginning with *i* such as *-ing*. If a word ends with *y* preceded by a vowel, then just add the suffix.

Copy these words. Say the words aloud as you write them. Remember there is no change made in the root word when adding the suffix **-ing**.

Root Word	-ed	-ing
play	played	playing
hurry	hurried	hurrying
empty	emptied	emptying
carry	carried	carrying

Day 1

f. slipped - When a one-syllable word ends with a short vowel followed by a consonant, the last consonant is doubled before adding a suffix beginning with a vowel.

Teacher's Note: Some exceptions to this rule are *paid, said, gaily,* and *gaiety.*

h. Add the suffixes **-ed** and **-ing** to the following words. Be sure to follow the rules for adding suffixes.

Root Word	-ed	-ing
Ex:fry	fried	frying
stay	stayed	staying
1) marry		
2) cry		
3) fray		
4) chop		
5) sneeze		
6) stray		
7) trade		
8) drip		
9) apply		
10) copy		

Day1
1.
h. 1) married, marrying
2) cried, crying
3) frayed; fraying
4) chopped, chopping
5) sneezed, sneezing
6) strayed; straying
7) traded, trading
8) dripped, dripping
9) applied, applying
10) copied, copying

Day 2

a. A sentence expresses a complete thought and has two parts, the complete subject and the complete predicate.

Ex: Three boys / were playing basketball.
(complete subject) (complete predicate)

b. The **simple subject** of a sentence is the noun or pronoun that is the focal point of the complete subject without any modifiers. (adjectives)

Ex: Three boys / were playing basketball.
(*boys* is the simple subject)

c. The **simple predicate** of a sentence is the verb or verb phrase that tells the action of the subject without any modifiers. (adverbs) A verb phrase is the main verb and one or more helping verbs.

Ex: Five girls / played tennis.
(*played* is the simple predicate or verb)

Three boys / were playing basketball.
(*were playing* is the simple predicate or verb phrase)

d. Look at the last sentence of the literature passage. Divide the complete subject and complete predicate with a vertical line. Underline the simple subject and circle the simple predicate.

e. Often sentences contain more than one simple subject. A **compound subject** consists of two or more subjects. Look at the following sentence:

Sara and Anna had a wonderful time at the park.

This sentence has a compound subject since both *Sara* and *Anna* are part of the complete subject.

Sentences with more than one verb (or simple predicate) have a **compound verb**.

Ex: Joe went to the store and bought some milk.

Since both the verbs, *went* and *bought*, are telling what action was taken by the subject, *Joe*, the sentence has a compound verb.

f. Find a sentence in the literature passage that contains a compound verb. Double underline the compound verb.

g. Write one sentence with a compound subject and one with a compound verb.

h. Review your spelling words.

Day 3

a. A **conjunction** is a connecting word used to connect words, groups of words, or sentences.

Common Conjunctions					
and	but	or	nor	so	yet

Day 2

d. His veins | swelled to bursting.

f. The whip snarled and cracked.

Day 3

c. Icicles were forming on Sham's feelers, (yet) his body was wet with sweat.

He lowered his head, (and) as the whip struck him, he made a snatching pull.

The load moved, (and) as if by some supernatural power Sham kept on going up the incline.

Teacher's Note: The word *however* in the literature passage also connects a compound sentence, but it is a conjunctive adverb, not a coordinating conjunction. This will be taught in a higher level book.

b. When two complete sentences are joined together by a conjunction, it forms a **compound sentence**.

Ex: The two girls went on a picnic together, but they had to return before dark.

The conjunction *but* connects the two complete sentences:
The two girls went on a picnic together.
They had to return before dark.

c. Read over the literature passage. Find three compound sentences connected by conjunctions, and circle those conjunctions.

d. In compound sentences, a **comma** is always used before the coordinating conjunction. Find the commas that appear before the coordinating conjunctions in the three compound sentences.

e. Read the compound sentences from the literature passage as two separate sentences leaving out the conjunction. Now read them as the author wrote them. Which way do you like better?

f. Read the literature passage again. Tell your teacher in your own words what is happening. What information is not given? What words give you a clear picture of the scene? Write a paragraph to add to the passage, explaining what may have happened next to Sham. Use words that enable the reader to envision a clear picture of the events. Try to use compound sentences.

g. Practice writing your spelling words. Keep in mind the rules for adding suffixes as you practice your words.

h. Optional: Enrichment (SAB)

Day 4

a. The author of the literature passage makes good use of adjectives, adverbs, and descriptive verbs to create a word picture that helps you to not only see, but feel and hear what was happening. For example, instead of just saying *The whip struck him*, the author describes it as *The whip snarled and cracked.* Reread the literature passage and examine the author's use of descriptive language.

b. Today you are going to write a paragraph describing a strenuous activity. You could describe a sport you enjoy, or describe an active animal such as a cat stalking prey.

c. Begin by brainstorming about your ideas. Choose your subject, such as the cat. Use your *Student Activity Book* or, draw a circle and place your subject in the middle. Make lines extending outward from the circle. On these lines you will write your ideas. You are drawing a circle word picture. Record anything that comes to mind. You will use some of the ideas but not all of them. Write down any descriptive words you could use in your paragraph.

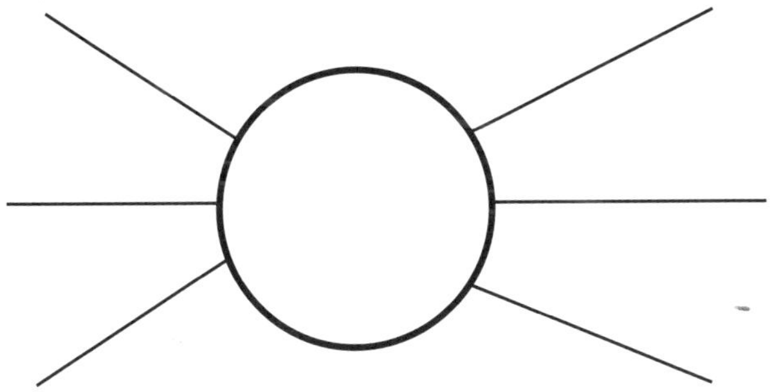

d. Beginning with a good topic sentence, take your ideas and form a good paragraph describing your subject. Create a word picture that will allow anyone who reads your paragraph to imagine he is observing or experiencing the activity.

e. Take an oral or written spelling pretest. Review words you found difficult to spell.

f. Optional: Enrichment

Day 5

a. Write the literature passage from dictation.

b. Continue to work on your descriptive paragraph from **4a-d**. Draw a picture illustrating the paragraph.

c. Take an oral or written spelling test.

d. Choose skills from the *Review Activities.*

Review Activities

Choose skills your student needs to review.

1. *Prefixes*
   Examine the words listed below that contain the prefix **fore-**. Guess the meaning of each word and then use your dictionary to check the definition. Does knowing the meaning of the prefix **fore-** help you in determining a word's meaning?

   a. foredoom
   b. forefather
   c. forecast

2. *Suffixes*
   Add the suffixes in parentheses to the following root words.

   a. plenty + (ful) =
   b. buy + (er) =
   c. hurry + (ing) =
   d. apply + (ed) =
   e. busy + (est) =

3. *Simple Subject and Verb*
   Underline the simple subject once and the verb twice in the following sentences.

   a. The tall plant waved in the breeze.
   b. The football player ran down the field for a touchdown.
   c. Mary can knit very quickly.
   d. The garden show will begin in ten minutes.
   e. The white flowers smell very sweet.

1.
a. foredoom: to condemn in advance
b. forefather: an ancestor, one who came earlier in a family line
c. forecast: to predict in advance

2.
a. plentiful
b. buyer
c. hurrying
d. applied
e. busiest

3.
a. The tall plant waved in the breeze.
b. The football player ran down the field for a touchdown.
c. Mary can knit very quickly.
d. The garden show will begin in ten minutes.
e. The white flowers smell very sweet.

4. *Conjunctions, Compound Subjects, Compound Predicates, and Compound Sentences*
Underline the conjunctions in the following sentences. On the line before each sentence, write if it contains a compound subject (**CS**), a compound verb (**CV**), or if it is a compound sentence (**CSent**). Also, add punctuation if the sentence is a compound sentence.

a. ______The daisies and marigolds made a lovely combination.
b. ______The *Nina*, *Pinta*, and *Santa Mari*a sailed to America.
c. ______We will walk to the park and catch the bus.
d. ______I will check with my mother but I do not think I will be able to go to the movie.
e. ______The children played games, ate lunch, and listened to a story.
f. ______We will go shopping at the mall or we can go to the shopping center.

5. *Adjectives*
In each sentence below, underline the adjectives.

a. We took a long walk through the beautiful magnolia trees.
b. The six geese glided across the blue lake.
c. The boys took three, big boxes of popcorn.
d. The book was scary at times.

4.
a. and, CS
b. and, CS
c. and, CV
d. I will check with my mother, but I do not think I will be able to go to the movie. CSent
e. and, CV
f. We will go shopping at the mall, or we can go to the shopping center. CSent

5.
a. long, beautiful
b. six, blue
c. three, big
d. scary

Assessment 1

(Lessons 1 - 9)

1. A simile is a form of figurative language. It compares two different things using the words **like** or **as**. Find the simile in the following sentence:

   The invaders struck like a lightning bolt.

2. Using the words **as** or **like**, write a simile.

3. Personification is a form of figurative language. It gives a thing or idea human characteristics. What is the personification used in the following sentence:

   The sun sighed as it set in the west.

4. Give an example of personification about the wind.

5. What is the prefix in the word **immobile**?

6. Write a word with the suffix **-ful**.

7. Write a word with the prefix **ex-**.

8. Tell your teacher what an adjective does.

9. Read the following poem and rewrite it in prose.

Who Has Seen the Wind?
by Christina Rossetti

Who has seen the wind?
Neither I nor you:
But when the leaves hang trembling
The wind is passing thro'.

Who has seen the wind?
Neither you nor I:
But when the trees bow down their heads
The wind is passing by.

10. Look at the literature passage in Lesson 5. What is the topic sentence?

1. like a lightning bolt (The two things being compared are *invaders* and *a lightning bolt.*)

2. Answers will vary.

3. The sun sighed.

4. Example: the wind whispered in my ear

5. a. im-

6. Possible answers: careful, joyful, etc.

7. Possible answers: example, exchange, etc.

8. Adjectives are words that describe nouns, the words which name persons, places, things, or ideas. Adjectives answer the following questions: Which one? What kind? How many? How much? Whose?

9. Possible answer: Has anyone seen the wind? You haven't; I haven't. But the wind makes the leaves move. Has anyone seen the wind? You haven't; I haven't. But the wind makes the trees bend.

10. For breakfast there were pancakes, and Ma made a pancake man for each one of the children.

11. Write the following phrases as contractions.

    a. he is
    b. they are
    c. we will

12. Rewrite the following holidays using correct capitalization.

    a. columbus day
    b. fourth of july
    c. new year's day

13. Use your thesaurus to find three synonyms for each of the following words.

    a. good
    b. say
    c. nice
    d. cold

14. Complete the following sentences by adding the correct ending to the adjectives.

    a. You are tall_ than he.
    b. Which of the three boys is the strong_?
    c. Bring me the long_ of the two ropes.
    d. I know which of the two children is the young_.
    e. Which of the four rooms is the warm_?

15. Give an example of an interrogative sentence. What puncuation would you use?

16. Rewrite the following imperative sentence with the subject (Sarah) understood but not stated.

    Sarah, put the dog out.

17. Write a word with the prefix **re-**.

18. Write a sentence with a compound subject.

19. Write a sentence with a compound verb.

20. Circle the conjunction in each of the following sentences.

    a. He ran down the beach and shouted for joy.
    b. We would like to come but cannot at this time.
    c. Sam or Sue could do the job.

11. **a. he's**
b. they're
c. we'll

12. **a. Columbus Day**
b. Fourth of July
c. New Year's Day

13. **Possible answers:**
a. kind, excellent, fair
b. speak, utter, declare
c. pleasant, delightful, fine
d. chilly, icy, shivering

14. **a. taller**
b. strongest
c. longer
d. younger
e. warmest

15. **Example:**
Where is the cat?
A question mark.

16. **Put the dog out.**

17. **Example:**
reread

18. **Example:**
Logan and Mary went to the park.

19. **Example:**
Olivia swam in the pool and dove from the diving board all day.

20. **a. and**
b. but
c. or

"At last the hole was cut, and I could push myself in. There was my father right below me, there on the wheel. The wheel was leaning against the side of the boat. With his last strength my father had climbed to the hub to be as close to me as possible while I sawed, to be within reach. I leaned in; I grabbed him under the arms; I lifted him out. I was small, but I was strong.

The Wheel on the School by Meindert DeJong. Used by permission, Harper and Row.

Day 1
a. This is a direct quotation.

c. gh is silent

Day 1

a. Look over the literature passage taking special notice of the punctuation. What do the quotation marks at the beginning and end of the passage tell you? Write the literature passage from dictation. Compare your copy to the model and correct any errors.

b. Make your own spelling list from any misspelled words in the dictation, or use the following list of suggested words.

climbed	strength	myself
possible	within	against

Write the spelling words, dividing them into syllables. Remember, each syllable has to contain a vowel.

c. It is important to be familiar with letters that are silent when they appear in certain letter combinations. Some words spell the long **/i/** sound with **igh** as in *light*. What letters are silent?

Spelling Tip
Some words spell the long /*i*/ sound with *igh* as in light.

Day 1
d. No

d. Copy the words and underline the **gh**. Say the words aloud as you write them. Do you ever hear a **/g/** sound?

1) freight	6) bright
2) light	7) sight
3) right	8) weight
4) might	9) might
5) height	10) twilight

e. Sometimes words can be tricky. In the first sentence, the word *hole* is used. How would the meaning change if the author had used the word *whole* instead? The words *hole* and *whole* are homonyms. **Homonyms** are words that sound the same, have different meanings, and are usually spelled differently.

Whole means entire, and *hole* means an opening. When writing, be careful to use the correct word.

Teacher's Note: Some grammar books refer to these words as homophones.

f. Listed below are five words from the literature passage that have corresponding homonyms. List the homonyms for each word. Be careful, some words have more than one homonym.

Ex: eight - ate

1) right	4) too
2) there	5) in
3) be	6) I

f. 1) write
2) their, they're
3) bee
4) to, two
5) inn
6) eye

g. Choose one set of homonyms and write a sentence using all the homonyms for that word in the sentence.

Ex: The *eight* of us *ate* supper at the deli.

Day 2

a. The person telling a story is called the **narrator**. The **point of view** is the angle from which the story is told. The point of view will depend upon who is telling the story, whether it is told from the point of view of one of the characters in the story or from the point of view of someone outside the story.

b. The **first person** point of view is when the story is told from the point of view of one of the story characters. One indication that a story is being told from the first person point of view is the use of the pronoun *I* in the telling of the story. Although the character is usually a person, the character telling the story could be an animal or even an object.

Ex: *I* was breathless with anticipation as the box was opened.

c. The **third person** point of view is used when the story is told from the point of view of someone outside the story. The use of the pronouns *he*, *she*, and *they* often indicate the use of third person.

Ex: *She* was breathless with anticipation as the box was opened.

d. Examine the literature passage. From what point of view is this story being told? Does the context of the passage let you know who the narrator is? Which words give you clues in identifying the narrator?

e. Examine some other stories and determine the point of view from which they are written.

f. Rewrite the literature passage into the third person point of view. Look over the two versions of the literature passage. Which version do you find more enjoyable to read? Why?

g. Review your spelling words.

Day 2

d. first person;
Yes, the son;
my father, myself, I

✎ Teacher's Note: **Often it is more enjoyable to read a story written from first person point of view because you feel more connected with the character in the story.**

f. Sample beginning:
"At last the hole was cut, and he could push himself in. There was his father right below him, there on the wheel...."

Day 3

a. Locate the three separate sentences joined together by semicolons (;) in the literature passage. The use of semicolons indicates that each part of the sentence is independent and could stand alone. An **independent clause** contains a complete thought which can stand alone as a sentence. **Semicolons** are used to join together independent clauses when they are not connected by a conjunction.

Ex: The wind blew through the trees; the leaves rustled.

Phrases that do not contain both subject and predicate are not independent. They are often listed together in a series with a conjunction joining the last phrase or item of the series. When three or more phrases or items are used together in a series, commas are used to separate the phrases or items, with a final comma used before the conjunction.

Ex: I will be driving to the store, shopping for some groceries, and coming home.
I love the peaches, plums, and nectarines that are ripe this time of year.

Find the three independent clauses in the literature passage that are joined by semicolons. Rewrite them into one good sentence containing phrases in a series. Some words will have to be omitted, but the meaning of the sentence should not change. Be sure to use commas to separate the phrases.

b. Having only one paragraph from an entire book restricts your information. However, there are certain things revealed in the literature passage. It can be determined there is a struggle taking place. Can you guess what is happening?

Teacher's Note: Some grammar books teach this skill by omitting the last comma before the conjunction.

Day 3

a. I leaned in, grabbed him under the arms, and lifted him out.

b. Allow your student to make any guess. The following is what actually took place: A son is rescuing his father who is trapped inside an overturned boat.

c. Possible answers: anxious, worried, hurried

The author succeeded in creating this mood by his dramatic description of each step of the rescue.

c. Reread the literature passage. Can you tell how the person telling the story feels? The emotion created by the author is called the **mood** of the story. A good author uses descriptions that draw the reader into the action happening in the story and allows the reader to share in the mood created. How would you describe the mood created in this paragraph? Discuss with your teacher how the author succeeded in creating this mood.

d. How would you feel if you were trying to rescue your father or a friend? Write a paragraph describing a tense situation. Use descriptions that create the mood you want and help the reader to feel what you feel.

e. Review your spelling words.

f. Optional: Enrichment (SAB)

Day 4

a. Every story has a plot. The **plot** is the sequence of events and actions that take place in the story. Every good plot contains five main elements:

Plot Line

1) **Opening**: This is the part of the story that introduces the characters, explains the background of the story, the setting, and the present situation.

2) **Rising Action**: This is a series of problems and struggles (the conflict) which are building toward a climax.

3) **Climax**: The climax is the turning point or action peak of the story. Usually this is the point at which the action and anticipation is at the fullest.

4) **Falling Action**: The point in the story at which the action of the turning point or high point is worked out and a solution is at hand.

5) **Conclusion**: The part of the story in which the solution comes to a conclusion and the problem is solved. This usually provides the story with its ending.

A graphic representation of the elements of the plot of a story is called a **plot line**. A plot line can help you envision the sequence of the elements and how they are put together to form the plot of a story.

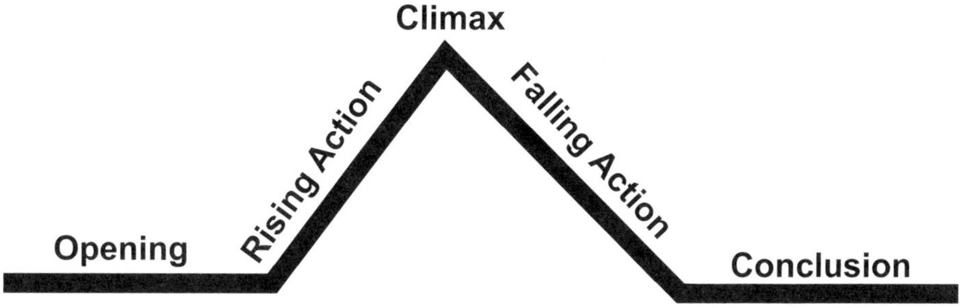

b. Which elements of the plot are present in the literature passage? Which sentence of the passage best describes the turning point or action peak?

c. Although the literature passage only supplies us with a small amount of information concerning the situation, it does allow us to speculate what problems might have occurred prior to the rescue. These problems would be considered part of the rising action of the story. Imagine what problems would lead up to the situation described in the literature passage. Write a paragraph or two describing events and problems that may have led up to the climax in the literature passage.

Read the paragraphs you have written with the literature passage. Does your version of the rising action supply a series of events that lead up to the climax?

d. Take an oral or written spelling pretest. Remember sounding out the syllables as you write them will help you spell them correctly.

e. Optional: Enrichment (SAB)

Day 4
b. Rising Action and Climax

I lifted him out.

Day 5

a. Write the literature passage from dictation.

b. Write a short story that contains the five elements of a plot. Map out your ideas on a plot line to make sure you have all the ingredients necessary for a effective plot.

c. Take an oral or written spelling test.

d. Choose skills from the *Review Activities*.

Review Activities

Choose skills your student needs to review.

1. *Homonyms*
   Choose the correct word in the parentheses to complete the sentence.

   a. (*There, Their*) will be a children's concert this evening.
   b. We will be going (*to, too*) the pottery class soon.
   c. I will (*right, write*) to my friend in Ireland.
   d. The (*be, bee*) kept buzzing around her head.
   e. The (*in, inn*) was already full because of the holiday.

2. *Narrator, Point of View, and Mood*
   Read the following paragraph. Who is the narrator? From what point of view is the story told? What mood has been created?

   > I surveyed all the land below me with a careful and calculated eye looking for the slightest possible movement. The rustle of a leaf, a shift of a blade of grass was all that was necessary to lead me to my prey. Suddenly, it happened! I detected movement! Quick as a flash I swooped from my treetop vantage point and clutched a small mouse in my talons.

3. *Commas*
   Add commas as necessary.

   a. On our summer vacation we will visit the seashore climb a mountain and ride a horse.
   b. I looked inside reached down and picked up the rabbit.
   c. For the party I need to buy balloons cake decorations and gifts.
   d. The bee buzzed flipped and dove around the flowers.
   e. My grandparents have visited England France and Spain.
   f. Bring your lunch a thermos and a blanket.

4. *Plot*
   What are the five main elements to a good plot?

1.
a. There
b. to
c. write
d. bee
e. inn

2.
Narrator: Hawk
Point of View: First Person
Mood: tense, anticipating

3.
a. On our summer vacation we will visit the seashore, climb a mountain, and ride a horse.
b. I looked inside, reached down, and picked up the rabbit.
c. For the party I need to buy balloons, cake decorations, and gifts.
d. The bee buzzed, flipped, and dove around the flowers.
e. My grandparents have visited England, France, and Spain.
f. Bring your lunch, a thermos, and a blanket.

4.
opening, rising action, climax, falling action, conclusion

Everybody laughed, but the teacher's eyes weren't pleased. "True, true," he said. "That's right, Eelka. We can't think much when we don't know much. But we can wonder! From now until tomorrow morning when you come to school again, will you do that? Will you wonder why and wonder why? Will you wonder why storks don't come to Shora to build their nests on the roofs, the way they do in all the villages around? For sometimes when we wonder, we can make things begin to happen."

The Wheel on the School by Meindert DeJong.
Used by permission, Harper and Row.

Day 1

a. Read the literature passage paying special attention to the punctuation marks. Write the passage from dictation. Proofread and correct your work.

b. The literature passage contains four contractions. Locate the contractions and circle them. List each of the contractions, and write the two words that make up each contraction next to it.

c. Find the word in the literature passage that is using an apostrophe (') to show possession and underline it. What is it showing possession of?

d. Make your own spelling list from any misspelled words in the dictation, or use the following list of suggested words:

tomorrow	villages	happen
wonder	around	morning

e. Look through the literature passage and find nouns that are plural (more than one). A noun is made plural by adding **s** or **es** to the word. The nouns in the literature passage have been made plural by adding just **s**.

Day 1

b. weren't - were not
that's - that is
can't - cannot
don't - do not

c. <u>teacher's</u> eyes - the eyes of the teacher

Spelling Tip

Most nouns form their plural form by just adding *s*. However, to form the plural of nouns ending in *sh*, *ch*, *x*, *s*, and *z*, add *es*.

In words that end in *y* preceded by a consonant, change the *y* to *i* and add *es*. If the word ends in *y* preceded by a vowel, then just add *s*.

Ex: beach - beaches wish - wishes box - boxes
glass - glasses waltz - waltzes puppy - puppies
ray - rays

f. Add **s** and **es** to your list of suffixes. Under parts of speech write *forms of plural nouns*. These suffixes have no meanings. Be sure to fill in some word examples.

g. Write each of the following nouns in its plural form.

1) cherry	6) dress
2) dish	7) perch
3) boy	8) daisy
4) fox	9) insect
5) rock	10) buzz

Day 2

a. As you learned in Lesson 10, every plot has at least one conflict or problem to be resolved. From reading the literature passage, can you identify the main conflict in *The Wheel on the School*?

b. Can you determine the mood of the teacher in the literature passage? What do you think the teacher was challenging the students to do?

Day 1

f. s, es: no meaning; forms plural nouns; Possible examples: pigs, beaches

g. 1) cherries
2) dishes
3) boys
4) foxes
5) rocks
6) dresses
7) perches
8) daisies
9) insects
10) buzzes

Day 2

a. The children try to find a way to get the storks to come back to Shora.

b. The mood of the teacher is serious, and he wants the students to be serious, too. The teacher is challenging the students to make a discovery and perhaps solve the problem.

c. Find the direct quotation in the literature passage.

The quotation is divided with the words *he said.* When the quotation is divided after a complete sentence, both parts of the quotation are completely enclosed by quotation marks.

Ex: "I love a rainy spring day," said Mary. "My mother can't wait until the flowers begin blooming."

If the quotation is divided within a sentence, then the second part of the quotation does not begin with a capital letter. This is called a **split quotation**.

Ex: "I need to finish my chores," answered Mark, "and then I will be able to join you."

d. Add capitalization and punctuation, including quotation marks, commas, question marks, exclamation points, and periods to the following direct quotations. (For information on punctuating direct quotations, refer to Lesson 7.)

1) I will finish my shopping said Jerri and meet you at the game
2) drive to the house slowly said Mary we don't want to arrive too early
3) when will the leaves begin to change color asked Jimmy
4) Marilyn smiled it is a wonderful feeling to know I have such good friend
5) stop playing and start working yelled Natalie with frustration we need to have the float finished by noon
6) spring is in the air. I see birds beginning to build their nests. a warm breeze is blowing from the south said Anne with a smile.

e. Read the literature passage carefully once again. What do you think possibly happened just before this scene? Use your imagination to write a paragraph describing what could have happened.

f. Review your spelling words.

Day 2

c. "True, true," he said. "That's right, Eelka. We can't...begin to happen."

d. 1) "I will finish my shopping," said Jerri, "and meet you at the game."
2) "Drive to the house slowly," said Mary. "We don't want to arrive too early."
3) "When will the leaves begin to change color?" asked Jimmy.
4) Marilyn smiled, "It is a wonderful feeling to know I have such a good friend."
5) "Stop playing and start working!" yelled Natalie with frustration. "We need to have the float finished by noon."
6) "Spring is in the air. I see birds beginning to build their nests. A warm breeze is blowing from the south," said Anne with a smile.

Day 3

a. **Declarative - Everybody laughed, but the teacher's eyes weren't pleased. "True, true," he said. That's right, Eelka. We can't think much when we don't know much. For sometimes when we wonder, we can make things begin to happen.**

Interrogative - From now until tomorrow morning when you come to school again, will you do that? Will you wonder why and wonder why? Will you wonder why storks don't come to Shora to build their nests on the roofs, the way they do in all the villages around?
Exclamatory: But we can wonder!

b. **From now until tomorrow morning when you come to school again, will you do that?**
Wonder from now until tomorrow morning when you come to school again.

Will you wonder why and wonder why?
Wonder why and wonder why.

Will you wonder why storks don't come to Shora to build their nests on the roofs, the way they do in all the villages around?
Wonder why storks don't come to Shora to build their nests on the roofs, the way they do in all the villages around.

Day 3

a. Sentences can ask a question (interrogative), make a statement (declarative), express strong feeling (exclamatory), or give a command (imperative). Find an example of an interrogative, declarative, and exclamatory sentence in the literature passage. Remember, the type of punctuation a sentence has can help you to identify it.

b. Find the three interrogative sentences in the literature passage again. Change these interrogative sentences into imperative sentences. Remember, the subject in an imperative sentence is often understood. Be sure to change the end punctuation.

Ex: Will you please close the door? (interrogative)
Please close the door. (imperative)

c. Look at the third sentence of the literature passage. In this sentence, Eelka is addressed by name. This is called a **direct address**. When a name is used in a direct address, set it off with **commas**. A pair of commas is used if the name appears within the sentence, but only one comma is necessary if the name appears at the beginning or end of the sentence.

Ex: Go to the kitchen, Nancy, and find my large platter.
Jack, please help me lift this box.
You do not have to come with me, Rick.

d. Punctuate the following sentences that use a direct address. Also, be sure to add the correct end punctuation.

1) Martha go see who is at the door
2) I really liked your part in the play William
3) The secret to success Lydia is to prepare for opportunity
4) Carol are you sure the meeting is today
5) Come here this minute Patrick

e. Review your spelling words.

f. Optional: Enrichment (SAB)

Day 4

a. Many important discoveries have been made or mysteries solved because someone was curious. Someone wondered, "What if? Why? How?" Think about how our lives have been enriched because someone wondered.

b. Eelka's teacher encouraged his students to think. One way to improve your thinking skills is to develop word analogies. A **word analogy** expresses a relationship between words. An analogy statement has two parts. In the first part of the statement two words are placed together that are in some way related, then in the second part of the analogy two different words are placed together that have a similar relationship.

Ex: eyes : sight :: ears : hearing

This word analogy would read: *Eyes are to sight as ears are to hearing.*

Day 3

d. 1) Martha, go see who is at the door.
2) I really liked your part in the play, William.
3) The secret to success, Lydia, is to prepare for opportunity.
4) Carol, are you sure the meeting is today?
5) Come here this minute, Patrick.

In the previous example the relationship is that as eyes provide the sense of sight; ears provide the sense of hearing. There are many different ways words can be related. Some of the relationships used in word analogies are:

antonyms good : bad :: happy : sad
synonyms yell : shout :: soaring : flying
part/whole fingers : hand :: toes : foot
characteristic leaves : green :: snow : white
function scissors : cut :: pencil : write
object/place car : garage :: furniture : house
representative/object teacher : student :: boss : employee
family mother : daughter :: father : son
grammar noun : adjective :: verb : adverb

Day 4
b. object to use

What type of relationship is used in our example analogy (eyes : sight :: ears : hearing)?

c. Fill in the second part of the word analogies listed below. First decide what the relationship of the first two words is and then apply that relationship to the second part of the word analogy to fill in the blank.

c. 1) pasture
2) mammal
3) sour
4) climbing
5) tree

1) fish : water :: cow:____________
2) ant : insect :: dog:____________
3) candy : sweet :: pickle: __________
4) beach : swimming :: mountain:__________
5) petals : flower :: leaves: _______________

d. Take an oral or written spelling pretest. Remember, sounding out the syllables as you write them will help you spell them correctly.

e. Optional: Enrichment (SAB)

Day 5

a. Write the literature passage from dictation. "Listen" for the punctuation as your teacher reads the paragraph.

b. Look at the paragraph below. Correct all errors in capitalization, punctuation, and other writing mechanics. When you are finished, compare to model and correct.

everybody laughed but the teachers eyes werent pleased. true true he said. thats right Eelka. we cant think much when we dont know much. but we can wonder. from now until tomorrow morning when you come to school again, will you do that. will you wonder why and wonder why. will you wonder why storks dont come to shora to build their nests on the roofs the way they do in all the villages around. for sometimes when we wonder, we can make things begin to happen.

c. What are some things that cause you to wonder? Name one thing and spend some time wondering about it. You can do this by thinking about it, talking about it, and/or looking up information about it.

d. Take an oral or written spelling test.

e. Choose skills from the *Review Activities*.

Day 5

b. See literature passage.

Review Activities

Choose skills your student needs to review.

1. *Plurals*
   Write the plural form of the following words.

   a. brush
   b. guess
   c. lily
   d. turkey
   e. ax

2. *Direct Quotations*
   Add quotation marks and punctuation to the following sentences.

   a. We will begin the canoe trip at this point announced Luke and then paddle downstream to the campgrounds
   b. Who is going to the concert asked Adam I will be leaving in an hour
   c. I do not know the answer to the problem said Anna Can you help me
   d. The soccer equipment is expensive at this store remarked Will
   e. Nicki shouted Catch the ball

3. *Direct Address*
   Add punctuation to the following sentences.

   a. Charlotte will you please open the door for me.
   b. I located the bird nest Kate in the old oak tree.
   c. Explain the bike safety rules to the club Lewis.

4. *Word Analogy*
   Fill in the word that correctly finishes the word analogy.

   a. black:white :: tall:_______
   b. run:sprint :: walk: _______
   c. uncle:nephew :: aunt:_______
   d. rabbit:hutch :: bird: _______
   e. ruler:measure :: spoon: _______

1.
a. brushes
b. guesses
c. lilies
d. turkeys
e. axes

2.
a. "We will begin the canoe trip at this point," announced Luke, "and then paddle downstream to the campgrounds."
b. "Who is going to the concert?" asked Adam. "I will be leaving in an hour."
c. "I do not know the answer to the problem," said Anna. "Can you help me?"
d. "The soccer equipment is expensive at this store," remarked Will.
e. Nicki shouted, "Catch the ball!"

3.
a. Charlotte, will you please open the door for me?
b. I located the bird nest, Kate, in the old oak tree.
c. Explain the bike safety rules to the club, Lewis.

4.
Possible answers:
a. short
b. stroll
c. niece
d. nest
e. stir

HOW TO CONDUCT

PERSONAL RESEARCH

Teacher's Note: The Personal Research unit continues in Lesson 13.

Day 1

a. In last week's lesson we discussed how our lives had been enriched by someone's curiosity. Many times curiosity naturally leads to research. Think of something that interests you. It could be something you desire to purchase: a pet, a bike, computer, or sports equipment. Perhaps you would even like to know which fast food chain offers the highest quality burger. For the next few days you will explore an enjoyable form of research written in the form of a story. Many times the purpose of research is extensive study of a topic with lots of library work. In your personal research story, however, you may use the library if you choose, but you will use a variety of resources as well.

b. First you must choose a topic. Imagine you are going to purchase a new bike. Think about possible questions to research. What is the purpose of the research? What information do you need to make a wise purchase? Where would you get the best price? Number and list your ideas.

Day 2

a. Decide the best way to gather the necessary information. If, for example, you choose to research the topic of bikes, planning a trip to several local bike shops would be a great starting point or find several sites online that specialize in bikes. Use the Internet to find bike shops that carry different brands. While visiting the shops, gather brochures and any other information they make available. Do a price comparison between bike shops. Prepare a standard list of questions to ask at each shop. Look at the following questions. Take notes and keep track of the information you gather.

1. Why do you carry this brand of bikes?
2. Tell me about the quality of your product.
3. Do your bikes have warranties?
4. What are your payment options? Could a purchase be made on layaway?
5. Do you ever have sales?

Day 3-5

a. Plan to interview several friends who own different brands of bikes. Make a list of questions for them. Use the rest of the week to thoroughly gather the following information.

1. Why did you choose this brand over another?
2. Have you enjoyed your bike?
3. Would you purchase this brand again?
4. Have you had any problems with your bike?

b. Optional: Enrichment

Day 1

a. Use a consumer report to read about different bikes. Check your library or online for a junior version of a standard consumer report.

b. Compare the prices you found in the bike shops to the prices in discount stores. Take notes.

Day 2-3

a. Check to see if you are satisfied with the information you gathered. If you are prepared to write your research story, follow the steps listed below in organizing your information.

Student Checklist

- ☐ 1) Make sure all your information is related to the topic you are writing about.
- ☐ 2) Make a list of the various ideas about your subject that you wish to write about.
- ☐ 3) Group your ideas into several main ideas and number these grouping as to the order in which you want them to appear in your paper.
- ☐ 4) Write an introductory paragraph for your research paper. This paragraph should explain the purpose of your research and give a brief summary of what your paper will be about.
- ☐ 5) Write your supporting paragraphs. Make sure that all the information presented supports the main topic presented in your introductory paragraph.
- ☐ 6) End your paper with a concluding paragraph that again summarizes your topic and ends with a closing sentence.

b. Spend two days compiling your research story. Since this is a research "story," it may be written informally and may include your own opinions and comments. Putting your story in a folder and adding sketches or pictures from brochures would add to the presentation of your research.

Day 4

a. Examine your research story. Was your research helpful in making a decision about your purchase? Would it be helpful to someone else making a similar choice?

b. After working hard to write your paper, you will want the final copy to be error-free. This requires that you read your paper several times, each time looking for specific errors. Follow these guidelines:

1) Underline any word you are not certain of the meaning. Check these words in a dictionary to make sure you are using the word correctly.

2) Using a thesaurus, replace words to avoid repetition and to add interest to your writing.

3) Review comma rules. Are you using commas correctly? Check for run-on sentences and separate or use a semi-colon.

4) Read your paper aloud. Do you use a variety of sentence types? Do you maintain an interesting rhythm by using a mixture of short and long sentences?

5) Check your verbs.

   Subject-verb agreement: for example, plural subjects need plural verbs.

   Verb tense consistency: do not shift from one tense to another if there is no change in the time frame.

6) Final reading for grammar and spelling errors. Most computer programs are capable of proofreading your work. Take advantage of this feature.

Day 5

a. Look over your research story once more. Make a final, neat copy for your teacher.

b. Opional: Enrichment

Notes

BOOK STUDY

on

The Bronze Bow

The Bronze Bow by
Elizabeth George Speare
Published by Houghton Mifflin

Readability level: 6th grade

Teacher's note:
This summary is intended for the teacher's use.

Introducing
The Bronze Bow

Elizabeth George Speare began writing after spending most of her years being a wife, mother, and teacher. Her first novel, *Calico Captive*, was based on the actual captivity of Susanna Johnson. It was recognized by the Children's Services Division of the American Library Association as a Notable Book in 1957. The following year, her second book, *The Witch of Blackbird Pond*, won the ALA's Newbery Medal as the most distinguished contribution to American literature for boys and girls. In 1961, she was once again honored with this award for *The Bronze Bow.*

Summary

Young Daniel Bar Jamin is driven by one passion: his hatred for the Romans who occupy his homeland. This hatred has grown steadily since the Romans executed his father and uncle and brought about the early death of his mother. His happy home life shattered, Daniel is apprenticed to a harsh master to train to be a blacksmith. He finally runs away to the mountains outside his village, leaving behind his elderly grandmother and deeply troubled younger sister, Leah.

On the mountain, Daniel is befriended by the outlaw, Rosh, who styles himself as a commander amassing a band of men who will one day overthrow the Romans. Daniel eagerly joins them until one day he meets Joel and his sister Malthace, twins who have come up on the mountain for a picnic. This meeting opens up a whole new world for Daniel. He realizes his longing for a home and friends. When his grandmother dies, Daniel must come down off the mountain and take care of his sister, Leah, who has never left the house since her father's death. She has lived in a world tormented by fear. Before Daniel can help his sister conquer her fears, he must first conquer the bitterness and hatred that controls him.

As Daniel enters into the world once again, he has several encounters with a Rabbi whose teaching is very hard for Daniel to understand. He speaks of liberty for the oppressed but doesn't call for the picking up of arms. Is he a Zealot? Is he the one they have been waiting for? The one who will lead them to freedom? In the end, Jesus gives Daniel the key that sets him free.

Vocabulary

Read the word in context. What do you think the word means? Look up the word in the dictionary, write a clear, simple definition, and use it in a sentence.

1. deliberately
   The teacher **deliberately** put him at a disadvantage with every question.

2. lumbering
   Her **lumbering** pace made everyone late for the party.

3. chagrined
   Chagrined, Daniel was made to go to the back of the line.

4. artisans
   The skilled **artisans** proudly displayed their beautiful creations.

5. derision
   He was embarrassed when his suggestion was greeted with **derision**.

6. glistened
   Her eyes **glistened** with unshed tears.

7. burly
   He felt secure as long as he was surrounded by his two **burly** bodyguards.

8. singed
   Escaping the fire, not a hair on her head was **singed**.

9. makeshift
   They attempted to mend their boat with **makeshift** tools.

10. disdain
   The queen looked with **disdain** at the lowly peasant.

1.deliberately - intentionally
2. lumbering - clumsy
3. chagrined - embarrassed
4. artisans - skilled craftsmen
5. derision - ridicule
6. glistened - sparkled
7. burly - sturdy
8. singed - slightly burned
9. makeshift - temporary substitute
10. disdain - despise

11. furtive - secret
12. pilfered - stolen
13. mottled - spotted
14. stupefied - stunned
15. coax gently persuade

11. furtive
Stealing a **furtive** look at the girl, he discovered that she was looking directly at him.

12. pilfered
All of the food had been **pilfered** from his neighbor's garden.

13. mottled
Fury **mottled** the man's face.

14. stupified
His opponent stole the ball, leaving him standing **stupified** on the court.

15. coax
He tried to **coax** the old woman to take a sip of the soup.

Discussion Questions

1. The conflict of a story is the problem that triggers the action. There are five basic types of conflict:

   1) **Man versus Man** - problems between characters in the story
   2) **Man versus Society** - problems with society
   3) **Man versus Himself** - problems with himself
   4) **Man versus Nature** - problems with natural happenings in nature
   5) **Man versus Fate (God)** - problems with strange or unbelievable coincidences

   What is the type of conflict in *The Bronze Bow*?

2. The **theme** of a story is the statement about life which the writer is trying to get across to the reader. It is sometimes called "the **moral** of the story." What would you say the theme is of *The Bronze Bow*?

3. What character do you most identify with in the book? Why?

Discussion Answers:

1. While *The Bronze Bow* does show conflict between man and man, conflict between man and society, and perhaps even conflict between man and fate, the main conflict in the story takes place within Daniel himself.

2. Love is stronger than hate.
Love your enemy.
Perfect love casts out fear.

3. Answers will vary.

4. In approaching the Roman soldier, Daniel was actually following Jesus in a truer sense than if he had physically walked after him. His gratitude to Jesus caused the hate to leave his heart and caused him to reach out to his enemy.

4. At the end of the story Daniel doesn't follow Jesus but walks across the street to the Roman soldier. In what way does this show how Daniel has changed?

5. Discuss with your teacher the meaning of the words *traitor*, *rebel*, and *patriot*. Could one person be viewed by different people as each one of these? Was Rosh a rebel or a patriot?

6. *"It's just that I don't want to face Jesus with a lie. I couldn't bear the way his eyes would look at me."*

   "If he understood the reason he wouldn't blame you."

   "Yes, I think he would," she said thoughtfully. "I think that for Jesus a lie is impossible, no matter what the reason."

   "In war a lie is a weapon," said Daniel. "We have to use what weapons we have. Even Jesus must see that."

   What do you think Jesus would think about Daniel's conclusion about lying?

7. *"Rosh is no bandit," he said. "When he robs it is for a good purpose."*

   "So, I've heard. Rob the rich to feed the poor. I'll be glad to see the poor that gets one penny of what he took last night."

   "There may be more important needs," said Daniel.

   Is there ever a good reason for stealing? Would it make a difference if the poor did receive what Rosh's band had stolen?

8. Who did Daniel think was his enemy? Who did Jesus say was Daniel's enemy? Why?

9. Discuss Daniel's reaction to discovering Marcus had been visiting his sister? Do you think he was justified? Can you understand why he felt the way he did? What reaction did it cause in Leah?

5. traitor - one who betrays his country by violating his allegiance
rebel - one who refuses allegiance to, resists, or rises in arms against the established or rightful government or ruler
patriot - one who loves his country zealously, supporting and defending it
Depending upon the viewpoint of the people making the judgment, a person could be perceived as all three of these at the same time by three different people.
Rosh was viewed as a rebel by the Romans and as a patriot by most of his countrymen.

6. discussion

7. discussion

8. Daniel thought the Romans were his enemies because they had destroyed his family and ruined his sister's life.
Jesus told him that hate was his enemy. He told him that hate is never satisfied and will destroy the person harboring it.

9. discussion

10. Daniel and Leah have both experienced healing. They have both been set free: Daniel from hate; and Leah from fear. This does not change the fact that their nation is under Roman rule and their lives will still be physically very hard, but they both can now continue on with their lives. Daniel will probably marry Malthace.

10. As the story ends, both Daniel and Leah have greatly changed. In what ways do you think their lives will be different now? In what ways will things still be the same?

Activities

The following activities are intended to help you explore Daniel's world and better understand his experience. Choose one or two activities to complete your study.

1. Stories can be set in many different places and times. Read about the world at the time Daniel lived. You may use your history book, an encyclopedia, or books from the library that will give you a picture of the times.

2. The setting of this story is Galilee at the time of Christ. Find a map of the area and locate the places mentioned in the story such as Capernaum, Tiberias, Jerusalem, etc.

3. Whenever an author chooses to write a fictional work that includes Jesus, he must treat the subject carefully. Do you think Mrs. Speare's portrayal of Jesus accurate to His character? Use passages from the book to support your argument.

4. Daniel was trained as a blacksmith. Research this skill. Are there still blacksmiths today?

5. In chapter 15, the author recounts the story of Jairus and his daughter. Read the account as recorded in Scripture (Luke 8:40-56). Do they agree? What information did the author add?

6. What do you think it was like to be a Roman soldier during this time? Research and write a short report.

7. One of the most compelling characters in the book is Samson. Although not much is told of him, his example of loyalty to Daniel is very moving. Using information provided, and filling in the missing details using your imagination, write a story around Samson.

8. Read *Calico Captive* or *The Witch of Blackbird Pond.*

I **C.A.N.** Assessment

The Bronze Bow Book Study B

After the *Carry On, Mr. Bowditch* Book Study is completed check off each I **C.A.N**. objective with your teacher.

_____	**C**	I can **complete** my work.
_____		I can be **creative**.
_____	**A**	I can be **accurate**.
_____		I can do my work with a good **attitude**.
_____	**N**	I can do my work **neatly**.

Jest 'Fore Christmas

by Eugene Field

Father calls me William, sister calls me Will,
Mother calls me Willie, but the fellers call me Bill!
Mighty glad I ain't a girl ruther be a boy,
Without them sashes, curls, an' things that's worn by Fauntleroy!
Love to chawnk green apples an' go swimmin' in the lake
Hate to take the castor-ile they give for belly-ache!
'Most all the time, the whole year round, there ain't no flies on me,
But jest 'fore Christmas I'm as good as I kin be!

Got a yeller dog named Sport, sic him on the cat;
First thing she knows she doesn't know where she is at!
Got a clipper sled, an' when us kids goes out to slide,
'Long comes the grocery cart, an' we all hook a ride!
But sometimes when the grocery man is worrited an' cross,
He reaches at us with his whip, an' larrups up his hoss,
An' then I laff an' holler, "Oh, ye never teched me!"
But jest 'fore Christmas I'm as good as I kin be!

Gran'ma says she hopes that when I git to be a man,
I'll be a missionarer like her oldest brother, Dan,
As was et up by the cannibuls that lives in Ceylon's Isle,

Where every prospeck pleases, an' only
man is vile!
But Gran'ma she has never been to see
a Wild West show,
Nor read the "Life of Daniel Boone," or else
I guess she'd know
That Buff'lo Bill an' cowboys is good
enough for me!
Excep' jest 'fore Christmas, when I'm
good as I kin be!

And then old Sport he hangs around,
so solemn-like an' still,
His eyes they keep a-saying': "What's
the matter, little Bill?"
The old cat sneaks down off her perch
an' wonders what's become
Of them two enemies of hern that used
to make things hum!
But I am so perlite an' 'tend so
earnestly to biz,
That Mother says to Father: "How
improved our Willie is!"
But Father, havin' been a boy hisself,
suspicions me
When, jest 'fore Christmas, I'm as
good as I kin be!

For Christmas, with its lots an' lots of
candies, cakes, an' toys,
Was made, they say, for proper kids,
an' not for naughty boys;
So wash yer face an' bresh yer hair, an'
mind yer p's and q's,
An' don't bust out yer pantaloons, and
don't wear out yer shoes;
Say "Yessum" to the ladies, an' "Yessur"
to the men,
An' when they's company, don't pass
yer plate for pie again;
But, thinkin' of the things yer'd like to
see upon that tree,
Jest 'fore Christmas be as good as yer
kin be!

Day 1

a. fellers, mighty glad, ain't, ruther, an', chawnk, swimmin', castor-ile jest, 'fore, kin

c. But jest 'fore Christmas I'm as good as I kin be!

Repetition gives the poem continuity and rhythm.

d. 1) before
2) can
3) and
4) laugh
5) polite
6) prospect
7) himself
8) just
9) thinking
10) worried
11) castor-oil
12) am not, are not

Day 1

a. Listen as your teacher reads the bolded section of the poem. Does the pronunciation of the words used in the poem sound different than the way you speak? Sometimes an author will use pronunciation peculiar to a certain region, called **dialect**, to express himself. This is an effective way to make his character seem true to life. What are some examples of regional dialect in the first stanza of this poem? Try reading the first two stanzas of the poem aloud.

b. Look over the poem. Note that the first word of every line of the poem is capitalized. Often in poetry the first word of every line is capitalized even when the word does not begin a sentence.

c. Find the phrase in the poem that is repeated in each stanza. The technique of repeating a phrase or word in a poem for emphasis or for rhythm is called **repetition**. What effect does the use of repetition have in this poem?

d. Look over your list of dialect words and pronounce them the way they are spelled. Sometimes words are purposely misspelled to allow for dialect pronunciation.

Listed below are some of the words in the literature passage which are misspelled for this purpose. Find the words in the literature passage, and use context clues to decide what the correct word for the dialect word would be. Opposite each of the words write the proper spelling.

Ex: ruther - rather

1) 'fore	7) hisself
2) kin	8) jest
3) an'	9) thinkin'
4) laff	10) worrited
5) perlite	11) castor-ile
6) prospeck	12) ain't

Day 2

a. Read the entire poem today.

b. Rewrite the first two stanzas in standard English. Read each version aloud. Which do you like better? Can you see how effective the use of dialect can be?

c. Look over the poem again. Circle any words that are capitalized other than at the beginning of a line poetry and the pronoun *I*. In Lesson 6 you learned that words were capitalized for two main reasons:

1) to indicate the beginning of a sentence
2) to help the reader quickly identify proper names and titles

Which of the reasons listed is the reason for the capitalization of the words you circled? Note that Christmas, the name of a holiday, is considered a proper name. The entire name of holidays are always capitalized.

Ex:	Fourth of July	Mother's Day
	Thanksgiving Day	Labor Day

d. Find the capitalized words that also indicate a family relationship. When a family relationship word is used in place of a name or in front of a person's name, the word is capitalized. However, when the word is not used to replace a name or is used with a personal pronoun such as *my*, *our*, or *her*, then the word is not capitalized.

Ex: Grandpa Joe came for a visit.
Grandpa came for a visit.
My grandpa came for a visit.

e. Correct any errors in capitalization in the following sentences as needed.

1) My Mother said I could go when I am finished.
2) Where is your Father going?
3) Aunt mary and uncle ralph will be visiting this week.
4) When will Grandma be arriving?
5) It will be wonderful to have all the Aunts and Uncles visit for christmas.

Day 2

b. Father calls me William, sister calls me Will, Mother calls me Willie, but the other boys call me Bill! I'm very glad I'm not a girl, I would rather be a boy, (continue)

c. William (2)
Will (2)
Willie (2)
Bill (2)
Fauntleroy (2)
Christmas (2)
Sport (2)
Oh (1)
Dan (2)
Ceylon's Isle (2)
Gran'ma (2)
Wild West (2)
Life of Daniel Boone (2)
Buff'lo Bill (2)
Sport (2)
What's (1)
Mother (2)
Father (2)
How (1)
Yessum (2)
Yessur (2)

d. Father, Mother, Gran'ma

Teacher's Note:
The word *sister* should also be capitalized but the author chose not to do so.

e. 1) My *mother* said I could go when I am finished.
2) Where is your *father* going?
3) Aunt Mary and *Uncle Ralph* will be visiting this week.
4) No change.
5) It will be wonderful to have all the *aunts* and *uncles* visit for *Christmas*.

Day 3
a. Yes

b. Where the Boats Go - abab
Autumn Fires - abcb

Day 3

a. Poetry that rhymes usually follows a certain pattern called a **rhyme scheme**. In order to identify the rhyme scheme, assign a letter to each line that rhymes. For example, the rhyme scheme for the first stanza of "Jest 'Fore Christmas" is **aabbccdd**, because the last word in the first two lines rhyme (**aa**), the last word in the next two lines is a new rhyme (**bb**), and so on. Does the second stanza follow the same rhyme scheme?

b. Read the following poetry selections by Robert Louis Stevenson. Assign a letter to each line that rhymes and identify the rhyme schemes of the stanzas of the poems.

(from) Where The Boats Go

Dark brown is the river,
Golden is the sand.
It flows along forever,
With trees on either hand.

(from) Autumn Fires

Sing a song of seasons!
Something bright in all!
Flowers in the summer,
Fires in the fall!

c. The poems you have been reading have only end rhyme. Other poems contain rhyme words within a line of poetry to create **internal rhyme.**

Ex: Jack *Sprat* could eat no *fat*.

Note that the words *Sprat* and *fat* rhyme within the same line of the poem creating an internal rhyme.

d. Read the selections below, find the internal rhymes, and underline them. Remember, in order for a poem to have internal rhyme the words that rhyme must be within one line of the poem.

Whisky Frisky
author unknown

Whisky Frisky,
Hippity-hop
Up he goes
To the treetop!

Whirly, twirly,
Round and round,
Down he scampers
To the ground.

Intery, Mintery, Cutery Corn
Mother Goose Rhyme

Intery, mintery, cutery corn,
Apple seed and apple thorn
Wire, brier, limber-lock,
Three geese in a flock;
One flew east, and one flew west,
And one flew over the cockoo's nest.

e. Write the end rhyme schemes for "Whisky Frisky" and "Intery, Mintery, Cutery Corn." Do you like the effect created when the poet combines end rhyme and internal rhyme?

Day 3

d. whisky, frisky;
whirly, twirly;

intery, mintery, cutery;
wire, brier

e. "Whisky Frisky" - abcb
"Intery, Mintery, Cutery Corn" - aabbcc

Day 4

a. Another device used in poetry is the repetition of beginning consonant sounds within a poem. This is called **alliteration**.

Ex: **D**iddle, **d**iddle, **d**umpling, my son John,

The consonant **d** is repeated in this example of alliteration. When alliteration is used often throughout the poem, it has a tongue-twisting effect. Read the following example:

Peter Piper

Peter Piper picked a peck of pickled peppers;
A peck of pickled peppers Peter Piper picked.
If Peter Piper picked a peck of pickled peppers,
Where's the peck of pickled peppers Peter Piper picked?

b. "Jest 'Fore Christmas" is about a rather naughty boy. Can you imagine him with a very good little sister? Using the poem below as a model, write another poem from the sister's point of view.

Father calls me Millicent, brother calls me Mills,
Mother calls me Milly, and dresses me in frills!
Mighty glad I'm not a boy, glad to be a girl,
Wouldn't touch a frog or toad for anything in the world!
Love to dress up pretty and have tea parties in the lane,
Hate to be a bother, or cause anyone the slightest pain.

c. Using the example poem in **4b**, complete the last two lines. Remember to follow the rhyme scheme and to use Mr. Field's poem as your model. After you have completed your poem read the original version and the poem from the sister's point of view. Which version do you like better?

d. The literature passage poem is fun to memorize and recite. Try to memorize just the first stanza of the poem. Follow these tips when reciting poetry or any oral presentation.

Tips on Poetry Recitation

1) Read the poem aloud several times. Try to understand the meaning and the mood of the poem.

2) Use your voice where emphasis is needed and pause accordingly.

3) Speak clearly and loudly.

4) Look at your audience as if you are speaking directly to them.

5) Stand straight; do not slouch.

Day 5

a. Continue rewriting the other stanzas of the poem from the sister's point of view.

b. Examine a book of poetry. Try to find examples of poems with internal rhyme and alliteration. Write the rhyme scheme for some of the poems with end rhyme.

c. Decide what rhyme scheme you like best and write an original poem that uses that rhyme scheme.

d. Choose skills from the *Review Activities*.

Review Activities

Choose skills your student needs to review.

1. *Poetry*
Read the following poem. What is the rhyme scheme? Identify the following elements: **alliteration**, **internal rhyme**, **end rhyme**, and **repetition**.

Roaring, rippling river races toward the sea.
Swirling, twirling waters laugh with joyful glee.
Listen to the waters, listen to them sing.

Whipping, whirling waves crashing on the shore.
Reeling, keeling ocean groans and moans its lore.
Listen to the waters, listen to them sing.

2. *Capitalization of Holidays*
Capitalize the names of the following holidays.

a. independence day
b. fourth of july
c. memorial day
d. thanksgiving day

3. *Dialect*
Identify the words and expressions in the following paragraph that indicate a regional dialect.

She ain't a purty horse, like sum are, but she shure is a strong one. Then again, them brown eyes of hers have a way of lookin' at ya that let ya know she's a smart one too.

4. *Edits*
Rewrite the above paragraph using correct spelling and grammar.

1.
rhyme scheme - aab

alliteration - roaring, rippling river races; whipping, whirling waves

internal rhyme - swirling, twirling; reeling, keeling; groans, moans

end rhyme - sea, glee; shore, lore

repetition - Listen to the waters, listen to them sing

2.
a. Independence Day
b. Fourth of July
c. Memorial Day
d. Thanksgiving Day

3.
ain't, purty, sum, shure, them, lookin', ya

4.
Example:
b. She isn't a pretty horse, like some horses, but she is strong. When she looks at you with her brown eyes, you know she is smart too.

At this moment the cocks crowed a sort of reproachful farewell to us; we had forgotten them. I immediately proposed to take our poultry with us: geese, ducks, fowls, and pigeons. For, as I observed to my wife, if we could not feed them, they would, at any rate, feed us. We placed our ten hens and two cocks in a covered tub. The rest we set at liberty, hoping the geese and ducks might reach the shore by water, and the pigeons by flight.

We waited a little for my wife, who came loaded with a large bag, which she threw into the tub that contained her youngest son. I concluded it was intended to steady him, or for a seat, and made no observation on it. Here follows the order of our embarkation. In the first division, sat the tender mother, the faithful and pious wife. In the second our amiable little Francis, six years old, and of a sweet disposition.

The Swiss Family Robinson by Johann Wyss.

Day 1

a. Read the literature passage. Write the bolded portion of the passage from dictation. Proofread your copy. Make any necessary corrections.

b. Find the word in the second sentence that contains the prefix **pro-**. The prefix **pro**- means *forward* or *in favor of.* Add this prefix to your prefix list along with the definition and word examples.

c. Make your own spelling list from any misspelled words in the dictation, or use the following list of suggested words.

reproachful	proposed	pigeons	observation
embarkation	pious	amiable	disposition

d. The word *wife* is a singular noun ending in **fe**. In order to make it plural change the **f** to **v** and add **es** because the /**f**/ sound in *wife* changes to a /**v**/ sound in *wives*.

To determine if the **f** or **fe** should be changed to **v** in order to form a plural, say the plural of the noun. If you hear a /**v**/ sound, then make the change; if you do not hear a /**v**/ sound, then just add **s**.

Ex: reef – reefs

Spelling Tip

When forming the plural of a word ending in *f* or *fe*, change the *f* or *fe* to *v* and add *es*. If the */f/* sound remains, just add *s*.

Day 1
d. 1) wives 5) selves
2) leaves 6) roofs
3) lives 7) chiefs
4) calves 8) wolves

Write the plural form of the following nouns.

1) wife	5) self
2) leaf	6) roof
3) life	7) chief
4) calf	8) wolf

Day 2

a. us (1); we (1); them (3); I (1); our (1); us (1); I (1); my (1); we (1); them (3); they (3); us (1); We (1); our (1); we (1); We (1); my (1); she (3); her (1); I (1); it (3); him (3); it (3); our (1); our (1)

Note: *Who, which,* and *that* are also pronouns but are classified separately from personal pronouns.

Day 2

a. Look over the literature passage and list the pronouns. Remember, pronouns are words that take the place of nouns. Refer to the Personal Pronoun Chart in Lesson 4 if you need help.

b. Personal pronouns may also be classified into persons; either **first**, **second**, or **third persons**.

Personal Pronouns			
First Person (The one speaking)	I we	my, mine our, ours	me us
Second Person (The one being spoken to)	you	you, yours	
Third Person (The one being spoken about)	he she it they	his her, hers its their, theirs	him her them

A **first person pronoun** is the one speaking.
Ex: I took the bus to town.
I is used as a first person pronoun.

A **second person pronoun** is the one being spoken to.
Ex: You come with me immediately!
You is used as a second person pronoun.

A **third person pronoun** is the one being spoken about.
Ex: Frequently, Bill visits his grandmother.
His is used as a third person pronoun. Bill is not the person speaking or being spoken to, but he is being spoken about.

c. Once again look at your list of personal pronouns from the literature passage. Indicate if they are first, second, or third person pronouns by writing 1, 2, or 3 by them.

d. You learned in Lesson 10 that a story is told from a first person point of view (when one of the characters of the story narrates the story from his point of view) or third person point of view (when someone from outside the story is narrating). Read over the literature passage and decide from what point of view this story is being told. The pronouns used can help you to identify the correct point of view.

Day 2
d. first person point of view

e. Review your spelling words.

f. Optional: Enrichment (SAB)

Day 3

a. Look at the first paragraph of the literature passage and underline all the plural nouns. Note that most plurals are formed by adding **s** or **es**. However, some nouns form plurals by changing the spelling of the word. These are called **irregular nouns**.

Ex: man – men

Locate the word in your list of plural nouns that follows this rule.

b. Look over the spelling rules for forming plurals.

c. Using these *Spelling Tips*, write the correct plural form for the following nouns.

1) shelf	6) woman
2) monkey	7) loaf
3) goose	8) mass
4) box	9) baby
5) sock	10) company

Spelling Tips for Plurals

1) To form the plural of most words just add **s**.
2) To form the plural of nouns ending in **ch**, **s**, **sh**, **x**, or **z** add **es**.
3) To form the plural of a noun ending in **y** preceded by a consonant, change the **y** to **i** and add **es**.
4) To form the plural of most words ending in **f** or **fe**, change the **f** to **v** and add **es**. If the plural word keeps the **/f/** sound, just add **s**.
5) Some words change their spelling to form the plural form.

Day 3

a. cocks, geese, ducks, fowls, pigeons, hens, cocks, geese, ducks, pigeons

c. 1) shelves
2) monkeys
3) geese
4) boxes
5) socks
6) women
7) loaves
8) masses
9) babies
10) companies

d. Make a list of the plural nouns in the following paragraph from *The Swiss Family Robinson.*

Supper was now ready. A tablecloth was laid over the butter-cask, and spread with the plates and spoons from the ship. The ham was in the middle, and the omelet and cheese at each end; and we made a good meal, surrounded by our subjects – the dogs, the fowls, the pigeons, the sheep, and the goats, waiting for our notice. The geese and ducks were more independent, remaining in their marsh, where they lived in plenty on the small crabs which abounded there.

e. Write the singular form of each of the plural nouns on your list.

f. Find the word *subjects* in the above literature passage. This word contains the prefix **sub-** which means *under.* Add this prefix to your prefix list along with its definition and some word examples.

g. Review your spelling words.

Day 4

a. Find the word **sat** in the literature passage. The verb **sit** means *to rest or be seated.* It is often confused with the word **set** which means *to place something.* When using the verb **set**, an object should be named that is being placed; the verb **sit** has no object.

Ex: Please sit in this seat.
Jim set his game on the table. (game is the object being placed)

b. Complete the following sentences with the correct form of sit or set.

1) Will you __________ with me during the concert?
2) ___________ your purse down and stay for a visit.
3) My dad always __________ in that chair.
4) Joanna likes to ___________ on the beach.
5) Would you _______ the package on the chair?

Day 3

d. plates, spoons, subjects, dogs, fowls, pigeons, sheep, goats, geese, ducks, crabs

e. plate, spoon, subject, dog, fowl, pigeon, sheep, goat, goose, duck, crab

Day 4

b. 1) sit
2) Set
3) sits
4) sit
5) set

c. Some other troublesome words are **to, too, two**. These words are homonyms, words with the same sound but different meanings. Again, being familiar with the meaning of each word will help you choose the correct word.

to – to move toward or in the direction of
We will be going *to* the park this afternoon.

too – also
He is on the team, *too*.

two – a number
I need to buy *two* apples.

Day 4
d. 1) too
2) to
3) two
4) two
5) too

d. Choose the correct word:

1) Do you want to see the movie (to, too).
2) What friend do you want (too, to) visit?
3) Do the (two, too) of you want to come along for the ride?
4) I have an appointment for (two, to) o'clock.
5) I would like a piece of pie (to, too).

e. Take an oral or written spelling pretest. Review any words you found difficult to spell.

f. Optional: Enrichment (SAB)

Day 5

a. Write the literature passage from dictation.

b. Imagine what it would be like to be shipwrecked with your family on an isolated, uninhabited island. Write a few paragraphs telling how you would feel and how you would prepare for living there.

c. Take an oral or written spelling test.

d. Choose skills from the *Review Activities*.

Review Activities

Choose skills your student needs to review.

1. *Prefixes*
   Add the prefix **pro**- to each of the following roots. If you are unsure of the meaning of the new word, look it up in the dictionary.
   a. ______jector
   b. ______tect
   c. ______pel

2. *Personal Pronouns and Point of View*
   Rewrite the following paragraph by substituting personal pronouns for the underlined words. Write 1 (*first person*), 2 (*second person*), or 3 (*third person*) above each pronoun to indicate which person the pronoun is. Also, tell from what point of view this story is being told.

   Marcy loved visiting Marcy's cousin, Jeanette at Jeanette's farm. Mary and Jeanette would wake up early in the morning because Jeanette needed to feed all Jeanette's animals. Jeanette had chickens, goats, pigs, and cows. However, Marcy's favorite animals were the horses. Jeanette had two horses named Thunder and Whisper. As soon as the chores were done, Marcy and Jeanette would ride for hours through the woods and pastures. Marcy and Jeanette had such fun together!

3. *Plurals*
   Circle the correct plural form in each of the following sentences.
   a. Many people dressed as (*elfs, elves*) at the party.
   b. We drove through many (*valleys, vallies*) on our trip.
   c. The meadow was full of (*daisys, daisies*).
   d. All the (*dishs, dishes*) must be washed before you can leave.
   e. We must finish putting the garden (*tools, tooles*) away before it starts raining.

1.
a. projector
b. protect
c. propel

2.
Marcy loved visiting her[3] cousin, Jeanette, at her[3] farm. They[3] would wake up early in the morning because Jeanette needed to feed all her[3] animals. She[3] had chickens, goats, pigs, and cows. However, Marcy's favorite animals were the horses. Jeanette had two horses named Thunder and Whisper. As soon as the chores were done, they[3] would ride for hours through the woods and pastures. They[3] had such fun together!

Point of view - third person

3.
a. elves
b. valleys
c. daisies
d. dishes
e. tools

4.
a) set
b) sit
c) set
d) sit
e) set

5.
a. to
b. too
c. two

6.
For example:
first person - I, me, my, we, us, our
second person - you, your
third person - he, his, him, she, hers, her, it, them, they

4. *Sit/Set*
   Choose the correct form of *sit* or *set* in the following sentences:

   a. She will (*sit, set*) the plant down on the table.
   b. We will (*sit, set*) here for lunch.
   c. Please (*sit, set*) the box down carefully.
   d. Jim likes to (*sit, set*) by the window.
   e. Did you (*sit, set*) my wallet here?

5. *To, Too,* and *Two*
   Underline the correct word.

   a. We will travel (*to, too*) Switzerland on the train.
   b. Will Henry be coming along (*to, too*)?
   c. The trip will cost (*two, too*) hundred dollars.

6. Write an example of a first, second, and third person personal pronoun.

RESEARCH ESSAY

Notes

Library Learning

Day 1

Public libraries will be very helpful as you learn to write and research. The librarian has been trained to assist you. If you can't find what you are looking for, ask for help. Most libraries are divided into sections or departments.

a. **Reference Department** - This is where you will find periodicals, pamphlets/fliers, newspapers, magazines, city/county directories, literary criticisms, consumer reports, and encyclopedias.

b. **Adult Department** - Here you will find adult literature, fiction/nonfiction, videos, books on audio tapes, large print books, science fiction, CDs and DVDs.

c. **Youth Department** - This is where you will find many of your resources. This department is almost like a library in itself containing much of what you find in the reference and adult departments. The books, however, are written for youth. You will find readers of all levels, nonfiction, audio books, encyclopedias, biographies, and a youth reference section.

d. **Computer** - Here you will find titles, authors, and their reference (call) numbers.

Plan a trip to your local library. Ask your librarian to help you become familiar with each department. Ask her to instruct you in using the computer.

Teacher's Note:
For the next three lessons your student will learn how to use the library for research.

Day 2

a. There are many books in each department. It would be an overwhelming task to search for a title without the help of the Dewey Decimal System. This system of numbers serves as a way to classify nonfiction books into ten major categories.

Dewey Decimal System

000-099 General Works - encyclopedias, computer information

100-199 Philosophy - conduct, manners

200-299 Religion - books about religion, religions of different countries

300-399 Social Science - Folk lore, fairy tales

400-499 Language - dictionaries, sign language, foreign language dictionaries, language helps

500-599 Science - experiments, animals, biology, chemistry, etc.

600-699 Technology - (how things work) health, body, medicine, etc.

700-799 Arts - fine arts, artists, crafts, sports, music, photography

800-899 Literature - (nonfiction) poetry, writing, books, plays

900-999 History/Geography - countries, states, U.S./World History

b. Using the Dewey Decimal System, write the correct number category where you would find the following books.

1) *Earth Science for Every Kid*, Janice Van Cleave
2) *The Teenage Book of Manners...PLEASE*, Fred Hartley
3) *How Things Work: The Physics of Everyday Life*, Louis Bloomfield
4) *The Thorndike Barnhart Children's Dictionary*, HarperCollins
5) *A Child's Treasury of Verse*, Eleanor Doan
6) *The Reader's Digest Children's World Atlas*
7) *Happy Hours in Storyland*
8) *World War II Day by Day*, Donald Sommerville

c. During a trip to your library use the Dewey Decimal System to find an example from each category.

d. Optional: Enrichment

Day 3

a. Fiction books (novels, mysteries, etc.) can usually be found in a special section of the library. They are arranged in alphabetical order by the author's last name. If the author has more than one title on the shelf, they are placed in alphabetical order by title.

Ex: *Summer of the Monkeys*; Rawls, Wilson
Where the Red Fern Grows; Rawls, Wilson

If the title begins with a small word like *A* or *The*, disregard it, and alphabetize according to the next word. For example, to look up the book title, *The Courage of Sarah Noble*, look under **C** for *Courage*.

Day 2

b. 1) 500-599 *Earth Science for Every Kid*, Janice Van Cleave

2) 100-199 *The Teenage Book of Manners... PLEASE*, Fred Hartley

3) 500-599 *How Things Work: The Physics of Everyday Life*, Louis Bloomfield

4) 400-499 *The Thorndike Barnhart Children's Dictionary*, HarperCollins

5) 800-899 *A Child's Treasury of Verse*, Eleanor Doan

6) 900-999 *The Reader's Digest Children's World Atlas*

7) 300-399 *Happy Hours in Storyland*

8) 900-999 *World War II Day* by Day, Donald Sommerville

Day 3

b. 9 *Call It Courage*; Sperry, Armstrong
4 *The Tale of Jeremy Vole*; Lawhead, Stephen
1 *Mr. Popper's Penguins*; Atwater, Richard and Florence
2 *The Big Wave;* Buck, Pearl S.
3 *The Tale of Anabelle Hedgehog*; Lawhead, Stephen
6 *Island of the Blue Dolphins*; O'Dell, Scott
5 *Rabbit Hill*; Lawson, Robert
8 *The Sign of the Beaver*; Speare, Elizabeth George
7 *The Road to Damietta*; O'Dell, Scott
10 *Farmer Boy*; Wilder, Laura Ingalls

d. 5 *Susanna Wesley* by Charles Ludwig
4 *Daniel Webster* by Robert Allen
2 *George Frideric Handel* by Charles Ludwig
3 *Robert E. Lee* by Lee Roddy
1 *Christopher Columbus* by Bennie Rhodes

b. Arrange the following 10 fiction titles in the order you would find them on the library shelf by placing the order number in the space provided.

____ *Call It Courage*; Sperry, Armstrong
____ *The Tale of Jeremy Vole*; Lawhead, Stephen
____ *Mr. Popper's Penguins*; Atwater, Richard and Florence
____ *The Big Wave*; Buck, Pearl S.
____ *The Tale of Anabelle Hedgehog*; Lawhead, Stephen
____ *Island of the Blue Dolphins*; O'Dell, Scott
____ *Rabbit Hill*; Lawson, Robert
____ *The Sign of the Beaver*; Speare, Elizabeth George
____ *The Road to Damietta*; O'Dell, Scott
____ *Farmer Boy*, Wilder; Laura Ingalls

c. Usually a library has a special section given to biographies and autobiographies. Do you know the difference between the two? If not, use a dictionary to look up the terms. You will find the books in this nonfiction section arranged in alphabetical order by the last name of the subject. If more than one biography has been written about a person, then the biographies are put in order by the author's last name.

Ex: *Benjamin Franklin*; d'Aulaire, Ingrid and Edgar Parin,
Meet Benjamin Franklin; Scarf, Maggi
Benjamin Franklin; Stevenson, Augusta

A **biography** is the story of a person's life written by someone other than that person. An **autobiography** is a person's life story that that person has written.

d. Arrange the following biographies in the order you would find them on the library shelf by placing the order number in the space provided.

_____ *Susanna Wesley*; Ludwig, Charles
_____ *Daniel Webster*; Allen, Robert
_____ *George Frideric Handel*; Ludwig, Charles
_____ *Robert E. Lee*; Roddy, Lee
_____ *Christopher Columbus*; Rhodes, Bennie

Day 4

a. In the General Works section of the library you will find reference books such as encyclopedias. Encyclopedias are arranged in alphabetical order by subject. Each volume has a reference to the range of the alphabet covered in that volume printed on the book for easy reference. For example;

1) Vol. 1 - A to Ameland
2) Vol. 2 - Amen to ArtilleryS

This method allows you to find your subject easily. In an encyclopedia set arranged as listed in the example, which volume would you find information about the American Revolution?

Which volume would you find information about the Amazon River?

b. Each year a special acknowledgment called the Newbery Award is made to certain books. Ask your librarian where you can find information on Newbery Award winners.

1) In what year was the first Newbery Award given?
2) How does a book win this award?
3) Who issues the award?
4) Why was it named "Newbery" Award?
5) What was the title and author of the 1949 award winner? The 1961 award winner? Last year's winner?
6) List some or all of the Newbery Award winners you would like to read.

Day 5

a. Use your library's computer to make a list of all the books your favorite author has written. How many have you read? Would you like to read some other books by this author?

b. Optional: Enrichment (SAB)

c. Use the reference area of your library to find out more information about your author. One good reference source is *Something About the Author*. Look for this or a similar reference book to research your author.

d. Choose skills from the *Review Activities*.

Day 4

a. Vol. 2 - American Revolution
Vol. 1 - Amazon River

b. 1) 1922
2) The Newbery Award is awarded to the American author contributing the finest book for children for the previous year.
3) Children's Services Division of the American Library Association (ALA)
4) It was named after John Newbery, an 18th century English bookseller.
5) 1949 - *King of the Wind* by Marguerite Henry
1961 - *Island of the Blue Dolphins* by Scott O'Dell
6) Answers will vary.

Notes

Review Activities

Choose only the skills your student needs to review.

1. *Departments of the Library*
   Refer to your list of library departments to answer the following questions.

   a. In what department would you find a magazine article on nutrition?
   b. In what department would you find young children's books?
   c. In what department would you go to locate a DVD on Spain?
   d. What department would help you in locating a book?

2. *Dewey Decimal System*
   Use the Dewey Decimal System to classify each of the following books. Write the correct number category next to each selection.

   a. *First Guide to the Universe*
   b. *Amazing Machines and How They Work*
   c. *Art Through the Ages*
   d. *Religions of Many Lands*
   e. *World Book Encyclopedia*

3. *Fiction*
   Arrange the following fiction books in the correct order they would appear on the library shelf of fiction by placing the number of their appearance on the space provided.

   a. _______ *Silver for General Washington*; Meadowcroft, Enid
   b. _______ *The Legend of Fire*; Roddy, Lee
   c. _______ *The Bronze Bow*; Speare, Elizabeth George
   d. _______ *Amos Fortune, Free Man*; Yates, Elizabeth
   e. _______ *Gift From the Midado*; Fleming, Elizabeth

1.
a. Reference
b. Youth
c. Adult
d. Help Desk or computer

2.
a. 500-599
b. 600-699
c. 700-799
d. 200-299
e. 000-099

3.
a. 2
b. 3
c. 4
d. 5
e. 1

4.
a. 2
b. 4
c. 5
d. 1 - autobiography
e. 3
f. 6

4. *Biographies/Autobiographies*
Arrange the following biographies in the correct order they would appear on the library shelf by placing the number of their appearance on the space provided. If the book is an autobiography, circle the number.

a. _____ *Michael Faraday, Father of Electronics*; Ludwig, Charles
b. _____ *Isaac Newton: Mastermind of Modern Science*; Knight, David
c. _____ *Inventor, Scientist & Teacher: Isaac Newton*; Tiner, John
d. _____ *Ben Carson*; Carson, Ben
e. _____ *Martin Luther: Hero of Faith*; Nohl, Frederick
f. _____ *The World of William Penn*; Foster, Genevieve

5.
a. 16
b. 16
c. 14
d. 15
e. 14

5. *Encyclopedia*
Indicate in which volume you would find the following information.

a. Vol. _____ - minerals
b. Vol. _____ - monarchy
c. Vol. _____ - Kitty Hawk
d. Vol. _____ - mathematics
e. Vol. _____ - library

6. *Research*
You did some research on the Newbery Award. Another special acknowledgment is the Caldecott Award. Use a computer search engine or other resource to answer the following questions.

1) In what year was the first Caldecott award given?
2) How does a book qualify to win the award?
3) What organization issues the award?
4) What was the title and author of the 1940 award winner? The 1963 award winner? Last year's winner?
5) Has any one person ever won the Caldecott medal more than once?
6) Has any one person ever won both the Newbery and Caldecott Awards?
7) For whom was the Caldecott medal named?
8) List some of the Caldecott winners you have read.

6.
1) 1938
2) The Caldecott Medal is awarded to the American artist/ illustrator contributing the finest picture book for children and exhibiting the most unique and distinctive style.
3) The American Library Association (ALA)
4) 1940 - *Abraham Lincoln* by Ingri and Edgar Parin d'Aulaire
1963 - *The Snowy Day* Ezra Jack Keats
5) Robert McCloskey; Marcia Brown
6) Robert Lawson
7) Randolph Caldecott, an English illustrator
8) Answers will vary.

✎ **Teacher's Note: The Research Essay unit continues in Lesson 18.**

"Prisoners walk to the side." It was the bored voice of the guard behind us. "Prisoners must not step on the matting."

Guiltily, we stepped off the privileged path.

Ahead of us in the corridor was a desk, behind it a woman in uniform. As each prisoner reached this point she gave her name for the thousandth time that day and placed on the desk whatever she was wearing of value. Nollie, Betsie, and I unstrapped our beautiful wristwatches. As I handed mine to the officer, she pointed to the simple gold ring that had belonged to Mama. I wriggled it from my finger and laid it on the desk along with my wallet and paper guilders.

The Hiding Place by Corrie Ten Boom.
Used by permission, Chosen Books, 25 Turner Dr., Chappaqua, NY 10514.

Day 1

a. Copy the literature passage. Compare your copy with the passage and correct any errors.

b. Make your own spelling list from any misspelled words in the dictation, or use the following list of suggested words.

guard	prisoners	privileged	corridor
guiltily	thousandth	wristwatches	wriggled

c. The words *wristwatches* and *wriggled* are spelled with a silent **w** and **r** to make the /**r**/ sound.

Spelling Tip

Some words spell the /r/ sound with *wr* as in write.

Copy the following words and underline **wr**. Say the words aloud as you write them.

write	wren
wreath	wreck
wrestle	wrinkle
wrong	wrap

Day 2

a. Many words are tricky and good writers must exercise extra care not to misuse them. Find the word *laid* in the last sentence of the literature passage. Locate this example and circle it. The use of the words *lay* and *lie* can be confusing. If you know the meaning of each word, it will help you to use the correct word when writing.

lay – to put or place something down
lay, laying, laid, (have) laid
Please *lay* the paper on my desk.

lie – to rest or recline
lie, lying, lay, (have) lain
It is time for you to *lie* down and go to sleep.

Although both words are verbs, only the word *lay* has an object. Look at this sentence again.

Please lay the paper on my desk.

The object is paper. The word *lay* usually has an object, but the word *lie* never has an object.

b. Choose the correct word.

1) My cat likes to (lay, lie) in front of the fireplace.
2) Make sure you (lay, lie) your clothes out for the next day.
3) (Lay, Lie) down and rest before the trip home.
4) (Lay, Lie) your books on the table.
5) Your game has been (laying, lying) on the floor all day.
6) The tiger was (laying, lying) in wait for its prey.

Day 2
b. 1) lie
2) lay
3) Lie
4) Lay
5) lying
6) lying

c. *The Hiding Place* is an autobiography written by Corrie Ten Boom telling of her experiences in an internment camp during War World II. An **autobiography** is the story of someone's life told by the person while a **biography** is the story of someone's life told by someone else. Although most of the information presented in *The Hiding Place* is based on firsthand experience, the author does present many facts about World War II that she obtained through research.

During the next two weeks, you will research the topic of your choice and write an essay about the subject. When various books, magazines, and other reference materials are used as sources of information for an essay that documents a subject, the resulting paper is referred to as a **research essay.**

d. Review your spelling words.

Day 3

a. This lesson will use World War II as a sample topic of research in order to guide you through the process of preparing a research essay.

b. Research requires proper planning. It is important that you follow the steps in the order presented without omitting any steps of research. Keep track of your research planning by using the student checklist in Lesson 18. Each time you complete a step on the checklist, mark the box and move to the next step.

c. Begin your research by first deciding the topic you want to research. Think of a subject you might like to know more about. Then take a trip to your library. Use books, magazines, or the Internet to help you choose an interesting topic. (Your librarian can help you with any questions you may have.) Your research paper will be only five or six paragraphs so you must narrow down your topic to a specific topic you would like to explore.

Ex: **General area of interest**: Battles of World War II
General topic: Battle at Pearl Harbor
Limited topic: The Destruction of the American Fleet at Pearl Harbor

d. Write a statement of purpose for your essay. This statement is called the **thesis statement** and should express the **main idea** of the essay in a sentence or two. Think of your thesis statement as your focus point. You want your research paper to center around what is said in your thesis statement.

Ex: The destruction of the American fleet at Pearl Harbor had more of an effect on the United States than any other event of World War II.

e. Look back at the Dewey Decimal System in Lesson 16. Write the number or name of the category you would find each of the following books.

1) Books on World War II
2) Online
3) A biography of a famous person involved in World War II

Day 3
e. 1) 900-999
2) 000-099
3) Biographies

f. What section would you find books on the subject of your choice?

f. Answers will vary.

g. Spend time today at the library gathering and deciding which books or reference you will use to research your topic. You may include pictures (drawn or otherwise) with your paper. In making your choices include at least one encyclopedia or reference book, one magazine or newspaper (if possible), and one book.

h. Review your spelling words.

Day 4

a. Once you have narrowed your broad topic to a more specific topic, begin reading the information you have gathered. You don't have to read the entire magazine article or book unless you want to. Focus just on the parts that deal with your specific topic.

b. Keep your ideas focused. Make a list of questions on 3 x 5 index cards. For example, with the topic, The Destruction of the American Fleet at Pearl Harbor, you might write the following questions. One question per card.

When did it happen?

Was there a warning of impending attack?

Who fired first?

How was the raid conducted?

Why was timing crucial in the attack?

How many battleships were lost?

What was the cost in human lives?

c. Begin answering your questions on the index cards. Be sure to use your own words. Do not copy information. This is against the law; it is called **plagiarism**.

When you use a reference, write where you got your information on the back of the card. You will need this when you make a list of references that goes on the last page of your research paper.

d. Review your spelling words. Remember to be careful of words with silent letters.

e. Continue gathering information and recording it on your note cards.

f. Take an oral or written spelling pretest. Review any words you found difficult to spell.

Day 5

a. Continue to gather information on your note cards.

b. As you continue your research, take a little time to investigate how the Japanese viewed Pearl Harbor. Compare that view with the view presented by American authors. You may do this research online, at home, or at the library. Ask a librarian to help you. How do the accounts differ? How are they the same?

c. Take an oral or written spelling test.

Day 1

a. Now you must put your notes in order. Focus first on your main idea and then follow with details. Look over your note cards and ask yourself these questions.

- [ ] Do all my note cards apply to my subject?
- [ ] Do I need to discard some that do not apply?
- [ ] Do I have enough information on my topic?

b. Decide what the main points of your essay will be and list them. Group the remaining ideas under these main points forming a **topical outline**. A topical outline uses words or phrases to express ideas; it does not use sentences. The most important points of your outline should be numbered with Roman numerals and the subheadings should be listed by capital letters. Any remaining supporting details should be listed numerically under the subheading they support. Be sure to place a period after each of the numbers and letters used in the outline formation and indent each level. One of the rules used in forming an outline is that you never have just one subheading or just one detail listed under a subheading. You always have at least two subheadings or at least two details. Often this rule is expressed: "You never have an ***A*** without a ***B*** and you never have a ***1*** without a ***2***." Look over the following sample topical outline and then create your own outline for the topic you have chosen.

The Destruction of the American Fleet at Pearl Harbor

I. The Japanese Attack on Pearl Harbor
   A. Situation Prior to Attack
      1. U. S. Naval base located on Oahu Island, Hawaii
      2. Bulk of the U.S. fleet was at its base
      3. Japanese diplomats in talks with U.S.
      4. American fleet not on a wartime alert
   B. The Attack
      1. Japanese planes attacked at 7:55 A.M.
      2. First destroyed planes
      3. Second attacked fleet in harbor
II. U.S. losses at Pearl Harbor
   A. Damage to U.S. Fleet

1. Battleships: 4 sunk; 4 damaged
2. Cruisers: 3 damaged
3. Destroyers: 3 sunk

B. Lives loss or wounded
1. Number of Americans killed: 3,581
2. Number of Americans wounded: 1,168

III. Results of Battle
A. Gave Japanese fleet temporary command of western Pacific
B. U.S. enters World War II

Day 2

a. Review your outline and notes. Pay special attention to any suggestions your teacher makes. Work on an opening paragraph developed from your thesis statement. The **opening paragraph** should contain your thesis statement.

Ex: World War II was raging, but the United States was still attempting to isolate itself from involvement. All this would change early the morning of December 7, 1941. The destruction of the American fleet at Pearl Harbor had more of an effect on the United States than any other event of World War II.

b. Use your outline to continue writing the body of your research paper. This is only your first draft. You may make changes without worrying about being neat.

c. In Lessons 12-13, your research included fact and opinion. The paper you will write now will be based on fact.

Fact: Information that is known to be true by experience or observation. Ex: The Japanese bombed Pearl Harbor on December 7, 1941.

Opinion: A personal view or judgement. Ex: The bombing of Pearl Harbor was a cowardly act.

d. This does not mean the paper will not reflect your opinion. Just make sure your opinion is reasonably supported by facts.

e. Read the paper you wrote in Lesson 13, noting what is opinion and what is fact.

Day 3

a. You must close your research paper. Develop a good **closing paragraph** concluding your research.

Ex: The attack at Pearl Harbor gave Japan temporary command of the Western Pacific. Japan thought it could defeat America before our military forces had time to fight back; instead their attack drew the United States into the war. America had just begun the road to victory.

b. Complete the **first draft** of your research paper.

c. If you choose to include sketches or pictures, neatly mount them onto paper.

d. Ask your teacher to look over your first draft.

Day 4

a. Discuss your essay with your teacher, and pay special attention to any suggestions that your teacher makes. Review your research essay using a red pencil to make corrections as you check your grammar and spelling. If there are any words you have used too often, use your thesaurus to find synonyms to replace them.

The process of revising and rewriting your work is called **editing**. All writer's have to edit what they write to improve it.

b. In checking over your essay it would be helpful to ask yourself the following questions:

- ☐ Did I follow my outline?
- ☐ Did I follow the main idea of my research essay?
- ☐ Are the opening paragraph and closing paragraph interesting?
- ☐ Did my thoughts flow well through the paper?
- ☐ Does it make sense?

c. Using the information on the back of your index cards, make a list of references to go on the last page of your research paper. This list is called a **bibliography**. List only the references you used in your research essay.

The general format for a book reference is:

Author's name (last name, first name). *Title* (italicized). Place of publication: Publisher's name in full, copyright date.

Ex: Prange, Gordon W. *At Dawn We Slept*: The Untold Story of Pearl Harbor. New York: Penguin Books. 1982

The general format for a periodical (magazine) is:

Author's name (last name, first name). "Title of Article" (in quotation marks). *Name of Magazine* (italicized). Date of publication: page reference.

Ex: Jones, Harold. "The Attack of Pearl Harbor." *History Chronicles* (6 July, 1997): pp. 14-18.

Citing an Internet source:

Name of author or authors (if known). "Title of the work" (if known). Title of the Web page (if applicable). Year article was published. Date accessed. URL (if the source cannot be easily found).

Ex: "Pearl Harbor, Oahu - The Attack: Facts and Information." Pearl Harbor Oahu: The Attack, Facts and Information. 2012. Web 05 Nov. 2012 <http://www.pearlharboroahu.com/attack.htm>

For additional examples, access an MLA site on the Internet or purchase a MLA handbook. Please note that different reference materials may have slightly different guidelines. The final authority is your teacher.

Day 5

Make a neat final copy. Look over your paper once more. When you are pleased with your work, put your paper in order: outline of the research essay, pictures/sketches, and bibliography. A nice way to end your work would be to place it in a folder with the title of your research essay on the front.

Student Checklist

- [x] Choose a subject.
- [x] Narrow topic.
- [ ] Select research materials.
- [ ] Prepare note cards/take notes recording any references used.
- [ ] Conduct interview (optional).
- [ ] Write a statement of purpose.
- [ ] Write an outline.
- [ ] Write first draft.
- [ ] Revise first draft.
- [ ] Add sketches or pictures (optional).
- [ ] Write reference list (bibliography).
- [ ] Write final copy.
- [ ] Place in order and put in a folder.

Assessment 2
(Lessons 10 - 18)

1. Combine the following two sentences to form one sentence.

   Bob opened the door. Bob stepped aside for his mother.

2. Copy the following sentence, adding the correct punctuation.

   Could you come over today Mary asked We could study together.

3. Use the verb *lie* correctly in a sentence.

4. Use the verb *lay* correctly in a sentence.

5. What is plagiarism?

6. Find the pronouns in the literature passage in Lesson 9.

7. Write the following singular nouns as plural nouns.

   a. book
   b. goose
   c. baby

8. Arrange the following authors' names in alphbetical order.

   Arthur Ransome, Laura Ingalls Wilder, Elizabeth George Speare, Meindert Dejong.

9 Write an example of alliteration using the consonant **t**.

10. Choose the correct word.

    a. The (to, too, two) boys played in the mud puddle.
    b. Please (sit, set) down.
    c. (Sit, Set) the book on the table.
    d. Would you like to go to the party (to, too, two)?
    e. Everyone was going (to, too, two) the play.

11. The list of references used to write a research paper is called the ________________.

Answers:

1. Bob opened the door and stepped aside for his mother.

2. "Could you come over today?" Mary asked. "We could study together."

3. Example: I want to lie down on the bed when we get home.

4. Example: Did you lay the book on the table?

5. Plagiarism is copying or using another author's work without giving him or her credit.

6. he, it, his, him, them

7. a. books
b. geese
c. babies

8. Meindert Dejong
Arthur Ransome
Elizabeth George Speare
Laura Ingalls Wilder

9. Example: two tall trees

10. a. two
b. sit
c. Set
d. too
e. to

11. bibliography

Notes

Suddenly a mottled green fish, a yard long, with a dark back and white underneath, came to the top. It lifted an enormous head right out of the water, and opened a great white mouth, and shook itself. A little perch flew high in the air. Roger's rod straightened. For a moment the great fish lay close to the top of the water, looking wickedly at the crew of the Swallow as they looked at it. Then, with a twist of its tail that made a great twirling splash in the water, it was gone.

Swallows and Amazons by Arthur Ransome.
Used by permission, David R. Godine Publishers Inc.

Day 1

a. Write the passage from dictation. Circle every word you are not sure is spelled correctly. Compare your copy with the passage.

Do you know why *Swallow* is underlined? The name of a ship is capitalized and underlined. (Use italics if computer-generated.) If you did not underline the ship's name in your dictation, do so now.

b. Make your own spelling list from any words you misspelled in the dictation or use the following list of suggested words.

mottled	underneath	enormous
straightened	twist	swirling

c. Try to imagine the scene described in the literature passage. Describe how you think the crew felt when the big one got away. If you'd like, draw a picture of what you think the fish looked like.

d. Find the word *underneath* in the literature passage. This word contains the prefix **under-** which means *beneath.* Although **under** is also a word which can stand alone, in this word it is acting as a prefix. Add the prefix **under-** to your list of prefixes and include the definition and some word examples.

Day 1
d. under-: beneath
Possible examples:
underneath, underline

e. Locate all forms of the pronoun *it* in the literature passage and draw a box around them. Remember, an antecedent is the noun that the pronoun stands for. What is the antecedent of *it* in the literature passage? What is the antecedent for the pronoun *they* in the literature passage?

f. Note that the pronoun *its* used in the last sentence of the literature passage is a possessive pronoun. What is the pronoun showing possession of in this sentence?

It is important not to confuse the possessive pronoun its with the contraction *it's*. If you are using the pronoun in a sentence, it should be showing possession and should not have an apostrophe. If you are using the contraction, the word should have an apostrophe. You can check to make sure you are using the correct form by substituting the words *it is* in the sentence. If the words *it is* make sense in the sentence, then the contraction form is correct.

g. Complete the sentences correctly with *its* or *it's*.

1) ________ going to be a beautiful morning.
2) I need to get the horse ________ bridle.
3) The peacock spread ________ tail in a breathtaking display.
4) When the alarm rings, ________ six o'clock.
5) The cat will let you pet ________ kittens.

Day 2

a. Look at the literature passage. Find and underline the adjectives (words that describe nouns) and circle the nouns they describe.

Ex: mottled, green fish

Day 1

e. it, its - the green fish
they - the crew of the *Swallow*

f. the fish having possession of its tail

g. 1) It's
2) its
3) its
4) it's
5) its

Day 2

a. dark back
white underneath
enormous head
great white mouth
little perch
great fish
great twirling splash

Day 2
c. suddenly - came
wickedly - looking

b. Read the paragraph aloud, leaving out the adjectives you underlined. Read it again with the adjectives. What difference do adjectives make? Which way does the paragraph sound better?

   Adjectives help you to picture the scene. Without adjectives it would be hard for you to envision what the author wants you to see. The paragraph would be dull and boring to read without adjectives.

c. Find the two words in the literature passage that end in the suffix **-ly**. These two words are adverbs, words that describe verbs. Most words ending in **-ly** are adverbs. Some exceptions are *friendly* and *lovely*; they are adjectives. Look at the sentences where these words are located. Identify the verbs they are describing.

d. Review your spelling words.

e. Optional: Enrichment

Day 3

a. Locate the word *perch* in the literature passage. Although it identifies a kind of fish, it is not capitalized. It is only when a particular variety of fish is identified that the name is capitalized, such as Yellow Perch.

   Ex: pine tree (not capitalized)
   Norfolk Pine (specific name - capitalized)

b. Read the following capitalization rules.

Capitalization Rules

1) Capitalize the name of a club, organization, association, team, or political party.
   Ex: Red Cross, Striker Soccer Team, Republican Party

2) Capitalize the names of languages, religions, races, and nationalities.
   Ex: French, Hindu, Indian, African

3) Specific school courses are capitalized, but a field of study is not.
   Ex: History 101 (specific course)
   history (field of study)

4) The brand name of a product is capitalized, but the common noun that appears after the brand name is not capitalized.
   Ex: Whirlpool oven

5) Capitalize the first and all important words in the titles and chapters of books, poems, plays, magazines, television programs, art works, movies, newspapers, musical compositions, articles, and stories.
   Ex: *The Last of the Mohicans* (book)
   My Fair Lady (movie)
   The New York Times (newspaper)

6) Capitalize the names of historical events and time periods.
   Ex: French Revolution (event)
   Middle Ages (time period)

7) Names of people, buildings, pets, boats, planes, trains, planets, bridges, monuments, and documents are capitalized.
   Ex: Statue of Liberty (monument)
   Jupiter (planet)
   Titanic (boat)

8) Capitalize the names of days of the week, months, holidays, and special events, but do not capitalize the names of seasons (spring, summer, fall, winter) unless they are part of the name of an event.
   Ex: Thursday (day of the week)
   September (month)
   Valentine's Day (holiday)
   Spring Livestock Show (event)
   spring rain storm (season)

9) Capitalize geographical places:
   Ex: bodies of water - Lake Superior, Mississippi River, Atlantic Ocean
   cities - Birmingham
   countries - Switzerland
   counties - Pinellas County
   continents - Asia
   islands - Hawaiian Islands
   mountains - Mount St. Helens
   parks - Yellowstone National Park
   provinces - Alberta
   sections of the country - the West (do not capitalize when referring to direction only - west of town)
   states - Florida
   streets, avenues, etc. - Grand Boulevard, Twenty- first Street (**Note:** The second part of the number is not capitalized.)

c. Review the literature passage and find proper nouns that are capitalized. Why are they capitalized?

d. Refer to the capitalization rules to help you choose the correct phrases.

		A	B
Ex:	B	the asian culture	the Asian culture
1)	____	a geometry assignment	a Geometry assignment
2)	____	Fifty-second Street	fifty-second street
3)	____	saturn's orbit	Saturn's orbit
4)	____	lake area 4-H club	Lake Area 4-H Club
5)	____	ocala national forest	Ocala National Forest
6)	____	Statue of Liberty	Statue of liberty
7)	____	Sony stereo	Sony Stereo
8)	____	the sound of music	The Sound of Music
9)	____	Lake Superior	lake superior

e. Review your spelling words.

Day 4

a. Adjectives are words that describe nouns. Look at the following sentence:

An elephant picked up the peanut with a spoon.

Look at the words that come before *elephant, peanut,* and *spoon. An, a,* and *the* are special adjectives called **articles**. Articles can be signals to tell you that a noun will follow. Usually, the nouns directly follow the articles. Sometimes other adjectives separate the article from the noun, but a noun always follows an article.

Ex: the round orange

The word *round* separates the article from the noun but the noun, *orange* still follows the article, *the.* Find all the articles in the literature passage, and locate the nouns they describe.

Day 3

c. Roger - name of a person
Swallow - name of a boat

d. 1) A
2) A
3) B
4) B
5) B
6) A
7) A
8) B
9) A

Day 4

a. *Articles are underlined once, nouns twice.*
a mottled green fish
a yard
a dark back
the top
an enormous head
the water
a great white mouth
a little perch
the air
a moment
the great fish
the top
the water
the crew
the Swallow
a twist
a great twirling splash
the water

Day 4
b. Possible Answers
dark - dusky (back)

white - pale (underneath)

enormous - immense (head)

great white - large blanched (mouth)

little - small (perch)

great - magnificent (fish)

great twirling - vast twisting (splash)

b. **Synonyms** are words that have the same or similar meanings. A **thesaurus** is a book of synonyms. Use your thesaurus to find synonyms for the adjectives you underlined in **2a**. Check to make sure your synonym makes sense in the context of the literature passage. For example, the word *great* appears three times as an adjective in the literature passage, but each time its meaning is a little different.

c. Rewrite the literature passage using the synonyms you found. Which way do you like better?

d. Take an oral or written spelling pretest. Remember, sounding out the syllables as you write them will help you spell them correctly.

e. Optional: Enrichment

Day 5

a. Write the literature passage from dictation again. Did you spell all the words correctly?

b. Read the literature passage again. Imagine you are Roger, and you have just battled with a great fish. Its tail makes a splash, and it's gone. How do you feel? Write down your thoughts on paper. Using these ideas, record a journal entry for Roger. A journal entry is written in the first person. This means you are the one speaking or telling the story. Use descriptive words to express how you feel. Edit your work. Check for errors in spelling, punctuation, and writing mechanics.

c. Take an oral or written spelling test.

d. Read each sentence below. Look for capitalization errors and correct them.

Ex: Many indians were moved to Reservations as people moved west.
Correct - Many Indians were moved to reservations as people moved West.

1) Christopher columbus crossed the atlantic ocean to find a new land.
2) Her High School schedule included geometry, biology, and word processing 102.
3) Their trip to New York city included visits to the statue of liberty and the empire state building.
4) She is considered bilingual because she can speak both english and spanish fluently.
5) He wasn't sure whether to purchase the Oldsmobile Station Wagon or the Ford Van.
6) There will be no classes on presidents' day and memorial day.
7) The directions tell us to turn left at the next Street and follow Bayview avenue to the auditorium.
8) I will be working on tuesday, thursday, and saturday of this Week.
9) We have short Winters and long Summers in the south.

e. Complete the *Review Activities*.

Day 5

d. 1) Christopher Columbus crossed the Atlantic Ocean to find a new land.
2) Her high school schedule included geometry, biology, and Word Processing 102.
3) Their trip to New York City included visits to the Statue of Liberty and the Empire State Building.
4) She is considered bilingual because she can speak both English and Spanish fluently.
5) He wasn't sure whether to purchase the Oldsmobile station wagon or the Ford van.
6) There will be no classes on Presidents' Day and Memorial Day.
7) The directions tell us to turn left at the next street and follow Bayview Avenue to the auditorium.
8) I will be working on Tuesday, Thursday, and Saturday of this week.
9) We have short winters and long summers in the South.

1.
a. underline - to draw a line beneath
b. undergrowth - small shrubs that grow beneath trees
c. underage - below the age required by law

2. The sun is at the center of our solar system. Its gravitational force holds the planets in their orbits. It's known that the sun is made of the gases hydrogen and helium, and that its surface temperature is about sixty times hotter than boiling water. The sun provides our planet with warmth and light, and it's impossible for life to exist without it.

3.
a. A beautiful border of flowers ran along the garden path.
b. The array of flowers made the garden a pleasant place to visit.
c. The visitors enjoyed the colorful butterflies that were attracted by the honeysuckle.
d. The tiny honeybees buzzed amongst the fragrant blossoms.
e. An afternoon spent in the lovely garden left you with a peaceful feeling.

Review Activities

Choose skills your student needs to review.

1. *Prefixes*
Add the prefix **under-** to the following root words. How does the addition of the prefix change the meaning of each word? If you are unsure of the meaning of the new word, look it up in the dictionary.

a. ____________line
b. ____________growth
c. ____________age

2. *Its and It's*
Complete the following paragraph by choosing the correct word.

The sun is at the center of our solar system. (*Its*, *It's*) gravitational force holds the planets in their orbits. (*Its*, *It's*) known that the sun is made of the gases hydrogen and helium, and that (*its*, *it's*) surface temperature is about sixty times hotter than boiling water. The sun provides our planet with warmth and light, and (*its*, *it's*) impossible for life to exist without it.

3. *Articles and Adjectives*
Underline any articles you find in the following sentences and draw an arrow to the noun that follows it. Circle any adjectives.

a. A beautiful border of flowers ran along the garden path.
b. The array of flowers made the garden a pleasant place to visit.
c. The visitors enjoyed the colorful butterflies that were attracted by the honeysuckle.
d. The tiny honeybees buzzed amongst the fragrant blossoms.
e. An afternoon spent in the lovely garden left you with a peaceful feeling.

4. *Adverbs*
Underline the adverbs in the following sentence. Circle the verb or verb phrase they modify.

a. She walked quickly down the sidewalk.
b. The ground quaked violently beneath their feet.
c. We seldom travel this road.
d. She rushed frantically into the room.
e. We will find the answer tomorrow.

5. *Capitalization*
Correct any errors in capitalization by placing a slash through any incorrect letters and placing the correct letter above it.

The Gainesville sun featured an article on the micanopy historical committee's plan to renovate many buildings of historical value in Micanopy. The old city hall located on twenty-second street will be the first project the committee will undertake. Also many houses built during the civil war are slated to be renovated. The renovations should begin this Spring.

6. *Personal Pronouns and Antecedents*
Underline each personal pronoun in the following sentences. Circle the noun that is its antecedent.

a. The mare whinnied at its young foal.
b. The youth group enjoyed their trip to the mountains.
c. Hannah and Megan went swimming, and then they played volleyball on the beach.
d. Mike usually played first base, but sometimes he played shortstop.

7. *Synonyms*
Write a synonym for each of these adjectives.

a. beautiful
b. tremendous
c. rigid
d. brittle

4.
a. She walked quickly down the sidewalk.
b. The ground quaked violently beneath their feet.
c. We seldom travel this road.
d. She rushed frantically into the room.
e. We will find the answer tomorrow.

5. The *Gainesville Sun* featured an article on the Micanopy Historical Committee's plan to renovate many buildings of historical value in Micanopy. The old City Hall located on Twenty-second Street will be the first project the committee will undertake. Also many houses built during the Civil War are slated to be renovated. The renovations should begin this spring.

6.
a. The mare whinnied at its young foal.
b. The youth group enjoyed their trip to the mountains.
c. Hannah and Megan went swimming, and then they played volleyball on the beach.
d. Mike usually played first base, but sometimes he played shortstop.

7. Possible answers
a. pretty, gorgeous
b. enormous
c. stiff, strict
d. fragile

Notes

The time I spent upon the island is still so horrible a thought to me, that I must pass it lightly over. In all the books I have read of people cast away, they had either their pockets full of tools, or a chest of things would be thrown upon the beach along with them, as if on purpose. My case was very different. I had nothing in my pockets but money and Alan's silver button; and being inland bred, I was as much short of knowledge as of means.

Kidnapped by Robert Louis Stevenson.

Day 1

a. Read the literature passage aloud paying close attention to punctuation. Notice the semicolon which joins the two parts of the last sentence. When you read the literature passage, be sure to pause at the semicolon as for a comma. Write the literature passage from dictation, then make any corrections.

b. The main character in the literature passage is also the narrator. What did the narrator in the literature passage think of stories of other castaways? What emotion or mood does the author create concerning the character's island experience? Did he have any practical experience in survival or even roughing it?

c. Explain what you think the first sentence of the literature passage means.

d. Make your own spelling list from any words you misspelled in the dictation or use the following list of suggested words:

horrible	either	different
inland	button	knowledge

e. The word *knowledge* is spelled with a silent **k** and **n** to make the /**n**/ sound. **Gn** also makes a /**n**/ sound. Words may begin with **kn** or **gn**, but **kn** will usually not end a word.

Day 1

b. The narrator thought stories of other castaways were unrealistic because they were always supplied with the tools or other means to survive.

The mood is one of frustration and concern.

No. The narrator indicates he is *inland bred* and has little knowledge of survival skills.

c. The memories are so unpleasant that he does not like to dwell on them.

Spelling Tip
Some words spell the /*n*/ sound with *kn* or *gn*; but *kn* will usually not end a word.

Copy the following words and underline **kn** and **gn**. Say the words aloud as you write them.

knee	gnaw
knight	gnat
knife	gnarl
knit	reign
knock	sign
knob	align
knuckle	design

Day 2
a. first person

b. Alan's; the use of 's

Day 2

a. Look at the literature passage again, paying special attention to the pronouns. In which person (first, second, or third) are the pronouns used?

b. Underline the noun that shows possession in the literature passage. How do you know it shows possession?

c. Another method of showing possession is the use of possessive pronouns. **Possessive pronouns** are words that take the place of nouns that show possession. The possessive pronouns most commonly used are:

Commonly Used Possessive Pronouns					
my	his	her	its	your	our
their	mine	hers	yours	ours	theirs

Hint
Possessive pronouns do not use an apostrophe to show possession.

d. Find and list the three possessive pronouns in the literature passage. Beside each one, write what each pronoun is showing possession of.

e. Usually possessive pronouns are used as adjectives in the structure of a sentence. All the possessive pronouns listed in the box above are used as adjectives.

f. Write the correct possessive pronoun in the space provided in the following sentences.

Ex: *Mary* went to _her_ Spanish lesson.

1) *Matthew and Lane* went to _____ favorite fishing spot.
2) The *car* slowed down to stay in ________ correct lane.
3) *I* want you to see ________ new shoes.
4) *Lydia* likes to finish ________ homework before going to softball practice.
5) *Mike* will achieve ________ goals because he believes in working hard.

g. Being cast away on a deserted island with just money and a silver button would put you in a very difficult situation. Think of some things you would need if you were stranded on a deserted island. Think about the reasons why you would need those particular things. Spend some time talking about it with your teacher to help you clarify your thoughts. Put your thoughts on paper and save it for tomorrow's work.

h. Review your spelling words.

Day 2

d. their pockets
my case
my pockets

f. 1) their
2) its
3) my
4) her
5) his

Day 3

a. **Essays** are used to explain an idea, describe how something is done, argue a point of view, or interpret something you read. In Lessons 18 and 19 you wrote a research essay. Today you will begin work on a different type of essay. It will be an essay in which you express your ideas and views about a survival situation. Use what you wrote yesterday in **2g** to guide you in formulating a thesis statement. Place your thesis statement at the top of your outline. This will help you remember to keep your thoughts focused on your main idea.

Ex: Although many items would be useful in a survival situation, I think the three items that would be crucial to my survival would be a knife, matches, and a first aid kit.

b. The next step in writing an essay is to complete a topical outline in order to better organize your thoughts. First list the three most important items you would need to survive on the island. Each of these main ideas will be numbered with a roman numeral.

c. Under each main idea list at least two reasons why this item would be important to your survival. Note these **supporting details** with a capital letter.

I. Knife
  A. Make weapons for hunting
  B. Cut up food to prepare for eating
  C. Make a shelter
II. Matches
  A. Cook food
  B. Keep warm
III. A First Aid Kit
  A. Cleanse wounds
  B. Bandage wounds

d. Any further supporting details should be listed in numerical order under the subheading shown with a capital letter. (See the outline in Lesson 18.) Save your outline for tomorrow.

e. Review your spelling words.

Day 4

a. Use your outline from yesterday to write the first draft of a short essay. Look over your outline. The first thing you need to do is develop a good opening paragraph. Just as you greet a friend "Hello!" on the telephone, you must introduce your reader to your idea of the essay. Use your thesis statement as a basis to build your opening paragraph. As you begin your writing, write on every other line. This will make revising your work easier.

b. Now take each main idea and supporting details to form three good paragraphs.

c. You now must close your essay. Just as you say "Goodbye" to a friend as you finish your telephone conversation, you now must conclude your thoughts on paper.

d. Today you have completed a rough draft of your essay. You are building a house, and the bricks are your words! It doesn't need to be perfect. You are working to get your thoughts down in an organized form.

e. Take an oral or written spelling pretest. Remember, sounding out the syllables as you write them will help you spell them correctly.

Day 5

a. All writers work to get their words just right. Today you will rearrange and add to your rough draft from yesterday. This is the process of editing, revising, and rewriting. This is an important step in writing your essay. Carefully look at each paragraph and decide what you want to change, rearrange, or reword. Perhaps you need to add more details or information.

b. Use your thesaurus to improve the quality of your words. Doing this will make your writing more interesting and increase your vocabulary.

c. Check your rough draft for spelling and punctuation. Read your composition aloud. Write a neat final copy.

d. Write the literature passage from dictation or take a final spelling test.

e. Choose skills from the *Review Activities*.

Review Activities

Choose skills your student needs to review.

1. *Possessive Pronouns*
   Underline the possessive pronouns in the following sentences.

   a. Their home near the creek is large and roomy.
   b. My teacher said I wrote an excellent essay.
   c. He grows a variety of different vegetables in his garden.
   d. Our family enjoys spending time together.

2. *Outline*
   Arrange the following information in outline form. The title of your outline is: *Eating a Healthy Diet.*

Vegetables	Foods You Should Eat
Candy	Cake
Fruit	Foods You Should Avoid
Carbohydrates	Whole-grain bread
Carrots	Fried foods
Broccoli	Apples
Fried chicken	High-sugar foods
French fries	Peaches
Cereal	

3. *Composition*
   Write a paragraph describing your favorite dessert. Be sure to use your first sentene to explain what the paragraph is describing.

1.
a. Their
b. My
c. his
d. Our

2.
Eating a Healthy Diet

I. Foods You Should Eat
A. Vegetables
1. Broccoli
2. Carrots
B. Fruit
1. Apples
2. Peaches
C. Carbohydrates
1. Cereal
2. Whole-grain bread
II. Foods You Should Avoid
A. Fried foods
1. French fries
2. Fried chicken
B. High-sugar foods
1. Candy
2. Cake

3. Example:
My favorite dessert is a hot fudge sundae.

After I had solaced my mind with the comfortable part of my condition, I began to look round me, to see what kind of place I was in, and what was next to be done. I soon found my comforts abate, and that, in a word, I had a dreadful deliverance, for I was wet, had no clothes to shift me, nor anything either to eat or drink to comfort me. Neither did I see any prospect before me but that of perishing with hunger or being devoured by wild beasts; and that which was particularly afflicting to me was, that I had no weapon, either to hunt and kill any creature for my sustenance, or to defend myself against any other creature that might desire to kill me for theirs. *In a word, I had nothing about me but a knife, a tobacco-pipe, and a little tobacco in a box. This was all my provisions, and this threw me into such terrible agonies of mind, that for a while I ran about like a madman. Night coming upon me, I began with a heavy heart to consider what would be my lot if there were any ravenous beasts in that country, as at night they always come abroad for their prey.*

Robinson Crusoe by Daniel DeFoe.

Day 1

a. Read the literature passage. Copy the bold print in the literature passage or write it from dictation.

b. When you complete your dictation, be sure to check your work for any spelling or punctuation errors. Make your own spelling list from any misspelled words in dictation or use the following list of suggested words:

solaced	deliverance	prospect	devoured
particularly	sustenance	provisions	ravenous

c. Two of the spelling words have the suffixes –**ion** and –**ous**. The suffix –**ion** means **the act of**, **state of**, or **result of**. This suffix can also be spelled –**sion or** –**tion**. The suffix –**ous** means **full of** or **having**. This can also be spelled –**ious** or –**eous**. Add each of these suffixes to your list, along with the definition and some word examples.

d. Suffixes make it possible to change a word from a noun to an adjective, from a verb to a noun, and from an adjective to an adverb. Use your list of suffixes to complete the following:

Ex: Change the noun *mathematics* to an adjective meaning *having an ability in mathematics*: mathematical

1) Change the noun *beauty* to an adjective meaning *full of beauty.*

2) Change the verb *inject* to a noun that means *the act of being injected.*

3) Change the verb *teach* to a noun that means *one who teaches.*

4) Change the adjective *quick* to an adverb that means *in the manner of being quick.*

e. How would you describe Robinson Crusoe? Was he happy or unhappy?

Day 2

a. Much of the story of Robinson Crusoe is written in the form of a **journal**. For example:

September 30, 1659. I, poor miserable Robinson Crusoe, being shipwrecked during a dreadful storm in the offing, came on shore on this dismal unfortunate island, which I called "the Island of Despair"; all the rest of the ship's company being drowned, and myself almost dead.

Many people write in journals or diaries to record their thoughts or events in their lives. Journals are written

Day 1

c. -ion, -sion, -tion - act of, state of, or result of
Possible examples: tension, graduation

-ous, -ious, -eous - full of or having
Possible examples: religious, gorgeous

d. 1) beautiful
2) injection
3) teacher
4) quickly

e. Robinson Crusoe was suffering and in great need. He was fearful and without hope.

Day 2
a. I, myself, my, me

in the **first person** because events are being recorded from the perspective of one of the characters in the story. Look over the above journal entry. What pronouns are used that indicate the passage is written in the first person?

b. The third sentence in the literature passage is quite long and is actually two complete sentences strung together by a **semicolon**. Semicolons are used when complete sentences containing one or more commas are linked together by coordinating conjunctions, such as *and, but, or, nor, for, yet, so.*

Day 2
c.
Neither did I see any prospect before me but that of perishing with hunger or being devoured by wild beasts.

That which was particularly afflicting to me was, that I had no weapon, either to hunt and kill any creature for my sustenance, or to defend myself against any other creature that might desire to kill me for theirs.

c. Rewrite the third sentence by removing the coordinating semicolon and the coordinating conjunction making separate sentences.

d. Pretend you are a historical person who lived long ago (George Washington at Valley Forge, a Pilgrim on the Mayflower, etc.). Take time today to gather some information on your character and an event which took place. Jot down notes to use tomorrow.

e. Review your spelling words.

Day 3

a. Taking the notes you gathered yesterday, create a journal entry for your historical character. Be sure to add enough detail to make it interesting and to understand how the narrator is feeling. Be sure to date your entry.

b. "…I soon found my comforts abate, and that, in a **word**, I had a dreadful deliverance;"

When spelling a word with a /**w**/ sound followed by the /**er**/ sound, the word is usually spelled **wor**.

Spelling Tip

Words like *word* with the */wer/* are usually spelled *wor.*

c. Copy these words and underline **wor**. Say the words aloud as you write them.

word	worth	world
worm	worse	worry

d. Review your spelling words.

Day 4

a. In the first part of the literature passage notice the phrase *with the comfortable part*. The word *with* shows the relationship between the noun (my mind) and the verb (solacing). This word is called a preposition. **Prepositions** show the relationship between a noun or pronoun and the other words in the sentence.
A preposition always begins a prepositional phrase. For example, *with the comfortable part* is the prepositional phrase. *With* is the preposition. The prepositional phrase will always contain a noun or pronoun which acts as the object of the preposition. The phrase may also contain modifiers of the object. In our example the words *the* and *comfortable* are modifiers of the word *part*.

b. Look over the list of some of the most commonly used prepositions.

List of Commonly Used Prepositions

aboard	at	during	off	under
about	before	except	on	until
above	behind	for	onto	up
across	below	from	outside	upon
after	beneath	in	over	with
against	beside	inside	past	within
along	between	into	since	without
among	beyond	like	through	
around	by	near	to	
as	down	of	toward	

There are twenty-one prepositional phrases in the literature passage. Using the list of prepositions, underline the prepositional phrases and circle the prepositions. **Caution:** Words that are used as

Day 4
b. with the comfortable part
of my condition
round me
of place
in a word
before me
with hunger
by wild beasts
to me
for my sustenance
against any other creature
for theirs
In a word
about me
in a box
into such terrible agonies
of mind
for a while
upon me
with a heavy heart
in that country
at night
for their prey

Day 4
c. Possible answers:
1) to, with
2) down, around
3) during

prepositions may also be used in other ways, such as adverbs or conjunctions. In order to be a preposition it must have a noun or pronoun as its object.

c. Complete the following sentences with a preposition.

1) We will walk ___________ Mary's house _________ the sewing class.

2) Joan's house is ____________ the road and __________ the corner.

3) It is important to be quiet ___________ the concert.

d. Take an oral or written spelling pretest. Remember, sounding out the syllables as your write them will help you spell them correctly.

Day 5

a. Take a final spelling test.

b. Add another entry to the journal you began in **3a**.

c. Think about how you would feel if you had been marooned on an island by yourself for a year. Write a journal entry telling how you would feel and what you would do on the one year anniversary of your arrival.

d. Choose skills from the *Review Activities*.

Review Activities

Choose skills your student needs to review.

1. *Suffixes*
   Add the correct suffix to the following words. Following each sentence write what part of speech (noun, verb, adverb, or adjective) each new word is.

   Ex: The singer sang a joy<u>ful</u> (*full of*) song.
   adjective________

   a. She lacked the motiva___ (*state of*) to finish the job.
   ____

   b. The stereo amplifi___ (*that which*) was turned up too loud. ________________

   c. She is very graci___ (*full of* or *having*) person to allow us to stay in her home. ________________

   d. The audience applauded loud___ (*like* or *manner of*) at the conclusion of the performance. ________________

2. *Prepositions*
   Underline the preposition and circle the object of the preposition in each of the following sentences:

   a. The girls walked under the bridge and across the street to the school.
   b. The car traveled through the tunnel before reaching its destination.
   c. Before you leave, turn off the light beside the door.
   d. Beyond this valley is the roadway to the campsite.
   e. Until the project is finished we will be inside the house.

3. *Journal Entry*
   Write a journal entry for a day in your own life. Be sure to date the entry and use descriptive words to tell about your day.

1. a. motivation, noun
b. amplifier, noun
c. gracious, adjective
d. loudly, adverb

2.
a. under - bridge
across - street
to - school
b. through - tunnel
c. beside - door
d. beyond - valley
to - campsite
e. until - project
inside - house

"You don't seem to see," continued Toad, "that this fine horse of mine is a cut above you altogether. He's a blood horse, he is, partly; not the part you see, of course – another part. And he's been a Prize Hackney, too, in his time – that was the time before you knew him, but you can still tell it on him at a glance, if you understand anything about horses. No, it's not to be thought of for a moment. All the same, how much might you be disposed to offer me for this beautiful young horse of mine?"

The Wind in the Willows by Kenneth Grahame.

Day 1

a. Look at the first sentence of the literature passage. Notice that this literature passage contains a split quotation. The quotation is interrupted with *continued Toad.* The comma is placed after the first part of the quotation, and after *continued Toad.* The quotation mark will always go outside the comma, period, exclamation mark, or question mark. Write the literature passage from dictation.

b. Proofread and check your work. Make a spelling list from any misspelled words or use the following suggested list.

altogether	understand	glance
disposed	thought	hackney

c. The word *thought* is spelled with **ough** to make the short **/o/** sound. Most of these words are followed by the letter **t** when making this sound.

Spelling Tip

Some words like *thought* are spelled with *ough* to make the short */o/* sound.

Copy these words and underline **ough**. Say the words aloud as you write them.

bought fought sought brought wrought

d. Look up the word *hackney* in the dictionary and find out its meaning and etymology. Is it a word that we would hear used today? Why or why not?

e. Make a list of all the contractions you find in the literature passage. Opposite each contraction write the two words that make up the contraction.

Ex: they're - they are

f. Read the literature passage aloud. Does it sound funny? Do you think Toad really wants to sell his horse? Describe Toad's personality.

Day 2

a. Look at the fourth sentence of the literature passage. A comma is used to set off introductory words when they begin a sentence. These words are called interjections. An **interjection** is a word or phrase expressing strong or sudden feeling.

Common Interjections
no yes well
wow oh my

An interjection may be separated by a comma or an exclamation mark. Be sure to capitalize the next word if using an exclamation mark.

Ex: Yes, I will help you.
Wow! Did you see that?

Day 1

d. a horse used for carriage driving or riding
etymology - Middle English

It is not used much today as horses are not used as a means of transportation and are rarely used to pull a carriage.

e. don't - do not
He's - he is
it's - it is

f. The passage is meant to be humorous. Yes, he wants to sell the horse, but you get the impression that Toad's representation of the horse is not quite truthful. From the literature passage we can guess that Toad is the type of character who exaggerates and is not quite truthful, but also that he is rather silly and not real clever.

b. Expressions used in a sentence for emphasis, to set off contrasting ideas, or to indicate an attitude by the speaker are called **parenthetical expressions**. These expressions are independent to the meaning of the sentence, and are set off by commas to separate it from the rest of the sentence. The sentence is independent if it is complete without the expression. Find two parenthetical expressions in the literature passage. Some of the most commonly used parenthetical expressions are listed below.

Common Parenthetical Expressions	
after all	incidentally
all the same	in fact
as a matter of fact	in my opinion
by the way	naturally
consequently	nevertheless
for example	of course
however	on the other hand
I believe (hope, suppose)	therefore

Day 2
b. of course, all the same

c. In addition to parenthetical expressions, a writer may choose to interrupt the narrative with **parenthetical commentary** or an aside. These comments are separated from the sentence by dashes.

Ex: And he's been a Prize Hackney, too, in his time — **that was the time before you knew him,** but you can still tell it on him at a glance, if you understand anything about horses.

c. Ex: He's a blood horse, he is, partly; not the part you see, of course — another part.

Teacher's Note: This author chose to use a dash at the beginning of the phrase only. Today's rules are that you use the dash before and after the phrase..

d. Find another example of parenthetical commentary in the dictation paragraph.

e. A dash is not the same thing as a hyphen. A hyphen is used to separate words and is shorter than a dash, while a dash separates words or sentences and is longer mark. If your word processor does not differentiate, type two hyphens to indicate a dash. Ex: —

f. Parenthetical commentary may also be punctuated with parentheses.

Ex: And he's been a Prize Hackney, too, in his time **(that was the time before you knew him)** but you can still tell it on him at a glance, if you understand anything about horses.

g. The overuse of dashes and parentheses can make the author look careless in his or her writing. Therefore, they should be used intentionally for effect.

h. Review your spelling words.

i. Optional: Enrichment (SAB)

Day 3

a. The literature passage is an example of humorous writing called **irony**. Irony always suggests something different from what is actually said.

Ex: My doctor said I needed an activity to help calm my nerves so I decided to go skydiving.

As we read the literature passage it is obvious that Toad's horse is not all he claims. What are some clues the author gives us in the passage to help us see this?

Day 3
a. not the part you see ....

that was the time before you knew him .....

b. Try writing a paragraph using the technique of irony. Look at Toad's example. Think of something amusing and make it have the opposite meaning.

c. Review your spelling words.

d. Optional: Enrichment (SAB)

Day 4

a. Read the literature passage aloud, pausing for commas and dashes. Add expression and read the passage again as if you were Toad trying to convince someone to buy this horse. Can you envision the humor of this scene?

b. Look at the classified advertisements section of your newspaper or online. Look over the advertisements for horses and other pets. Male horses are either called *stallions* or *geldings*. A female horse is called a *mare*. If you do not have a newspaper available, use the following example.

FOR SALE: Chestnut Gelding, 12 years old, 14 hands, gentle for anyone to ride. Good-looking horse. $800. Call 1-437-555-8436 anytime.

Notice that the height of a horse is described in *hands*. Each hand measurement is approximately 4 inches. If a horse is described as being 14 hands, then the horse is approximately 56 inches tall.

c. When you have read a few ads, think of how Toad might describe his horse in a newspaper ad. Write an advertisement for Toad's horse as he might have written it.

Day 4
c. Possible answer: FOR SALE: Prize Hackney Horse, young and beautiful, great blood lines, gentle disposition. A real steal at $5,000. Call Toad at (843)-555-8712.

d. Take an oral or written spelling pretest. Review any words you found difficult to spell.

Day 5

a. Write the literature passage from dictation. Compare it with the model and correct any mistakes.

b. Write another ad for an object you would like to sell. For example, you might write an ad to sell a bicycle, a skateboard, or a dog.

c. Take an oral or written spelling test.

d. Choose skills from the *Review Activities*.

Review Activities

Choose skills your student needs to review.

1. *Punctuation and Capitalization (Quotations and Interjections)*
   Rewrite the following paragraph correcting any mistakes in capitalization and adding any needed punctuation.

   yes there are many different breeds of horses continued the instructor some breeds are known for the size and strength of the horses while other breeds are known for their speed.

2. *Irony*
   Which of the following sentences contains an example of irony?

   a. It was a beautiful day, so Marie decided to go to the beach.
   b. The one time Jack arrived at work on time the store was closed.

3. Write a sentence with an interjection.

4. Write a sentence with a parenthetical expression.

1. "Yes, there are many different breeds of horses," continued the instructor. "Some breeds are known for the size and strength of the horses while other breeds are known for their speed."

2. b

**3. Example:
No! I don't think I can sing that high.**

**4. Example:
Snowboarding, in my opinion, is more fun than skiing.**

Notes

BOOK STUDY C

Big Red

Big Red by Jim Kjelgaard
Published by Bantam Skylark

Readability level: 7th grade

Teacher's note:
This summary is intended for the teacher's use.

Introducing *Big Red*

Jim Kjelgaard spent his childhood years in a country setting much like what is described in *Big Red*. He enjoyed exploring the vast wilderness that surrounded him.

Summary

It was love at first sight. "Spellbound, Danny returned the dog's gaze ... never before had he seen any dog that revealed at first glance all the qualities a dog should have." Danny's love was a sleek and silky Irish setter named Cheapen Sylvester's Boy, but Danny simply called him Red. Danny's first thought on seeing Red was how much he wanted to own him. He found out that Mr. Haggin, the wealthy man who owned thousands of acres in the Wintapi, had paid seven thousand dollars for the dog. That was more money than Danny and his father, Ross, had made in their entire lives hunting, trapping, and doing odd jobs.

Mr. Haggin was a man who made his fortune sizing up men. He knew Danny had what it takes to become a good dog handler and also knew that like himself, Danny could love and understand a great dog. That is how Danny ended up as caretaker for Red. He wanted to start Red's education by training him to hunt partridge, knowing Red had the makings of an exceptional partridge dog, if he could only be cured of his interest in other varmints. This was taken care of by a close encounter with a skunk.

Red and Danny spend an eventful winter together, where both grow in knowledge and strength. Not only does Red help to save Ross' life, but he and Danny have an exciting encounter with a wolverine and end up in the biggest contest of their lives battling the cunning and dangerous bear, Old Majesty. One of Danny's dreams begins to come true as Red acquires a mate and begins a family which Danny hopes to see as the first in a long line of champions. Finally, the best dream of all comes true as Danny becomes the owner of Red.

Jim Kjelgaard wrote an exciting story of courage and sense of duty in both man and beast. His childhood was spent in much the same way as Danny's and he brings his love of the wilderness to each of his books.

Vocabulary

As you read the book, use the sentences before and after each word to determine its meaning. Then use your reference materials to locate a definition for the word.

1. ravenous - (Chapter 1)
2. profoundly - (Chapter 2)
3. varmints - (Chapter 4)
4. careening - (Chapter 6)
5. indispensable - (Chapter 9)
6. surreptitiously - (Chapter 10)
7. hypodermic - (Chapter 11)

1. ravenous - very hungry
2. profoundly - with deep feeling
3. varmints - troublesome animals
4. careening - moving swiftly
5. indispensable - necessary
6. surreptitiously - secretively
7. hypodermic - introduced under the skin

Choose the correct word from the words listed above to complete the following sentences.

1. A carpenter's tools are _____________ for his work.
2. He winked at her ____________.
3. Mother is ___________ against the use of pesticides.
4. The patient grimaced as the doctor placed the _______ needle in his arm.
5. The race car went ____________ into the stands.
6. The young boy had a __________ appetite.
7. Pesky ____________ made a mess in the barn.

1. indispensable
2. surreptitiously
3. profoundly
4. hypodermic
5. careening
6. ravenous
7. varmints

Optional: Enrichment (SAB)

Discussion Questions

Find sections of the book that tell you the answers to these discussion questions. Be prepared to read some of them aloud in the discussion.

1. Mr. Haggin entrusts Danny with his valuable dog. What does he see in Danny's character that makes him do this?

2. What are some examples of his character traits found in Chapter 1?

3. Examine your own character. How do you think people see you? What strengths can you identify? What weaknesses?

4. Mr. Haggin explains why people exhibit their dogs. The reason he gives is "he ... will know that he has built on what competent men have declared to be the very best. He will know also that he, too, can go one step nearer the perfection that men must and will have in all things." Is there such a thing as perfection? Why would men seek for perfection?

5. There are two major conflicts between Danny and Ross in the story. Are they resolved? If so, how?

---

1. **Danny has proved himself to be hard working, thoughtful, dependable, loyal, and truthful.**

2. **Possible answers:**
   1) **He tracks a bull for Mr. Haggin and completes the job.**
   2) **He goes beyond what was asked of him by acting to prevent the dead bull from spoiling.**
   3) **He bravely hunts Old Majesty, which he has done since he was 12 years old.**
   4) **Mr. Haggin comments that he will call Danny next time anything goes astray.**
   5) **Mr. Haggin appreciated Danny's perceiving the value of Big Red and protecting him from possible injury.**

3. **Answers will vary.**

4. **Allow for discussion.**

5. **The first conflict had to do with Red's education. Ross' solution to the problem of Red running after every varmint he encountered was to give him a licking. Danny felt that Red was too sensitive and he would lose Red's trust if he struck him. The conflict was resolved when Red chased a skunk and was sprayed. This made him stop chasing varmints.**

   The second conflict arose over Red's being trained as a partridge dog. Ross thought this was a waste of a good dog and made him look down on Red. This was resolved when Red saved Ross' life by finding him in the snow, causing Ross to love and appreciate Red.

6. Do you think Danny lied to his father about how Red found Ross in the snow?

7. What made Danny change his mind about taking Big Red to hunt Old Majesty?

8. "He was young, but old enough to know that life was seldom easy. And it seemed to him that in the future there would be a great many bears to meet. How he met them depended in great measure on what he did now with Old Majesty." Could Danny have been thinking of something other than real bears that he would have to meet in the future? What kind of bears do you think he meant?

   Can you apply this to your life? In what ways?

9. Danny made the choice to take Mr. Haggin's valuable dog into the forest to meet Old Majesty. What was Mr. Haggin's reaction? Do you think he made the right decision?

10. Foreshadowing in literature is a suggestion of what is to come later in the story by giving hints or clues. What is the major event that is foreshadowed in this book?

---

6. **Allow for discussion.**

7. **After Old Majesty had killed their animals and attacked Ross, Danny felt that Old Majesty was asserting his supremacy over all the Wintapi. No animal or man would ever be safe there again unless this challenge was met. Danny also realized that how he met this challenge would determine how he would meet other challenges that were sure to come to him in life.**

8. **Allow for discussion.**

9. **Mr. Haggin agreed with Danny's decision. He felt that a man's life was worth more than an animal's, even such a valuable animal as Red.**

   Allow for discussion.

10. **In the beginning of the book, Danny and Big Red have a confrontation with Old Majesty which is not resolved because Danny is afraid of hurting Big Red. This conflict is resolved at the end of the book.**

Activities

The following activities are intended to help you understand the friendship that Danny and Red formed as well as what Danny's life was like. Choose two or three activities to complete your study.

1. If you have a dog, sign up for dog training classes. These are usually held at community centers or you can call your local veterinarian. Even if you do not have a dog, you can attend these classes and observe the relationship between a dog and his owner.

2. Go to the library or look online to look for pictures of different dog breeds. How are dogs grouped? What characteristics determine the different groups?

3. Research the American Kennel Club. What is it? When and why was it formed? What purpose does it serve?

4. Attend a dog show. Talk to the owners and find out what characteristics judges look for in each breed of dog represented.

5. Since money was scarce, Danny and Ross were used to doing things for themselves. For instance, they knew basic first aid and could treat small injuries and illnesses. Think about things around your house that you could do yourself that would save your family money.

6. Ross and Danny made their living hunting and trapping animals. Do you know anyone who hunts? Most hunting today is for the purpose of sport. There are arguments against this as well as arguments in favor. What do you think? Write a paper defending your position.

7. Read other books about Irish setters written by Mr. Kjelgaard, *Irish Red* and *Outlaw Red*, as well as his other books about the wilderness.

I **C.A.N.** Assessment
Big Red Book Study C

After the *Big Red* Book Study is completed check off each I **C.A.N**. objective with your teacher.

______	**C**	I can **complete** my work.
______		I can be **creative**.
______	**A**	I can be **accurate**.
______		I can do my work with a good **attitude**.
______	**N**	I can do my work **neatly**.

Before they had gone half a mile, the storm broke with all its strength. Lightning and thunder crashed and flashed together in a perfect fury! Stunned by the force of it, the children ran for shelter under the great oak tree that marked the halfway point between home and school. Its branches lashed and creaked, but it was something sturdy to cling to. Caddie and Warren and Hetty clung together under the tree, but Tom urged them on.

Caddie Woodlawn by Carol Ryrie Brink.
Used by permission, Macmillan Publishing Company.

Day 1

a. Write the literature passage from dictation. Compare your copy to the passage and correct any errors. Make your own spelling list from any words you misspelled in dictation or use the following list of suggested words:

strength	lightning	stunned
sturdy	thunder	shelter

b. Look at the spelling words *thunder* and *shelter*. The letter combination **er** is the most common way words make the /**er**/ sound.

Three other ways to spell the /**er**/ sound is **ir**, **ur**, and **ear**.

Spelling Tip

The /*er*/ sound may be spelled *er, ir, ur* or *ear*.

Copy these words and underline **er**, **ir**, **ur**, and **ear**. Say the words aloud as you write them.

term	sir	hurt	earth
serve	first	purse	early
fern	bird	burn	learn
certain	dirt	curl	pearl

c. Underline the prepositional phrases in the literature passage. Circle the prepositions. Review the list of prepositions from Lesson 21 if you need help.

d. Find and draw a box around the possessive pronoun *its* each time it appears in the literature passage. What is the antecedent of *its* in the first sentence of the literature passage? What is the antecedent of *its* in the fourth sentence?

e. Find two words in the literature passage with the prefix **be-**. Review your list of prefixes and find its meaning.

f. Using your prefix list, add a prefix to each of the following underlined root words to correctly complete each sentence.

1) The cat is _____active if it is sleeping.
2) If you broke the vase, you will have to _____place it.
3) I hope the weatherman's _____cast is correct for this weekend.
4) We will _____port this product for sale in France.

Day 2

a. It is important not to confuse the possessive pronoun *its* with the contraction *it's*. Write two sentences using the words *its* and *it's* correctly.

b. Look at the first sentence in the literature passage.

Before they had gone half a mile, the storm broke with all its strength.

This sentence contains a comma separating a phrase from the remaining sentence.

Read the first part of this sentence: *Before they had gone half a mile.* This phrase does not express a complete thought and cannot stand alone as a sentence. This is called a **dependent clause.**

Day 1

c. (with)all its strength
(in) a perfect fury
(by) the force
(of) it
(for) shelter
(under) the great oak tree
(between) home and school
(under) the tree

d. 1st - the storm
4th - the oak tree

e. be- on or away;
Possible examples: before, between

f. 1) inactive
2) replace
3) forecast
4) export

Now read the second part of the sentence: *the storm broke with all its strength.* This phrase expresses a complete thought and can stand alone as a sentence. This is called an **independent clause**.

When a dependent clause begins a sentence, it is separated from the independent clause by a comma.

Ex: *Although the wind had blown hard*, there was no damage done to the house.

c. Look at the third sentence in the literature passage. Is the first part of the sentence a dependent or independent clause? Is the second part of the sentence a dependent or independent clause?

d. Underline the dependent clauses in the following sentences. If the sentence begins with a dependent clause, be sure to place a comma between the dependent and independent clause.

1) Since I started jogging I have been steadily losing weight.
2) If you wish to attend the meeting you must be ready at 9:00 A.M.
3) I will practice playing the piano until I have mastered the skill.
4) When other people have needs we should try to help them.
5) Everyone rejoiced when he arrived home safely.

e. Read the literature passage aloud with expression. Be sure to pause at the commas and emphasize the second sentence of the passage.

f. What do you think will happen next? Write the next sentence as if you were the author.

g. Review your spelling words.

Day 2

c. 1st part - dependent clause;
2nd part - independent clause

d. 1) <u>Since I started jogging</u>, I have been steadily losing weight.
2) <u>If you wish to attend the meeting</u>, you must be ready at 9:00 A.M.
3) I will practice playing the piano <u>until I have mastered the skill.</u>
4) <u>When other people have needs</u>, we should try to help them.
5) Everyone rejoiced <u>when he arrived home safely</u>.

Day 3

a. Read the literature passage again. Make a list of the things in the order which they happened in the story. When we write about events in the order in which they happened, we are placing the events in correct **sequence**.

Ex: The storm broke.
Lightning and thunder crashed and flashed.

b. Use your list to tell the story to your teacher. Did you have enough information? Are the events listed in the correct sequence? Add to your list if you need to.

c. Using your list, write a paragraph about the literature passage without looking at it. Be sure to write the events in correct sequence. Compare your work with the model. Did you include everything? Are the events in the correct order?

d. Review your spelling words.

e. Optional: Enrichment (SAB)

Day 3

a. 1) The storm broke.
2) Lightning and thunder crashed and flashed.
3) Children ran for the tree.
4) Branches lashed and creaked.
5) They clung together under tree.
6) Tom urged them on.

Day 4

a. The use of expressive verbs in the writing process allows the writing to come alive for the reader. It can be the difference between the writing being drab and uninteresting, or being captivating and exciting. Read the following sentences. Decide which of the sentences makes use of expressive verbs.

1) As I walked down the beach, I saw the waves come ashore.
2) As I strolled down the beach, I watched the waves crash ashore.

b. Note that the only difference in the two sentences above is the verbs that were used. Look over the literature passage. What verbs would you consider expressive?

Day 4

a. the 2nd sentence

b. Possible answer: broke, crashed, flashed, stunned, lashed, creaked, clung, urged

c. Read over the paragraph you wrote in **3c**. Are there any verbs you can change to more expressive verbs? Use a thesaurus to help you find expressive verbs to add to your writing. Edit until you have done your best. Make a neat copy of your paragraph.

d. Take an oral or written spelling pretest. Review any words you found difficult to spell.

e. Optional: Enrichment (SAB)

Day 5

a. Write the literature passage from dictation. Be sure to use correct punctuation and spelling.

b. Using the sentence you added to the literature passage in **2f**, continue writing the story as if you were the author. Be sure to make use of expressive verbs.

c. Take an oral or written spelling test.

d. Choose skills from the *Review Activities*.

Review Activities

Choose skills your student needs to review.

1. *Prepositions; Its and It's; and Antecedents*
   Underline the prepositions. Draw a box around the contraction for *it is*. Circle the possessive pronoun *its,* and draw an arrow to the antecedent.

   The Privet Hawk Moth hides on tree bark or under leaves during the day, but after the sun sets, it flies around the area looking for nectar. The moth uses its long proboscis to drink nectar from flowers; it's similar to a straw. After the sun rises, the moth grabs onto a tree and remains there until dusk comes again.

2. *Dependent Clauses*
   Write one sentence with a dependent clause at the beginning of the sentence, and another sentence with a dependent clause at the end of a sentence. Be sure to punctuate the sentences correctly.

3. *Correct Sequence*
   Read over the following sentences. Decide the correct sequential order and place the correct order number in front of the sentence. The first one is done for you.

   _____ The thaw causes the streams and rivers to swell.
   __1__ Spring brings amazing change to the land.
   _____ As winter ends, the hours of daylight grow longer and the temperature grows warmer.
   _____ Finally, new buds begin to appear on the trees.
   _____ The land has completed its change, and a new season has begun.
   _____ The increased temperatures cause the winter snows to melt.
   _____ As the thaw continues, wildflowers and green grasses begin to bloom.

1. The Privet Hawk Moth hides <u>on</u> tree bark or <u>under</u> leaves <u>during</u> the day, but <u>after</u> the sun sets, it flies <u>around</u> the area looking <u>for</u> nectar.

The moth uses (its) long proboscis to drink nectar <u>from</u> flowers; [it's] similar <u>to</u> a straw. <u>After</u> the sun rises, the moth grabs <u>onto</u> a tree and remains there <u>until</u> dusk comes again.

2. Examples:
Before the sun set, we walked to the lake.

They ran in the marathon before the sun rose.

3. 4
1
2
6
7
3
5

4. Possible answers:
a. squat, perch
b. step, march, amble, stroll
c. sprint, bound, dart, scamper
d. tell, state, announce, declare
e. observe, inspect, examine, gaze

5. Use synonyms listed for activity 4.

4. *Expressive Verbs*
   Using research material, write expressive verbs that could be substituted for the following verbs.

   a. sit
   b. walk
   c. run
   d. say
   e. see

5. *Edits*
   Rewrite each sentence below, using a more expressive verb than the underlined one.

   a. I will sit in the tree while I read my book.
   b. She began to walk around the room.
   c. Joey likes to run onto the field.
   d. I like to say my name loudly.
   e. Did you see the bull in the parade?

THE GETTYSBURG ADDRESS

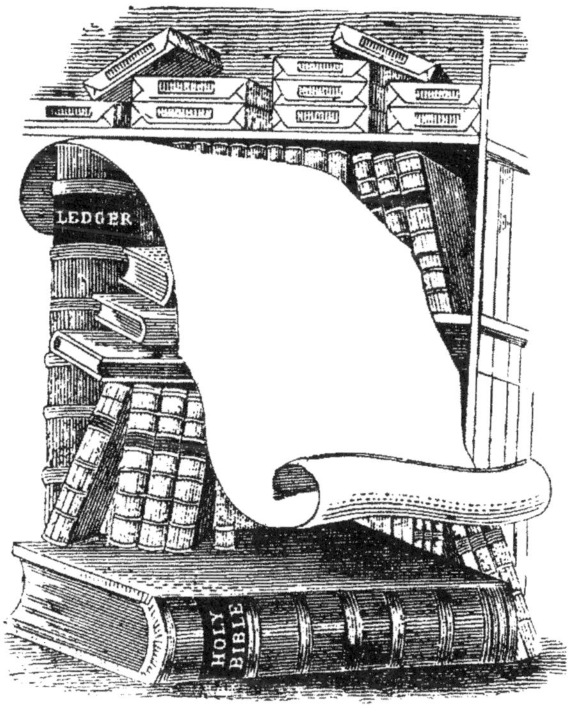

✎ **Teacher's Note: Your student will continue with the Gettysburg Address in Lesson 25.**

Fourscore and seven years ago our fathers brought forth on this continent a new nation, conceived in liberty, and dedicated to the proposition that all men are created equal. Now we are engaged in a great civil war, testing whether that nation, or any nation so conceived and so dedicated, can long endure. We are met on a great battlefield of that war. We have come to dedicate a portion of that field as a final resting place for those who here gave their lives that that nation might live. It is altogether fitting and proper that we should do this.

Gettysburg Address by Abraham Lincoln.

Day 1

a. Read this portion of the *Gettysburg Address*. Write it from dictation. Compare your dictation copy to the model to see if you made any mistakes. Correct any errors you find. Make a spelling list from any misspelled words or use the following suggested list.

conceived	portion	endure
proposition	continent	nation

b. Most words spell **/shun/** as in nation with **-tion**. Other words spell it with **-sion**.

Spelling Tip

Most words spell the */shun/* sound with *-tion*. Other words spell it with *-sion*.

Copy these words and underline **-tion** and **-sion**. Say the words aloud as you write them.

emotion	division
lotion	lesion
caption	pension
sensation	vacation
tension	vision

c. The speech in the literature passage contains a number of prefixes. Find the words that contain the prefixes **con-** and **en-.**

Add these prefixes to your prefix list along with their definitions and word examples. The prefix **con-** means *together* or *with*, and the prefix **en-** means *in* or *into.*

d. Add either the prefix **con-** or **en-** to complete the following words. Use the definitions provided to help you choose the correct prefix.

1) _____compass (*to shut in all around*)
2) _____struct (*to build by fitting parts together*)
3) _____stellation (*a gathering of stars*)
4) _____gage (*to draw into, to involve*)
5) _____gregate (*to meet together*)

Day 2

a. Although the *Gettysburg Address* is a famous speech, there may be several words that you are unfamiliar with. Look up the following words in the dictionary and write a definition for each.

1) conceived	4) fourscore
2) dedicate	5) engaged
3) proposition	6) endure

b. Using the same words from **2a**, use your thesaurus to find synonyms for each word.

c. Rewrite the passage using the synonyms you found in **2b**. Does this help you to better understand the speech?

d. Review your spelling words.

Day 1

c. continent, conceived, engaged

con-: together or with
Possible examples: confirm, continue

en-: in or into
Possible examples: enrich, enact

d. 1) encompass
2) construct
3) constellation
4) engage
5) congregate

Day 2

a. 1) to form a concept or idea
2) to set apart for a special purpose
3) a purpose or plan that is set forth
4) four times twenty (80)
5) become involved in
6) endure - remain in existence

b. Possible answers:
1) conceived - created
2) dedicate - appropriate
3) proposition - proposal
4) fourscore - eighty
5) engaged - undertook
6) endure - last

Teacher's note:
***a. There* can also function as a pronoun:**
***There* will be a concert at the park.**
Or a noun:
He will take it from *there*.

b. 1) There
2) Their
3) They're
4) there
5) Their

c. 1) Nov. 19, 1863
2) It was given as a dedication speech at a ceremony dedicating the battlefield of Gettysburg as a national cemetery for soldiers who were killed in that battle during the Civil War.
3) The speech was remembered because it set forth the highest purposes of the Civil War and a statement of democracy.
4) It was given at the battlefield of Gettysburg.
5) five copies

Day 3

a. Find the word *their* in the last sentence of the literature passage. The word *their* is a possessive pronoun, but it also has two homonyms. Remember, homonyms are words that sound the same but have a different meaning and usually a different spelling.

Ex: We will travel to *their* house.
(*Their* is a possessive pronoun.)

I will meet you over *there*.
(*There* is usually an adverb.)

They're good friends of ours.
(*They're* is a contraction for they are.)

b. Complete the following sentences with *their*, *there* or *they're*.

1) ____________ are many miles more to travel before we reach our destination.
2) _____________ ideas really helped to make this project a success.
3) _____________ very surprised they have been chosen to receive the award.
4) The ball flew over ______________.
5) ____________ dog loves to romp in our yard.

c. The *Gettysburg Address* is a powerful, moving speech. Research Abraham Lincoln or Gettysburg to find information about the background of the speech. You may use the following questions as a guide.

1) When was the speech made?
2) Why was it given?
3) Why is it so powerful and remembered?
4) Where was it given?
5) How many copies did Lincoln make of the speech?

d. Begin to study this portion of the *Gettysburg Address*. Plan to have it memorized by the end of next week's lesson.

e. Review your spelling words.

Day 4

a. Take your notes from **3c** and write two to three paragraphs sharing something that you found interesting about the *Gettysburg Address*.

b. Take an oral or written spelling pretest. Remember, sounding out the syllables as you write them will help you spell them correctly.

c. Optional**:** Enrichment (SAB)

Day 5

a. Write the text of the literature passage from dictation. This will also help you to memorize the speech. Check your copy for any mistakes in spelling or punctuation.

b. Practice saying the literature passage aloud paying special attention to the punctuation. Be sure to pause for the commas.

c. Take an oral or written spelling test.

Day 2
a. Introduction - first sentence
Body - the sentences in between
Conclusion - last sentence

Day 1

a. One method that will help you memorize the *Gettysburg Address* is to prepare index cards with key words or pictures to help you remember specific parts of the speech. For example, you might draw a picture of North America to give you a clue to the word *continent.* After you have finished preparing your cards, number them by placing a small number in the right hand corner. This will help you keep the cards in the correct order.

b. Continue to study and memorize the beginning of the *Gettysburg Address* using your index cards.

Day 2

a. Read the *Gettysburg Address* slowly and carefully. Every good speech has several parts: the **introduction**, the **body**, and the **conclusion**. Identify these parts of the *Gettysburg Address* with your teacher.

b. Continue memorizing the speech.

c. Optional: Enrichment (SAB)

Day 3

a. Prepare to make an oral presentation. Use your index cards to practice your speech. Record your speech with a tape recorder, then play it back and listen to yourself. Are there any parts you need to improve?

b. Follow these guidelines when preparing an oral presentation.

Oral Presentation Checklist

__ 1) Read the speech aloud several times. Try to understand the meaning and the mood of the speech.
__ 2) Use your voice where emphasis is needed and pause accordingly.
__ 3) Speak clearly and loudly. Be sure not to rush through the speech.
__ 4) Look at your audience as if you are speaking directly to them.
__ 5) Stand straight; do not slouch.
__ 6) Practice in front of a mirror.

Day 4

a. Give an oral presentation of the speech to your group or family.

b. Ask them for any advice as to how you could improve your presentation.

Day 5

a. You are now familiar with the beginning of the *Gettysburg Address*. Write a paragraph telling about the speech. This will show how well you understand what was said. A retelling of a speech (or any written material) in your own words is called a **paraphrase**.

Ex: Eighty-seven years ago our forefathers formed a new government in this land, based on freedom etc.

b. Which speech do you think would be most effective to today's audience?

c. Give an oral presentation of the paraphrased speech to your group or family. Which speech did they prefer? Why?

The dog-wanting disease never did leave me altogether. With the new work I was doing, helping Papa, it just kind of burned itself down and left a big sore on my heart. Every time I'd see a coon track down in our fields, or along the riverbanks, the old sore would get all festered up and start hurting again.

Just when I had given up all hope of ever owning a good hound, something wonderful happened. The good Lord figured I had hurt enough, and it was time to lend a helping hand.

It all started one day while I was hoeing corn down in our field close to the river. Across the river, a party of fishermen had been camped for several days. I heard the old Maxwell car as it snorted and chugged its way out of the bottoms. I knew they were leaving. Throwing down my hoe, I ran down to the river and waded across at a place called the Shannon Ford. I hurried to the camp ground.

Where the Red Fern Grows by Wilson Rawls.
Used by permission, Doubleday Books, Dell Publishing Group.

Day 1

a. The boy wanted a dog so badly that his heart ached not to have one.

Day 1

a. Read the literature passage. This boy had a "dog-wanting disease" that left a big sore in his heart. Tell your teacher what you think this means.

b. Write the bold part of the literature passage from dictation. Check your copy with the passage and make a list of any misspelled words or use the following list of words:

hoeing	waded	snorted
leaving	chugged	hurried

c. Each of the suggested spelling words has a suffix. Write the root word next to each word. What changes were made in each of the root words in order to add the suffix? Which spelling word is an exception to the rule concerning adding a suffix beginning with a vowel to a root word ending with a silent **e**?

d. Look at the literature passage. List all the words that are capitalized that are not the first word of a sentence or the pronoun *I*. Determine why each word is capitalized. If you are not sure, check with the capitalization rules in Lessons 6 and 19.

Day 2

a. Find the contraction in the first paragraph of the literature passage. Write it as two words.

b. Find the word *its* in the third paragraph of the literature passage. Is it a possessive pronoun or a contraction? If it is a possessive pronoun, what is its antecedent?

c. Read the first sentence of the second paragraph of the literature passage. What do you think happened? Often the author gives us hints as to what is going to happen in the story. This is called **foreshadowing**. What hints do you find in the literature passage that help you to predict what will happen in this story?

d. Write the next paragraph of the story telling what you think happened.

e. Review your spelling words.

Day 3

a. Looking at the last paragraph of the literature passage, draw a box around all the prepositions. There are nine. If you are unsure of the prepositions, refer to your list of common prepositions in Lesson 21.

Day 1

c. hoe (exception - just add *ing*),

leave (drop the silent e before adding *ing*),

wade (drop the silent e before adding *ed*),

chug (double the last consonant before adding *ed*),

snort (just add *ed*),

hurry (change the *y* to *i* before adding *ed*)

d. Papa - proper name
Maxwell - brand name of a product
Shannon Ford - geographical place

Day 2

a. I'd - I would

b. its - possessive pronoun
antecedent - the old Maxwell car

c. The dog-wanting disease never did leave me altogether. Just when I had given up all hope of ever owning a good hound, something wonderful happened. Across the river, a party of fishermen had been camped for several days.
I hurried to the camp ground.

Day 3

a. in, to, Across, of, for, of, to, at, to

Day 3
b. In-field,
to-river,
across-river,
of-fishermen,
for-days,
of-bottoms,
to-river,
at-place,
to-camp ground

c. 1) (to) - neighbor
2) (in) - bookcase
3) (for) - types
(of) - birds; (by) - river
4) (across) - bridge; (into)
- county
5) (outside) - lines

b. For each preposition you boxed ask, "What?". Underline the noun that answers that question.

Ex: [in] our field
Ask yourself, "In what?" In field.

Each word you underlined is called the **object of the preposition**. Some words that are used as prepositions can also be used as other parts of speech. Remember, for a word to be a preposition, it must have an object.

c. Circle the preposition and underline its object in the following sentences.

Ex: We will spend the day swimming (at) the pool.

1) Mary delivered fresh bread to her neighbor.
2) I found the novel in the bookcase.
3) We will look for different types of birds by the river.
4) We must travel across the bridge and into the next county.
5) The ball bounced outside the boundary lines.

d. Review your spelling words.

e. Optional: Enrichment (SAB)

Day 4

a. Have you ever wanted anything as badly as this boy? Did you receive what you wanted?

b. Write a friendly letter explaining your experience to a friend. Follow the format for a friendly letter found in Lesson 5. Be sure to include how you felt.

c. Take an oral or written spelling pretest. Review any words you found difficult to spell.

d. Optional: Enrichment

Day 5

a. Write the bolded part of the literature passage from dictation. Were you able to spell all the words correctly? Did knowing the root of a word help you with your spelling?

b. Take an oral or written spelling test.

c. Choose skills from the *Review Activities*.

Review Activities

Choose skills your student needs to review.

1. *Capitalization and Conjunctions*
   Add capitalization and punctuation to the following paragraph. Underline any conjunctions.

   in europe during the middle ages falconry or hawking as it was sometimes called was a favorite sport. hawks falcons and eagles were trained to respond to their owners commands and hunt small prey. the bird was hooded and sat on his owners gloved arm. the hood was removed when small game was spotted and the bird would swoop down on its prey. the bird would catch the animal return to his owner with the prey and receive its reward of a piece of meat.

2. *Foreshadowing*
   Write a paragraph that uses foreshadowing to give the reader a hint of what is going to happen next.

3. *Object of the Preposition*
   Write two sentences that contain a preposition and its direct object.

4. *Friendly Letter*
   Write a letter to someone who has done something nice for you recently telling that person how much you appreciate it.

1. In Europe during the Middle Ages falconry, <u>or</u> hawking as it was sometimes called, was a favorite sport. Hawks, falcons, <u>and</u> eagles were trained to respond to their owner's commands <u>and</u> hunt small prey. The bird was hooded <u>and</u> sat on his owner's gloved arm. The hood was removed when small game was spotted, <u>and</u> the bird would swoop down on its prey. The bird would catch the animal, return to his owner with the prey, <u>and</u> receive its reward of a piece of meat.

2. Example:
As Alicia pulled up to her house she looked in the rearview mirror. She didn't look a year older. She assumed she would be spending her birthday with her family and friends, but strangely all of her friends seemed to have other plans. She sighed as she walked up to her door. The house was so dark. Not even her family had remembered what day it was. She was feeling sorry for herself as she put her key in the door. Suddenly, there was a blinding light and voices singing, "Happy Birthday."

3. Example:
He never could find anything to eat in the refrigerator.
The kitten was sleeping under the chair.

It was always a pleasure to prowl where fishermen had camped. I usually could find things: a fish line or a forgotten fish pole. On one occasion, I found a beautiful knife stuck in the bark of a sycamore tree, forgotten by a careless fisherman. But on that day, I found the greatest of treasures, a sportsman's magazine, discarded by the campers. It was a real treasure for a country boy. Because of that magazine, my entire life was changed.

Day 1
a. sportsman, fisherman
man

b. ex:
<u>Where the Red Fern Grows</u> - handwritten
***Where the Red Fern Grows* - computer generated**

c. careless
care - root word
The suffix changes the meaning from care to without care.

-less: without
Possible examples: motionless, helpless

Day 1
d. dis-: apart, away, reverse;
Possible examples: discarded, disappear

Day 1

a. Write the literature passage from dictation. Compare your copy with the passage and make a list of any misspelled words or use the following suggested list.

sycamore	occasion	magazine
discarded	sportsman	fisherman

Which of the suggested spelling words are compound nouns? What word is common to both compound nouns?

b. Look at the title of the literature passage. Copy the title paying close attention to the capitalization. Capitalize the first word and every other important word of a title. If handwritten, underline the entire title; if computer generated, use italics.

c. This literature passage contains the suffix **-less**. Find the word in the passage that contains this suffix. What is the root of this word? The suffix **-less** means *without*. How does the suffix change the meaning of the root word? Add this suffix to your list along with its definition and word examples.

d. Find the prefix **dis-** in the literature passage. This prefix means *apart, away, reverse.* Add this to your prefix list along with its definition and word examples.

Spelling Tip

When adding a prefix to a word do not add or drop any letters. If the last letter of the prefix and the first letter of the root word are the same, the word will contain a double letter.

1) dis + satisfied =
2) dis + appear =
3) un + necessary =
4) im + mature =
5) dis + similar =

1) dissatisfied
2) disappear
3) unnecessary
4) immature
5) dissimilar

e. Many times a prefix added to a word changes the meaning of the word to mean the opposite. Refer to your prefix list to make words of opposite meaning.

Ex: sufficient (not sufficient) - insufficient

1) necessary (not necessary) =
2) expensive (not expensive) =
3) correct (not correct) =
4) fair (not fair) =
5) ripe (not ripe) =

e. 1) unnecessary
2) inexpensive
3) incorrect
4) unfair
5) unripe

Day 2

a. Look at the first sentence of the literature passage. The subject *it* is a singular subject, therefore the singular verb *was* is used. A verb must agree with the subject in number. If the subject is singular, then the verb must be singular. If the subject is plural, then the verb must be plural. The following information will help you in determining whether a verb is singular or plural.

Singular Verbs

1) A verb ending in **s** is usually considered singular.
   Ex: He looks. Susan writes. The dog runs.
2) The verbs *am, is, was, does,* and *has* are singular.

Plural Verbs

1) Plural verbs usually do not end in *s*.
   Ex: They look. Susan and Jim write. The dogs run.
2) The verbs *are, were, do,* and *have* are plural.

b. The subject of a sentence determines whether a singular or plural verb is used. Look at the following guidelines for choosing a singular or plural verb.

A singular verb is used when:

1) The subject is singular.
   Ex: The cricket is chirping.

2) The subject is e*ach, nobody, anyone, everyone, either*, or *neither*. These are singular words.
   Ex: Everyone agrees with your choice.

3) The singular subjects are connected by the words *or* or *nor*.
   Ex: Linda or Mary is babysitting.

4) The subject is a collective noun (one that names a group).
   Ex: My family volunteers at the library every Saturday.

5) The subject expresses an amount of money.
   Ex: Two dollars is the amount I owe.

A plural verb is used when:

1) The subject is plural.
   Ex: The kittens are cute.

2) The subject is *you*.
   Ex: Are you coming with us?

3) The subjects are connected by *and*.
   Ex: Jim and Tom are working together.

4) Plural subjects are connected by *or* or *nor*.
   Ex: Horses or ponies are fun to ride.

c. Often word phrases separate the subject and verb in a sentence. Do not let these word phrases confuse you when determining subject/verb agreement.

Ex: The *rabbits* in the meadow *eat* the clover.
(The prepositional phrase *in the meadow* does not affect the subject/verb agreement of *rabbits eat*.)

Day 2
d. 1) sleeps
2) take
3) drinks
4) is
5) are
6) were
7) do
8) work
9) loves
10) travel
11) was
12) is
13) Have
14) are
15) agree

d. Underline the verb that agrees with the subject in number in the following sentences.

1) Our dog often (*sleep*, *sleeps*) under the porch.
2) The students in the class (*take*, *takes*) their notebooks home.
3) The hummingbird (*drink*, *drinks*) from our feeders.
4) Three dollars (*is*, *are*) the price of admission.
5) Several runners (*is*, *are*) entered in this race.
6) The fish of the coral reef (*was*, *were*) very beautiful.
7) The leaves on this tree (*do*, *does*) not change color in the fall.
8) The members of the club (*work, works*) on projects together.
9) The squirrel outside gathering acorns (*love*, *loves*) to jump through the trees.
10) People (*travel*, *travels*) on this roadway daily.
11) Each of the workers (*was*, *were*) capable of completing the job.
12) Either John or Hank (*is*, *are*) going to drive to the store.
13) (*Has*, *Have*) Martha and Deanna finished the assignment?
14) I hope you (*is*, *are*) coming with us to dinner.
15) Neither the boys nor the girls (*agree*, *agrees*) that the game was played fairly.

e. 1) The Princess and Curdie
2) The House of Sixty Fathers
3) Trail of Apple Blossoms
4) The Cabin Faced West

e. Capitalize and underline the following titles of books.

1) the princess and curdie
2) the house of sixty fathers
3) trail of apple blossoms
4) the cabin faced west

f. Review your spelling words.

Day 3
a. it, I, my

Day 3

a. Pronouns are used to replace nouns. Find the three different pronouns in the literature passage.

b. The literature passage is written in the first person. This means that the author is writing from his point of view, using the pronoun *I.* Most stories, however, are written in the third person, using the pronouns *he, she,* and *they.* Rewrite the literature passage in the third person.

Ex: It was always a pleasure to prowl where fishermen had camped. He usually could find . . .

c. You have learned to capitalize and underline titles of books. Here is a list of other titles that are also underlined.

magazines	works of art	movies
newspapers	music albums	plays
television programs	ships	trains
aircraft		

d. Capitalize and underline titles in the following sentences.

Ex: The Gainesville Sun is a source for daily news.
The *Gainesville Sun* is a source for daily news.

1) where the red fern grows is an excellent book for young boys and girls to read. (book)
2) The space shuttle, columbia, is orbiting the earth at this time. (aircraft)
3) I am cooking a recipe I cut out of the family circle. (magazine)
4) The doulos will be docking here today. (ship)
5) Shakespeare's hamlet will be performed by the actors of the Community Theater. (play)

e. Review your spelling words.

Day 4

a. An adverb describes a verb, adjective, or another adverb. They tell us how, when, where, or to what extent or degree. Find two adverbs in the literature passage.

Day 3

b. It was always a pleasure to prowl where fishermen had camped. He usually could find things: a fish line or a forgotten fish pole. On one occasion, he found a beautiful knife stuck in the bark of a sycamore tree, forgotten by a careless fisherman. But on that day, he found the greatest of treasures, a sportsman's magazine, discarded by the campers. It was a real treasure for a country boy. Because of that magazine, his entire life was changed.

Teacher's Note: Titles may be underlined if handwritten; italicized if computer generated.

d. 1) Where the Red Fern Grows OR *Where the Red Fern Grows*
2) Columbia OR *Columbia*
3) Family Circle OR *Family Circle*
4) Doulos OR *Doulos*
5) Hamlet OR *Hamlet*

Day 4

a. always, usually

b. Locate the punctuation mark used in the literature passage before the list of things the boy found. This mark is a **colon**. The colon (**:**) is used to introduce a list. Often the colon is preceded by summary words such as *things, as follows, the following,* or *these.*

Ex: Be sure to bring the following things: drawing paper, soft lead pencils, and erasers.

c. Colons are also used as follows:

1) After the salutation of a business letter
Ex: Gentlemen:

2) Between the hour and minute when referring to time
Ex: 2:45

Day 4
d. 1) These are the items we need for the trip: coolers, snacks, sleeping bags, and sheets.
2) The meeting will begin at exactly 8:00 P.M.
3) The children chosen for the team are as follows: James, Karen, Robert, Todd, and Sandy.
4) Dear Mr. Jones:

d. Add colons and commas as needed in the following sentences. Remember that items in a series are separated by commas. (Refer to Lesson 10, **3a** if you need further review of this punctuation rule.)

1) These are the items we need for the trip coolers snacks sleeping bags and sheets.
2) The meeting will begin at exactly 8 00 P.M.
3) The children chosen for the team are as follows James Karen Robert Todd and Sandy.
4) Dear Mr. Jones

e. Pretend you are the young boy described in the literature passage. Write a business letter to *Field and Stream,* 2147 Bird Dog Avenue, Spokane, WA 63458, requesting information on purchasing a hunting dog. This letter will not be mailed; it is only for the purpose of acquainting you with the format of a business letter. Use the following model as an example for your letter. The parts of the business letter are labeled in italics for your information. Do not copy these words when you are writing your letter.

(*Heading)*
1234 Main Street
Seattle, WA 63782
April 8, 2013

(*Inside Address*)
Field and Stream
2147 Bird Dog Avenue
Spokane, WA 63458

(Salutation or Greeting)
Gentlemen:

(Body)

I read your article on purchasing hunting dogs in the March edition and would like to have the additional information you offer along with the list of breeders. Please send this information to me at the address listed below:

Mr. Logan Harris
1234 Main Street
Seattle, WA 63782

Thank you for your attention in this matter.

(Closing)
Sincerely,

(Signature)
Logan Harris

Teacher's Note: **There are many styles of business letters. This is the commonly used block style.**

f. Take an oral or written spelling pretest. Review any words you found difficult to spell.

Day 5

a. Write the literature passage from dictation and check your copy.

b. Write a paragraph describing your favorite magazine. Use adverbs to help describe why you find it so interesting. Remember to underline the title of the magazine and capitalize the first word and every important word in the title.

c. Take an oral or written spelling test.

d. Choose skills from the *Review Activities*.

Review Activities

Choose skills your student needs to review.

1. *Suffix*
   Add a suffix from your list of suffixes to the following root words to fit the definition given. If you are not sure about a word, check your dictionary.

   a. heart__________ (*without heart or compassion*)
   b. thank______ (*full of thanks*)
   c. quick_______ (*manner of quick*)
   d. connect_____ (*the state of being connected*)
   e. paint_____ (*one who paints*)

1. a. heartless
b. thankful
c. quickly
d. connection
e. painter

2. *Prefixes*
   Add the prefixes to complete the following words.

   a. dis + solve =
   b. im + material =
   c. im + practical =
   d. un + written =
   e. un + navigable =

2. a. dissolve
b. immaterial
c. impractical
d. unwritten
e. unnavigable

3. *Subject/Verb Agreement*
   Choose the correct verb to complete the following sentences:

   a. Everyone (*is*, *are*) going to the lecture tonight.
   b. The panther (*run*, *runs*) swiftly through the underbrush.
   c. (*Do*, *Does*) Rick and Mary know where to meet us?
   d. James or John (*has*, *have*) the skill to play the piano.
   e. The paintings on the wall (*contain*, *contains*) beautiful colors.

3. a. is
b. runs
c. do
d. has
e. contain

4. *First, Second, and Third Person*
   Read each of the following sentences. Indicate whether the sentence is written in first (**1**), second (**2**), or third person (**3**). Underline the pronouns that help you in making your decision.

   a. _____He drove into the placid pool of water and broke through the surface of the water with a shout.
   b. _____I ran as I had never run before; my lungs were ready to burst.
   c. _____You must pay attention if you hope to succeed in mastering this skill.

4. a. 3 - He
b. 1 - I, my
c. 2 - You

5. *Titles*
   Capitalize and underline the titles in the following sentences.

   a. The miami herald printed a story about the many boating accidents in their area. (newspaper)
   b. little women is based on the life of author, Louisa May Alcott. (book)
   c. The mona lisa is on display at the Louvre in Paris. (painting)
   d. I read an article about the future of the economy in time. (magazine)
   e. The television program, christy, is based on the novel by Catherine Marshall. (television program)

5.
a. Miami Herald OR *Miami Herald*
b. Little Women OR *Little Women*
c. Mona Lisa OR *Mona Lisa*
d. Time OR *Time*
e. Christy OR *Christy*

6. *Colon*
   Add colons to the following sentences.

   a) We will begin hiking the trail at 800 A.M.
   b) The following things were littering the ground cans, newspapers, and bottles.
   c) You will be taking these subjects this fall Earth science, literature, and algebra.

6. a) 8:00 A.M.
b) the ground:
c) fall:

7. *Business letter*
   Write a business letter to the company of your choice.

8. *Capitalization and Punctuation*
Rewrite this paragraph and add punctuation and capitalization.

what do you feel is our nation's greatest resource water is the greatest natural resource our country has we most often think of water in terms of drinking water and water for household needs there are many other ways that water is valuable some of these uses are as follows transportation irrigation and hydroelectric power the united states would not be the rich nation it is today without the ability to transport its goods down the mississippi river or use the waters of the colorado river to water farmland in the west much of the electrical power in the west is generated by hydroelectric power plants no other natural resource is as valuable to our nation as our water supply

8. What do you feel is our nation's greatest resource? Water is the greatest natural resource our country has. We most often think of water in terms of drinking water and water for household needs. There are many other ways that water is valuable. Some of these uses are as follows: transportation, irrigation, and hydroelectric power. The United Sates would not be the rich nation it is today without the ability to transport its goods down the Mississippi River or use the waters of the Colorado River to water farmland in the West. Much of the electrical power in the West is generated by hydroelectric power plants. No other natural resource is as valuable to our nation as our water supply.

Assessment 3
(Lessons 19 - 27)

1. Circle the adjectives in the following sentence:

   The ragged, dirty shirt hung on the line.

2. Using your thesaurus, rewrite the above sentence replacing the adjectives with synonyms.

3. Arrange the following in outline form.

   Cars, Motorcycles, Places People Live, Condominiums, Apartments, Trucks, Vehicles, Houses

4. Rewrite the first two sentences of the literature passage in Lesson 20 as if someone else were telling the story (third person).

5. Write a sentence using *to, two, too.*

6. How are pronouns used?

7. List at least three pronouns that show possession (ex: his). Do possessive pronouns ever need an apostrophe?

8. Rewrite the following phrases using possessive nouns:

   a. the book that belongs to John
   b. the bikes that belong to the boys
   c. the sister of Pat

1. ragged dirty

2. Example:
The torn, filthy shirt hung on the line.

3. I. Places People Live
A. Houses
B. Apartments
C. Condominiums
II. Vehicles
A. Cars
B. Trucks
C. Motorcycles

4. The time he spent upon the island is still so horrible a thought to him, that he must pass it lightly over. In all the books he had read of people cast away, they had either their pockets full of tools, or a chest of things would be thrown upon the beach along with them, as if on purpose.

5. Possible answer:
Give this *to* Bob.
I have *two* cats.
Bill will come with us, *too*.

6. Pronouns are used to replace nouns.

7. Possible answers:
my, mine, your, yours, his, her, hers, its, our, ours, your, yours, their, theirs
Possessive pronouns never use an apostrophe.

8. a. John's book
b. boys' bikes
c. Pat's sister

9. Find at least three prepositional phrases in the literature passage in Lesson 20. Underline the preposition in each.

10. Copy the following making corrections in capitalization and punctuation:

    In fact john said all we have to do is read the directions i am sure we will be able to build the model ourselves

11. Write a word with the prefix **con-.**

12. Write a word with the suffix –**tion.**

13. Choose the right word to complete these sentences:

    1) We all went to (their, there, they're) house after the game.
    2) (Their, There, They're) was no reason for me to continue.
    3) (Their, There, They're) coming to pick Jane up in an hour.

14. Write a word with the prefix **pre-.**

9. <u>upon</u> the island, <u>to</u> me, <u>In</u> all the books, <u>of</u> people, <u>of</u> tools, <u>of</u> things, <u>upon</u> the beach, <u>with</u> them, <u>on</u> purpose, <u>in</u> my pockets, <u>of</u> knowledge, <u>of</u> means

10. "In fact," John said, "all we have to do is read the directions. I am sure we will be able to build the model ourselves."

11. Possible answers: convex, convoluted

12. Possible answers: election, reaction

13. 1) their
2) There
3) They're

14. Possible answers: preface, pretext

It was almost quite dark, the girls were getting tired, and as Bobbie said, it was past bedtime, when suddenly Phyllis cried, "What's that?"

And she pointed to the canal boat. Smoke was coming from the chimney of the cabin, had indeed been curling softly into the soft evening air all the time – but now other wreaths of smoke were rising, and these were from the cabin door.

"It's on fire – that's all," said Peter, calmly. "Serve him right."

"Oh – how **can** *you?" cried Phyllis. "Think of the poor dear dog."*

The Railway Children by E. Nesbit.

✎ **Teacher's Note: You may want to reassure your student that as the story continues, you find that the dog is unharmed.**

Day 1

a. Read the literature passage paying close attention to how quotation marks are used. Written conversation is called **dialogue**. Also, note the author's use of dashes. In Lesson 22 **2c** you learned that dashes can be used to set off parenthetical statements. Dashes can also be used in place of other punctuation, such as a comma or semicolon.

b. The last part of the literature passage is a conversation. When writing dialogue, begin a new paragraph when there is a change in speaker.

c. Write the literature passage from dictation. Proofread and correct your work. Make a spelling list from the words you misspelled or use the following suggested list.

bedtime	chimney	wreaths
suddenly	pointed	softly

d. Some words, like *chimney* are spelled with the ending **ey**. Other words, like *candy* are spelled with just **y**. It is helpful to know the correct spelling of these words so you can spell the plural form correctly.

To form the plural of words ending with a consonant before the **y**, change the **y** to **i** and add **es**. To form the plural of words ending with a vowel before the **y**, just add **s**.

Ex: chimney - chimneys
candy - candies

Spelling Tip

To form the plural of words ending in *y* preceded by a consonant, change the *y* to *i* and add *es*. Otherwise, just add *s*.

e. Copy these words and write its plural form.

chimney	monkey	donkey
candy	pony	sky

f. Which words from the suggested spelling list are used as adverbs in the literature passage? What suffix helps to identify these words as adverbs?

Day 2

a. Locate the word *poor* in the literature passage. What does this word mean? The word *poor* has two meanings. If you are unsure, look the word up in the dictionary. The word *poor* also has two homonyms (words that sound the same but have different meanings and spellings). The homonyms are *pore* and *pour.* Look up the meanings in the dictionary for each of these words. You will find the word *pore* also has two definitions. Write one sentence for each homonym.

Day 1

e. chimneys, monkeys, donkeys, candies, ponies, skies

f. suddenly, softly the suffix -ly

Day 2

a. poor - penniless or pitiful
pore - to gaze intently or a small opening in the skin
pour - to flow freely

Teacher's Note: Depending on the regional accent, these words may sound slightly different.

Day 2
b. a comma

b. Note the dashes (—) in paragraphs two, three, and four. What other punctuation mark could be used instead to tell the reader to pause in these places? While a dash can be used to indicate a pause or break in thought, it also is used to emphasize and set apart a word or phrase. Sometimes a dash is used to indicate an interruption in speech by another person.

Ex: There is something — actually many things — that we need to accomplish this afternoon. (break in thought)

At this meeting — this private meeting — we will discuss our future plans. (emphasis)

c. Look at the last sentence in the literature passage. Since both a dash and a comma causes the reader to pause, a comma could replace the dash following *Oh*. Words like *oh* used at the beginning of a sentence to express strong emotion or a sudden feeling are called **interjections**. Usually a comma or an exclamation point follows an interjection. If a comma is used, do not capitalize the next word; if an exclamation point is used, remember to capitalize the next word.

Ex: Well, I hope my cousins come to visit this year.
Oh! What a pretty dress!

Write two sentences; one using an interjection followed by a comma and another using an exclamation point.

d. Look at the word *can* in the first sentence of the last paragraph in the literature passage. It is printed in a different type for emphasis. Try reading the literature passage aloud using good expression.

e. The way we emphasize words can change the entire meaning of a sentence. Try reading the literature passage again, emphasizing different words. For extra fun, try recording your reading.

f. Review your spelling words.

Day 3

a. What do you think about Peter's attitude? Let your imagination take you to the scene depicted in the literature passage. What would you tell Peter?

b. Write what you think happened next. Be sure to write it in conversational form (dialogue) and remember to use quotation marks around all direct quotations. Everytime someone different is speaking make sure you indent. You can review the quotation rules in Lesson 7.

c. Quotation marks are also used around the titles of songs, short stories, chapters of a book, magazine articles, and short poems. Capitalize the first word and every other important word.

Ex: "The Eagle" (short poem)
"A Mighty Fortress" (song)
"The Real Thing" (short story)

d. Add quotation marks and punctuation to the following sentences.

Ex: You must go with us to the museum said James
"You must go with us to the museum," said James.

1) Which dog is best for a pet in an apartment asked Jim
2) If you will come with me pleaded Myra we will ask Mrs. Jimson together
3) There are many ways to solve the problem said Kelly
4) Run quickly or they will catch you exclaimed Janice
5) The teacher assigned the poem The Charge of the Light Brigade to read for discussion in class tomorrow

e. Review your spelling words.

Day 3

d. 1) "Which dog is best for a pet in an apartment?" asked Jim.
2) "If you will come with me," pleaded Myra, "we will ask Mrs. Jimson together."
3) "There are many ways to solve the problem," said Kelly.
4) "Run quickly or they will catch you!" exclaimed Janice.
5) The teacher assigned the poem, "The Charge of the Light Brigade," to read for discussion in class tomorrow.

Day 4

a. Pretend you are a television reporter sent to get the "scoop" on a fire. Write out your report being sure to include the four essential information points of any news article.

1) Who is the story about?
2) What is the story about?
3) When did the story take place?
4) Where did the story take place?

b. Once you have completed your report, practice saying it aloud. Record your version of the news report.

c. Take an oral or written spelling pretest. Review any words you found difficult to spell.

d. Optional: Enrichment (SAB)

Day 5

a. Write the literature passage from dictation. Proofread and make any corrections. If you still have questions about the use of quotation marks, ask your teacher to explain.

b. Try acting out the literature passage plus the part you added in **3b**.

c. Take an oral or written spelling test.

d. Choose skills from the *Review Activities*.

Review Activities

Choose skills your student needs to review.

1. *Homonyms (Pore, Pour and Poor)*
   Underline the correct homonym in each of the following sentences.

   a. He used (*pore*, *pour*, *poor*) judgment in choosing a fishing spot.
   b. Please (*pore*, *pour*, *poor*) yourself some lemonade.
   c. The sweat flowed from every (*pore*, *pour*, *poor*) of his body.
   d. He will often (*pore*, *pour*, *poor*) over old documents at night trying to unlocked their secrets.
   e. The (*pore*, *pour*, *poor*) cat looked terrible after falling into the puddle.

2. *Interjections*
   Underline the interjections and add punctuation.

   a. Oh What a lovely dress
   b. Well so you did decide to come
   c. Hurrah We won the championship
   d. My what a lovely daughter you have

3. *Dialogue and Quotation Marks*
   Rewrite the following sentences of dialogue. Begin each new paragraph by indenting, and add quotation marks and punctuation where needed. Be sure to punctuate any interjections.

   Mary it was a great concert last night exclaimed Ginger. I wish you could have come. Well it was hard to stay home and babysit last night, but I had already promised Mrs. Wilson I would watch her children while she went to a meeting said Mary with a shrug. How many kids from school came? Everyone came but Sam and John answered Ginger. The band sang my favorite song. It was great! Oh well I sat around and read an article in Horses magazine sighed Mary but I know I made the right decision to be faithful to my promise.

1. a. poor
b. pour
c. pore
d. pore
e. poor

2. a. <u>Oh</u>! What a lovely dress!
b. <u>Well</u>, so you did decide to come.
c. <u>Hurrah</u>! We won the championship!
d. <u>My</u>, what a lovely daughter you have.

3.
"Mary, it was a great concert last night!" exclaimed Ginger. "I wish you could have come."
"Well, it was hard to stay home and babysit last night, but I had already promised Mrs. Wilson I would watch her children while she went to a meeting," said Mary with a shrug. "How many kids from school came?"
"Everyone came but Sam and John," answered Ginger. "The band sang my favorite song. It was great!"
"Oh well, I sat around and read an article in <u>Horses</u> magazine," sighed Mary, "but I know I made the right decision to be faithful to my promise."

4. *News Report*
   Write a news report about something that has happened in your life. It could be about a sport, a trip, a concert, an accomplishment, etc. Be sure to include the who, what, when and where points in your story.

Pooh was thoughtful when he heard this, and then he murmured to himself:

But whatever his weight in pounds, shillings, and ounces,
He always seems bigger because of bounces.

"And that's the whole poem," he said. "Do you like it, Piglet?"
"All except the shillings," said Piglet. "I don't think they ought to be there."
"They wanted to come in after the pounds," explained Pooh, "so I let them. It is the best way to write poetry, letting things come."
"Oh, I didn't know," said Piglet.

The House at Pooh Corner by A. A. Milne.

Day 1

a. Read the literature passage. Why do you think the shillings wanted to come into Pooh's poem? Look up *shilling* in the dictionary to find its meaning.

b. Look at the literature passage paying special attention to punctuation. This literature passage contains written conversation known as dialogue. In what ways does the writer let the reader know a new person is speaking?

c. Write the literature passage from dictation. Proofread and correct any mistakes. Make a spelling list of any misspelled words or use the following suggested list:

thoughtful	murmured	weight
pounds	shilling	ounces

d. Look at the words *pounds* and *ounces* in the suggested spelling list. Words with the /**ow**/ sound are usually spelled with **ow**. Some words are spelled **ou**, but **ou** will usually not end a word.

Day 1

a. Pounds is a unit of money as well as a unit of weight. Shillings is also a unit of money.

b. The writer begins a new paragraph by indenting each time a new person speaks.

Spelling Tip

Most words spell the */ow/* sound with *ow*. Some words are spelled *ou*.

e. Locate the word in the literature passage with the suffix **-ful**. The suffix **-ful** means *full of.* This suffix usually changes a word into an adjective. Add **-ful** to your suffix list. Also fill in the definition, part of the speech, and word examples.

f. Find an adjective in comparative form and an adjective in superlative form in the literature passage. Refer to Lesson 7 if you need any review.

g. In the literature passage, what punctuation separates the text from the poem which Pooh composed? Why do you think the writer chose this punctuation?

Day 2

a. Look at the literature passage. What do you notice about the use of quotation marks? Write two rules about the use of the quotation marks. Refer to Lesson 7 if you need any review.

b. Underline the sentence in the literature passage which contains a split quotation.

Day 1

e. thoughtful
thoughtful - full of thought
part of the speech - adjective
Possible word examples:
restful, beautiful

f. comparative form: bigger
superlative form: best

g. colon; to set off the poem from the rest of the text

Day 2

a. Refer to Lesson 7, Quotation Rules

b. "They wanted to come in after the pounds," explained Pooh, "so I let them.

c. Add correct punctuation to the following direct quotations. Refer to the quotation rules in Lesson 7 if needed.

Ex: Come with us to the rally begged Alicia
"Come with us to the rally," begged Alicia.

1) We need to find a way for the whole group to take the canoe trip explained Jim
2) Janice replied I'm not sure I'll be able to afford the cost
3) One way to help cover the cost interjected Seth is to have a car wash
4) What a great idea exclaimed Jim That would help reduce everyone's cost.
5) Where would we have the car wash asked Sara.

d. Review your spelling words.

e. Optional: Enrichment

Day 3

a. Dialogue is used in a story to bring the characters to life. Good stories usually contain some element of dialogue. Look through some stories you have available. Do they all contain dialogue?

b. Write a short conversation between you and your teacher. Remember to indent each time the speaker changes. Be sure to identify the speaker when necessary so the reader is clear about who is speaking.

c. Check your punctuation. Did you use the quotation marks correctly?

d. Optional: Enrichment (SAB)

e. Review your spelling words.

Day 4

a. Pooh is very good at making up poetry. The poem he composes in the literature passage is a **couplet**, a two-lined stanza of poetry ending in words that rhyme. What two words in Pooh's poem rhyme?

Day 2

c. 1) "We need to find a way for the whole group to take the canoe trip," explained Jim.
2) Janice replied, "I'm not sure I'll be able to afford the cost."
3) "One way to help cover the cost," interjected Seth, "is to have a car wash."
4) "What a great idea!" exclaimed Jim. "That would help reduce everyone's cost."
5) "Where would we have the car wash?" asked Sara.

4.

a. ounces, bounces

b. In Pooh's poem he is describing his friend, Tigger. Write a list of words that describe someone you know or an animal. Write two or three couplets about this person or animal. Make sure the ending words of each stanza rhyme.

c. Take an oral or written spelling pretest. Review any words you found difficult to spell.

Day 5

a. Write the literature passage from dictation. Compare your copy with the passage and correct any errors. Were you able to correctly punctuate all the direct quotations?

b. A play is similar to a short story with dialogue. You can write dialogue in the form of a one-act play. This form of a mini-play is called a **duolog**. Plan your basic plot and decide on your characters. Most stories have a problem of some kind which the characters must overcome. Try to provide the reader with some insight into the personalities of your characters. When writing in play form, quotation marks are not used. When your play is complete, find someone to act it out with you. Look at the following example:

SETTING: A hiking trail that follows a creek in a forest wilderness

NANCY: I don't know how you talked me into this hiking experience. You know how I hate bugs!

JOANNA: Come on Nancy! The bugs aren't that bad. Look at the beauty around you.

c. Take an oral or written spelling test.

d. Choose skills from Review Activities page.

Review Activities

Choose skills your student needs to review.

1. *Punctuation (Dialogue)*
   Rewrite the following dialogue adding punctuation.

   Do you feel the judging team is ready for the competition asked Martha. I really don't think we are. We need to spend some more time practicing and studying answered Mike. Well, the competition is only two weeks away said Martha and everyone's schedule is full. Then we will have to practice the best we can individually and hope we can still do well as a team at the competition said Mike with a shrug.

2. *Poetry - Couplet*
   Write a couplet describing an animal.

3. *Edits*
   Rewrite the following paragraph correcting spelling, grammar, and punctuation.

   Unce upon a tyme there were three pigs these pigs desided to leaf home and build there own homes won wanted to build a home from straw won from sticks and won from bricks witch house do you think waz the stronger

1.

"Do you feel the judging team is ready for the competition?" asked Martha.

"I really don't think we are. We need to spend some more time practicing and studying," answered Mike.

"Well, the competition is only two weeks away," said Martha, "and everyone's schedule is full."

"Then we will have to practice the best we can individually and hope we can still do well as a team at the competition," said Mike with a shrug.

2. Example:
The turtle never needs to pack.
He carries his home on his back.

3. Once upon a time, there were three pigs. These pigs decided to leave home and build their own homes. One wanted to build a home from straw, one from sticks, and one from bricks. Which house do you think was the strongest?

Red took three uncertain steps forward and stopped again. Danny rushed angrily toward him. He reached down to grasp Red's collar, but the toes of his snowshoes crossed and he stumbled forward again. His bare hands plunged deeply into the snow. They hit something soft and yielding, something that gave before them. It was a man's trousered leg. Danny dug frantically, and lifted Ross Pickett from his snowy bed. His hand went under Ross's shirt. His father was warm and his heart still beat.

Day 1

a. Look over the literature passage making note of punctuation and spelling, and then write the passage from dictation. Proofread your copy and correct any errors in punctuation and spelling.

b. Make a spelling list of any misspelled words or use the following suggested list.

angrily	snowshoes	stopped
yielding	frantically	trousered

c. What spelling rule applies to the word *angrily*?

What spelling rule applies to the word *stopped*?

Day 1

c. When a word ending in y is preceded by a consonant, the y is changed to i before adding a suffix, except a suffix that begins with i such as -ing.

When a one-syllable word ends with a short vowel followed by a consonant, then the last consonant is doubled before adding a suffix beginning with a vowel.

d. Find the word *frantically* in the literature passage. When a word ending in **ic** is an adjective, the adverb is usually formed by adding **-ally** rather than just **-ly**.

Ex: energetic - energetically

e. Add the suffix **-ally** to the following words.

1) pathetic_________
2) realistic________
3) enthusiastic______

f. Underline the words in the literature passage that show ownership. What has been added to each of these words to show they are possessive?

Day 2

a. Find and circle all the words in the literature passage that end with the suffix **-ly**. These words tell *how*, *when*, *where*, *how often* or *to what extent*. Note that although most words ending in **-ly** are adverbs, some are adjectives, such as *friendly* and *lovely.* If you need to review adverbs, refer to Lesson 5.

b. Draw an arrow from the adverbs you have circled to the verb it tells about. Tell your teacher what each adverb tells about the verb.

Ex: Danny rushed (angrily) toward him.
(The adverb *angrily* tells how he rushed.)

c. Not all adverbs end in **-ly**. Adverbs modify not only verbs, but sometimes adjectives or other adverbs.

Ex: The car sped around the curb (too) rapidly.
(The adverb *too* is modifying the adverb *rapidly*.)

The players were (very) happy after winning the game.
(The adverb *very* modifies the adjective *happy.)*

Look at the literature passage. Find four adverbs that do not end in **-ly** and indicate the verb being modified.

Day 1

e. 1) pathetically
2) realistically
3) enthusiastically

f. Red's collar
man's trousered leg
Ross's shirt

an 's has been added

Day 2

a. angrily, deeply, frantically

b. angrily (rushed); how
deeply (plunged); to what extent
frantically (dug) how

c. Any four of the following:
forward (took)
again (stopped)
down (reached)
again (stumbled)
under (went)
still (beat)

Teacher's note:
forward can be considered either an adverb or a direct object in this sentence:
...he stumbled forward again.

d. Write four sentences using adverbs to answer how, when, where, how often, or to what extent.

Ex: The rabbit hopped *merrily* through the field. (how)
The plumber called *yesterday*. (when)
The toddler fell *down*. (where)
He ate apples regularly for lunch. (how often)
Mother is *very* happy. (to what extent or degree)

e. Review your spelling words.

Day 3

a. Every verb has four principal parts: the **present**, the **present participle**, the **past**, and the **past participle**.

Ex: present - look
present participle - (is) looking
past - looked
past participle - (have) looked

Note that the present participle and past participle are used with helping verbs such as *is, are, am, have, has, had,* etc.

b. Regular verbs form the past and past participle by adding **-ed** to the present form. The present participle is formed by adding **-ing** to the present form. Write the principal parts of the following regular verbs. The first one is done for you.

Present	Present Participle	Past	Past Participle
1) change	changing	changed	(have) changed
2) ask			
3) fill			
4) love			
5) rush			
6) climb			

Day 3
b. 2) ask, asking, asked, (have asked)
3) fill, filling, filled, (have) filled
4) love, loving, loved, (have) loved
5) rush, rushing, rushed, (have) rushed
6) climb, climbing, climbed, (have) climbed

c. Irregular verbs form the past and past participle in different ways. Because there is no single rule that applies to irregular verbs, it is important to familiarize yourself with them. Look at the list on the next page for the most common irregular verbs. The present participle form has not been included in the list because it is always formed by adding **-ing** to the present form.

Irregular Verbs

Present	Past	Past Participle
beat	beat	(have) beaten or beat
become	became	(have) become
begin	began	(have) begun
bite	bit	(have) bitten
blow	blew	(have) blown
break	broke	(have) broken
bring	brought	(have) brought
burst	burst	(have) burst
catch	caught	(have) caught
choose	chose	(have) chosen
come	came	(have) come
do	did	(have) done
draw	drew	(have) drawn
drink	drank	(have) drunk
drive	drove	(have) driven
eat	ate	(have) eaten
fall	fell	(have) fallen
fight	fought	(have) fought
fly	flew	(have) flown
forget	forgot	(have) forgotten
freeze	froze	(have) frozen
get	got	(have) got or gotten
give	gave	(have) given
go	went	(have) gone
grow	grew	(have) grown
hang	hung	(have) hung
hit	hit	(have) hit
know	knew	(have) known
lay	laid	(have) laid
lead	led	(have) led
leave	left	(have) left
lie	lay	(have) lain
lose	lost	(have) lost
pay	paid	(have) paid
ride	rode	(have) ridden
ring	rang	(have) rung
rise	rose	(have) risen
run	ran	(have) run
say	said	(have) said

Present	Past	Past Participle
see	saw	(have) seen
set	set	(have) set
shake	shook	(have) shaken
shine	shone, shined	(have) shone, shined
shrink	shrank	(have) shrunk
sing	sang	(have) sung
sink	sank	(have) sunk
sit	sat	(have) sat
speak	spoke	(have) spoken
spring	sprang	(have) sprung
steal	stole	(have) stolen
swear	swore	(have) sworn
swim	swam	(have) swum
swing	swung	(have) swung
take	took	(have) taken
tear	tore	(have) torn
think	thought	(have) thought
throw	threw	(have) thrown
wear	wore	(have) worn
weep	wept	(have) wept
win	won	(have) won
weave	wove	(have) woven
write	wrote	(have) written

d. Underline the verbs in the literature passage. What is the tense of each verb? Remember to watch for helping verbs that indicate past participle. Also indicate which of the verbs are irregular. How can you tell?

Day 3

d. took, stopped, rushed, reached, crossed, stumbled, plunged, hit, gave, was, dug, lifted, went, was, beat.

All the verbs are in the past tense.

Irregular verbs: hit, gave, dug, went, beat.

You can tell they are irregular verbs because the past is formed by some other change than the addition of the suffix -ed.

e. Complete the following sentences with the correct verb form.

Ex: *come* She <u>came</u> from India to study in our country.

1) We have _____ *(do)* the majority of the work for this project.
2) I _____ *(choose)* this subject for my experiment because it was interesting.
3) They _____ *(leave)* the movie early because Joshua did not feel well.
4) Jeremiah had _____ *(think)* over his plans for the future carefully.
5) They _____ *(build)* the house for a family whose house had burned down.
6) Have we _____ *(buy)* enough supplies for the trip?
7) Only a few people have _____ *(swim)* that distance.
8) We have _____ *(speak)* to Hannah about becoming a member of our soccer team.
9) The garden _____ *(grow)* quickly in the summer heat.
10) She _____ *(take)* the letter to the post office to purchase a stamp.

f. Review your spelling words.

Day 4

a. Imagine you work for your local newspaper. You have been assigned to report what happened to Danny and his father. A news story should be written in a short, crisp, direct form. Use your imagination and make up your own details to create a newspaper account of this story. Follow these guidelines:

1) The first paragraph of a story usually has very important information in it. It answers the questions *who, what, when*, and *where*.

2) The paragraphs in the story usually tell why something happened and how it happened. These paragraphs usually have details about the event. Sometimes quotes from the people involved are included.

Day 3

e. 1) done
2) chose
3) left
4) thought
5) built
6) bought
7) swum
8) spoken
9) grew
10) took

Day 4

a. **Snowy Town - On Saturday, Ross Pickett, his son, Danny, and their dog, Red, went on a cross country trek across the Snowy Mountain Banks. Little did they know that by Sunday afternoon, Danny and Red would be heroes.**

Authorities say circumstances are still unclear as to what took place. However, it is known that Ross and Danny became separated just as an unexpected blizzard came upon them. Danny told authorities that as he searched for his father, Red insistently nudged him in the opposite direction. Danny tried to pull Red the other way, but he lost his footing and fell down. As his hands reached down into the snow, he felt a man's trousered leg. Frantically, Danny dug and lifted his father from the snowy bed. "I put my hand under his shirt, and he was warm and his heart still beat," Said Danny with joyful tears.

Father and son are in good condition at Hope Hospital. Red is in excellent health, enjoying his new found attention.

Read some newspaper articles to see how they organize their information.

b. Create a headline for your story that will catch the attention of the reader.

c. Take an oral or written spelling pretest. Review any words you found difficult to spell.

d. Optional: Enrichment (SAB)

Day 5

a. Write the literature passage from dictation. Proofread and correct any errors in punctuation and spelling.

b. Use your thesaurus to revise your news story. Edit carefully. Be sure to use good descriptive words. Rewrite it neatly and give it to your teacher.

c. Take an oral or written spelling test.

d. Choose skills from the *Review Activities*.

Review Activities

Choose skills your student needs to review.

1. *Suffixes*
   Look at the following words and decide if you add the suffix **-ly** or **-ally** to form the adverb.

   a. basic
   b. serious
   c. sweet
   d. drastic
   e. eager

2. *Adverbs*
   Circle the adverbs in the following sentences. Write the question the adverb answers: *how*, *when*, *where*, *how often*, or *to what extent*.

   Ex: The German shepherd ran *swiftly* beside the bicycle.
   How

   a. The keys were found inside the car. __________
   b. We will be attending the concert today. __________
   c. We often take a walk after dinner. __________
   d. Laura laughed cheerfully at the joke. __________
   e. He is very concerned about his test scores. __________

3. *Principal Parts of a Verb*
   Underline the correct verb form in the following sentences. Indicate whether the verb form is present (**Pr**), past (**Past**), or past participle (**PP**).

   a. Anne (*swimming*, *swam*) in the second race.
   b. Greg and Don have (*decide*, *decided*) to stay for dinner.
   c. I (*fills*, *filled*) the pool with water last night.
   d. Jenny and Mark (*draw*, *drawn*) very detailed drawings.

1. a. basically
b. seriously
c. sweetly
d. drastically
e. eagerly

2. a. inside - where
b. today - when
c. often - how often
d. cheerfully - how
e. very - to what extent

3. a. Past - swam
b. PP - have decided
c. Past - filled
d. Pr - draw

4. a. sang
b. stolen
c. sank
d. rung
e. sprang

4. *Irregular Verbs*
   Underline the correct form of the irregular verb in the following sentence.

   a. She (*sang*, *sung*) beautifully in the recital.
   b. The shirt was (*stole*, *stolen*) from the store.
   c. The large ship (*sank*, *sunk*) when the torpedo hit it.
   d. The bell has (*rang*, *rung*); please go to your class.
   e. Martha (*sprang*, *sprung*) forward to catch the little boy who was falling.

5. *Writing a Newspaper Article*
   Read an article in your local newspaper. Find the answers to the *who*, *what*, *when*, and *where* questions.

Marilla was a tall, thin woman, with angles and without curves; her dark hair showed some gray streaks and was always twisted up in a hard little knot behind with two wire hairpins stuck aggressively through it. She looked like a woman of narrow experience and rigid conscience, which she was; but there was a saving something about her mouth which, if it had been ever so slightly developed, might have been considered indicative of a sense of humour.

Matthew dreaded all women except Marilla and Mrs. Rachel; he had an uncomfortable feeling that the mysterious creatures were secretly laughing at him. He may have been quite right in thinking so, for he was an odd-looking personage, with an ungainly figure and long iron-gray hair that touched his stooping shoulders, and a full, soft brown beard which he had worn ever since he was twenty. In fact, he had looked at twenty very much as he looked at sixty, lacking a little of the grayness.

A child of about eleven, garbed in a very short, very tight, very ugly dress of yellowish gray wincey. She wore a faded brown sailor hat and beneath the hat, extending down her back, were two braids of very thick, decidedly red hair. Her face was small, white and thin, also much freckled. Her mouth was large and so were her eyes, that looked green in some lights and moods and gray in others.

Anne of Green Gables by L. M. Montgomery.

Day 1

a. Read the three character descriptions. Can you visualize these people? An author tells about a character by describing him physically, but he also describes his personality. Some description is usually given when a character is first introduced to the reader, as in these paragraphs. This is commonly referred to as a **character sketch**. Look through some books on your shelf and find other character sketches. How does the author make you "see" the person?

b. Write the third paragraph of the literature passage from dictation. Compare your copy with the passage and correct any errors in spelling and punctuation. Make a spelling list of any misspelled words or use the following suggested list:

garbed	wincey	freckled
decidedly	yellowish	sailor

c. ish - adjective
ex: childish, reddish

d. able, ible - adjective
ex: likeable, audible

e. Teacher's note: While there are exceptions, if the main part of the word is a complete word by itself, then the suffix -able is usually used or when the main part of the word ends in a hard c or g.
ex: payable, amicable

Fewer words end in -ible. The In this case, the main part of the word is less likely to be recognizable.
ex: eligible

c. The word yellowish contains the suffix **-ish**, meaning *origin, nature*, or *resembling*. Add this to your list of suffixes along with the definition and word examples.

d. Locate the word *uncomfortable* in the literature passage. This word contains the suffix **-able** which means *able* or *can do.* This suffix can also be spelled **-ible** in words such as *invisible* and *sensible.* Add these suffixes to your list along with the definition and word examples.

e. Spelling words with the suffixes **-able** and **-ible** are often confused with one another. Because the suffix **-able** is used more often, the suffix **-ible** is often misspelled. Copy the following words and underline the suffix noting which suffix is used. Say each word aloud as you write them. Listen for the short **/a/** sound or the short **/i/** sound in the suffix.

eligible	indispensable
legible	edible
flexible	reversible
predictable	dependable
acceptable	irritable

f. Locate the phrase *with an ungainly figure* in the second paragraph of the literature passage. Why is the article *an* used in this phrase instead of the article *a*?

Day 2

a. An adjective is a word that modifies or describes a noun or pronoun and answers the questions *what kind, how much,* or *which one.* Circle the adjectives in the third paragraph of the literature passage.

b. Look at this simplified sentence from the literature passage.

Her face was small.

Adjectives usually come before the noun or pronoun they are describing, but in this sentence the adjective, *small*, comes after the noun, *face*. These are called predicate adjectives. **Predicate adjectives** follow a verb and describe the subject. The verb that links the subject to the predicate adjective is called a **linking verb**.

Ex: The rising sun is *beautiful.*

Beautiful is the predicate adjective; it follows the linking verb *is*.

c. Find the predicate adjective in this simplified sentence from the literature passage.

Her mouth was large.

What linking verb does it follow? Draw an arrow from the predicate adjective to the noun or pronoun it describes.

d. Sometimes a noun is described by an adjective of two or more words. When two or more words act together as a single adjective, it is called a **compound adjective.** Sometimes these adjectives are compound words (two words joined together) or hyphenated words.

Find the two compound adjectives in the second paragraph of the literature passage that are joined together by a hyphen.

Day 1

f. The article *an* is used with a word beginning with a vowel sound.

Day 2

a. (about) eleven
(short, tight, ugly) dress
(yellowish, gray) wincey
(faded, brown, sailor) hat
(two) braids
(thick, red) hair
(small), (white), (thin) face
(much) freckled
(large) mouth

Teacher's Note:
***Of about eleven* is a prepositional phrase; *eleven* is therefore the object of the preposition making it a noun. *Freckled* is a noun. *Green* and *gray* are nouns.**

c. Predicate adjective - large
Linking verb - was

d. odd-looking, iron-gray

✎ **Teacher's Note: Dictionaries will vary in hyphen use of compound words.**

Day 2

e. 1) <u>beautiful</u>, floor-length
2) <u>well-liked</u>
3) soft-spoken
4) chocolate-covered
5) <u>mind-boggling</u>

Predicate adjectives follow being verbs and modify the subject of the sentence. Predicate adjectives can also follow linking verbs. Since *had* is not a linking verb, examples 3 and 4 in 2(e) do not have predicate adjectives. *Gentle* is an adjective modifying the noun *smile* and *good* is an adjective that modifies the noun *supply*.

e. Add hyphens to compound adjectives where needed in the following sentences. Underline any predicate adjectives.

1) She looked beautiful in her floor length dress.
2) The new student was well liked.
3) He had a soft spoken manner and a gentle smile.
4) The theater had a good supply of chocolate covered raisins.
5) The idea you expressed in class was mind boggling.

f. Review your spelling words.

Day 3

a. Think of a person you know or create a fictitious character that you would like to describe in a character sketch. Write down words that you feel would be descriptive of him. Remember, don't just describe the physical features; also describe the person's personality. You can include details about how the person speaks, moves, or dresses. In order to give more insight into his personality you can include details about the person's surroundings, hobbies, plans for the future, viewpoint, and background.

b. Once you have completed your list, write a character sketch about the person you have chosen. Be sure to make use of adjectives in your description. Read the following example of a character sketch.

She looked up expectantly at the entrance way to the college. Her wavy blonde hair encircled her youthful freckled face as her blue eyes glimmered with the spark of determination. A faded flowered dress caressed her slender frame in the breeze as she stood momentarily with her one suitcase of possessions. She knew she must succeed; she had worked too hard for this day.

c. Review your spelling words.

d. Optional: Enrichment (SAB)

Day 4

a. To tell the difference between an adjective and an adverb, remember that an adjective always describes a noun or pronoun. An adverb can describe a verb, adjective, or another adverb. It answers the questions *how, where, how often, when,* and *to what extent.* When an adverb describes an adjective it usually appears just before the adjective and tells *how* or *to what extent.* If the adverb is describing an adverb, it usually appears just before the adverb and usually tells *how.*

b. List the six adverbs found in the third paragraph of the literature passage. One adverb is used four times. Beside each adverb listed, write the word it describes and indicate whether it is describing a verb, adjective, or another adverb.

c. Look up the word *garbed* in the dictionary to find the definition. Use the word correctly in a sentence.

d. Take an oral or written spelling pretest. Review any words you found difficult to spell.

e. Optional: Enrichment (SAB)

Day 5

a. Write the third paragraph of the literature passage from dictation. Correct any errors in spelling and punctuation.

b. Using the three descriptive paragraphs of the literature passage, draw a picture of one or more of the characters. Pay attention to details.

c. Take an oral or written spelling test.

d. Choose skills from the *Review Activities.*

Day 4

b. ***very*** **short - modifies adjective** ***short***

very **tight - modifies adjective** ***tight***

very **ugly - modifies adjective** ***ugly***

extending ***down*** **- modifies verb** ***extending***

very **thick - modifies adjectiv** ***thick***

decidedly **red - modifies adjective** ***red***

c. **garbed - clothed; Answers will vary.**

Review Activities

Choose skills your student needs to review.

1. *Suffixes*
   Add suffixes from your list that match the definition of the following words.

   a. fool + (*having the nature of a fool*) =
   b. sneak + (*inclined to sneak*) =
   c. like + (*able to like*) =
   d. life + (*without life*) =

2. *Adjectives and Adverbs*
   Underline the adjectives and circle the adverbs in the following sentences. Draw an arrow to the word each is modifying.

   a. The sun rose quickly over the steep mountaintops and chased the dark shadows from the lush meadows.
   b. The fierce waves break against the rugged shore before the storm.
   c. The very agitated boy struck the hard ground with his small fist.
   d. Yesterday we decided we can never know which team will win the game.
   e. The orange frisbee was expertly caught by the clever dog as the wide-eyed group of children watched.

1. a. foolish
b. sneaky
c. likeable
d. lifeless

Teacher's Note: Assist your student if there is any confusion between adverbs and prepositions.

2. a. The sun rose quickly over the steep mountaintops and chased the dark shadows from the lush meadows.

b. The fierce waves break against the rugged shore before the storm.

c. The very agitated boy struck the hard ground with his small fist.

d. Yesterday we decided we can never know which team will win the game.

e. The orange frisbee was expertly caught by the clever dog as the wide-eyed group of children watched.

BOOK STUDY D

The Horse and His Boy

The Horse and His Boy **by C.S. Lewis**
Published by Macmillan Publishing

Readability level: 7th - 8th grade

Teacher's note:
This summary is intended for the teacher's use.

Introducing
The Horse and His Boy

This fifth book in *The Chronicles of Narnia* series by C.S. Lewis deals with some of the events that took place during the time of the first book, *The Lion, the Witch, and the Wardrobe.* Mr. Lewis once again weaves deep truths into the excitement and high adventure of the skillfully told story.

Summary

Narnia and the North! This becomes the cry of young Shasta's heart after overhearing the man who calls himself his father, telling a visiting nobleman the story of how Shasta came to live with him. It seems some years ago a boat had washed up on the shore containing only a small baby and a man who had obviously starved himself to death keeping the baby alive. Thinking this was a fortunate gift of free labor, the man took the baby as his own and named him Shasta. Over the years, Shasta was treated as a slave, not knowing his origin. After learning this, Shasta runs to the stable to plan what to do when Bree, the horse belonging to his "father's" guest, speaks to him and convinces him that he is not a Calormene. Because of his fair coloring, he must have come from the North, from either Narnia or Archenland. Bree had been kidnapped as a pony and had served the Tarkaan as a war horse, keeping his ability to speak a secret. So the two decide to set off for Narnia and for freedom.

On the way, they meet a young Tarkheena who is fleeing a forced marriage. She, too, is riding a talking horse, Hwin. Hwin has told Aravis about Narnia, where they do not force young ladies to marry. Aravis and Hwin decide to join Shasta and Bree. Their journey takes them through the great city of Tarkaan, where they become separated when Shasta is mistaken for the prince of Archenland. Meanwhile, Aravis, in trying to escape through the palace of the Tisroc, finds herself hiding behind a sofa listening to the Tisroc agree to Prince Rabadash's plan to lead a surprise attack on the country of Archenland.

Finally, Shasta and Aravis are reunited with Bree and Hwin, and push onward to Archenland in order to sound the alarm before Prince Rabadash's army attacks. Almost there, they feel they can not go on. A lion chases them and proves they have more strength than they thought. Happily, Shasta is in time to give the cry of alarm and the Narnians go to the aid of the Archelanders in a brief but fierce battle with the Calormenes. After a decisive victory, Shasta learns that he is indeed an Archenlander and a very special one. Prince Rabadash learns what it is to be judged for his foolishness and Aravis, Bree, and Hwin learn what it means to find freedom at last.

Vocabulary

As you read the book, use the sentences before and after each word to determine its meaning. Then use your reference materials to locate a definition for the word.

1. dappled - (Chapter 1)
2. jostled - (Chapter 4)
3. queue - (Chapter 6) /kyoo/
4. prudence - (Chapter 8)
5. besieged - (Chapter 12)
6. appalling - (Chapter 13)
7. noisome - (Chapter 15)

1. dappled - spotted
2. jostled - pushed or shoved
3. queue - a group of people waiting in line
4. prudence - good judgement
5. besieged - surrounded
6. appalling - causing dismay
7. noisome - smelly

Choose the correct word from the words listed above to complete the following sentences.

1. He chose the _________ horse instead of the white one.
2. The theater manager asked the crowd to form a _________ to purchase tickets.
3. She showed _____________ in choosing good friends.
4. Ryan's ______________ lack of manners was unfortunate.
5. The ______________________ odor indicated there may have been a gas leak.
6. Everyone was _____________ when the concert doors were opened.
7. As the city was _____________, no one could get in or out.

1. dappled
2. queue
3. prudence
4. appalling
5. noisome
6. jostled
7. besieged

Discussion Questions

Find sections of the book that tell you the answers to these discussion questions. Be prepared to read some of them aloud in the discussion.

1. Who was your favorite character in this book. Why?

2. What parts made you laugh? Cheer? Afraid for the characters?

3. Were the characters believable? Have you ever known anyone like them?

4. We see pride and humility contrasted in the four main characters. Which were proud? Which were humble? How did this change by the end of the story?

5. How did you feel about the arranged marriage Aravis' father had planned for her? What did it tell you about her father? Do you think arranged marriages are always wrong?

6. Would you describe Rabadash's punishment as "poetic justice" (getting what he deserved)? Why?

7. Shasta felt that he was a most unfortunate boy; that everything went right for everyone else but him. Have you ever felt like Shasta? When? How did you deal with these feelings?

---

1. **Answers will vary.**

2. **Answers will vary.**

3. **Answers will vary.**

4. **Bree and Aravis are both full of pride, mainly because of the way others have treated them.**
   Hwin and Shasta are very humble because of the way they have been viewed by others.
   At the end of the book, as Bree is lecturing in a rather superior tone, he encounters Aslan and sees himself as he really is. Aravis has learned to think more highly of others than she does herself, especially of Shasta, who bravely rushed to defend her. Shasta, while still humble, has to start thinking of himself as a prince instead of a slave and Hwin remains her own sweet self.

5. **Allow for discussion.**

6. **Allow for discussion.**

7. **Allow for discussion.**

8. As Shasta walks through the darkness getting colder, feeling alone, and very sorry for himself, he begins to cry. What put a sudden stop to this? What emotions did Shasta experience as he walked though the mist with "The Thing" beside him? As the mist clears, how does Shasta feel?

9. When Aravis exclaims that being in the battle must have been wonderful, Cor replies that it wasn't at all like what he thought. Have you ever experienced anything that turned out to be very different than you thought? Explain.

10. Characters can be either round (changing) or static (unchanging). Round characters develop and change as a result of facing conflict. Static characters do not experience any significant growth or change throughout the story. Discuss the characters Aravis and Rabadash. Which one is round? Which is static? Give examples from the text.

---

8. A sudden fright put a stop to his tears. He felt fear because someone or something was walking beside him in the darkness. He was shocked to realize that he didn't know how long the creature had been there. His fear intensified to terror as he remembered stories of giants living in those parts. He began to hope he only imagined it.

Then in desperation, he finally spoke to it. He was relieved to find that it was not a giant, but immediately was even more terrified to think that it might be a ghost. He was told that was not the case and encouraged to tell of his sorrows. This reassured him a little and he felt relief in telling of all he had suffered.

When Shasta found out who was walking by him he was no longer afraid of being eaten or being accompanied by a ghost. Then a new and different sort of trembling came over him, and along with this, gladness. The mist evaporated and revealed his companion. Shasta looked into the Lion's face, slipped out of the saddle, and fell at its feet.

9. Answers will vary.

10. Aravis is a round character. At the beginning of the book she is arrogant, stubborn, and self-important. For example, read how she relates her history in the beginning of Chapter 3. Notice her lack of concern for the beaten slave. In Chapter 14, Aslan tells Aravis that the scratches he gave her were the same as the lashes the servant received because of her. Aravis shows remorse and concern for the servant. Upon meeting with Shasta again, she tells him that she is sorry she was such a pig and wants him to know that she changed before she knew he was a prince.

Rabadash also suffers from self-importantance. He is a static character because he is introduced as being ridiculous and by the end of the book he has not changed. We first meet Prince Rabadash in Chapter 8. He is having a temper tantrum because he has not gotten what he wants. In Chapter 15, aptly titled "Rabadash the Ridulous," he is still having temper tantrums.

Activities

The following activities are intended to expand your understanding and enjoyment of this wonderful book. Choose two or three activities from this list.

1. Since authors always bring part of themselves to their work, it is interesting to find out something about them when you read their books. Find some information about C.S. Lewis and his life.

2. Have you ever ridden a horse? If possible, visit a stable and go for a ride. Do you have to hold on with your knees like Bree told Shasta?

3. The Calormenes are known for their story-telling capabilities. Practice telling an exciting story by choosing an incident from the book, *The Horse and His Boy*.

   Suggestions:

   Shasta gets separated from the horses and Aravis in Tarkaan

   the battle scene where Prince Rabadash is defeated

4. *The Horse and His Boy* is a type of literature called *fantasy*. What makes it so?

5. The Calormenes love to quote their poets.

   Ex: Natural affection is stronger than soup and offspring more precious than carbuncles.

   This could also be called a proverb. Benjamin Franklin is famous for his proverbs.

   Ex: A penny saved is a penny earned.

   Find some other examples of proverbs and then try writing your own.

6. The idea of mistaken identity is intriguing to authors. Some examples are found in books such as Charles Dickens' *The Prince and the Pauper* and Anthony Hope's *The Prisoner of Zenda*. Try writing a story about twins or look-alikes being mistaken for each other.

7. Mr. Lewis uses analogies throughout *The Chronicles of Narni*a series. An **analogy** is a comparison of two similar things. The main analogy is Aslan as a picture of Jesus. What other analogies did you notice in reading *The Horse and His Boy*?

8. Read the other books in this series:

   The Lion, the Witch, and the Wardrobe
   Prince Caspian
   The Voyage of the Dawn Treader
   The Magician's Nephew
   The Silver Chair
   The Last Battle

I **C.A.N.** Assessment
The Horse and His Boy Book Study D

After *The Horse and His Boy* Book Study is completed check off each I **C.A.N**. objective with your teacher.

______	**C**	I can **complete** my work.
______		I can be **creative**.
______	**A**	I can be **accurate**.
______		I can do my work with a good **attitude**.
______	**N**	I can do my work **neatly**.

The Crow and the Pitcher

A crow perishing with thirst saw a pitcher, and hoping to find water, flew to it with delight. When he reached it, he discovered to his grief that it contained so little water that he could not possibly get at it. He tried everything he could think of to reach the water, but all his efforts were in vain. At last he collected as many stones as he could carry and dropped them one by one with his beak into the pitcher, until he brought the water within his reach and thus saved his life.

Aesop's Fables

Day 1

a. Before writing this literature passage, look at the title. Why are certain words in the title capitalized and others not? Write the literature passage from dictation, then compare with the model. Correct any errors you find.

b. Make a list of any misspelled words or use the following suggested spelling list:

perishing	delight	discovered
possibly	contained	grief

c. What spelling rule will help you remember how to spell *grief*?

d. Look at the word *discovered* from your suggested spelling list. Note how the suffix **-ed** is added to the word. The last consonant, **r**, is not doubled because it is preceded by a vowel.

Day 1

a. Capitalize the first word and every other important word in a title.

c. i before e except after c, and in words that say /a/ as in *neighbor* and *weigh*.

Spelling Tip

Words with more than one syllable that end with a consonant preceded by a vowel do not double the final consonant when adding a suffix beginning with a vowel unless the last syllable is accented.

Ex: travel - traveled (The last syllable is not accented.)
commit - committed (The last syllable is accented.)

Day 1
e. 1) beginning
2) referred
3) recoiled
4) admitting
5) trapped
6) benefited
7) shipping
8) marveled
9) transferring
10) shopping

e. Add suffixes to the following words applying this *Spelling Tip*. Also remember that one-syllable words ending with the one vowel and one consonant doubles the last consonant before adding a suffix beginning with a vowel.

1) begin + ing	6) benefit + ed
2) refer + ed	7) ship + ing
3) recoil + ed	8) marvel + ed
4) admit + ing	9) transfer + ing
5) trap + ed	10) shop + ing

f. dis- reverse, apart
con- together, with
de- down, from

1) converged
2) discouraged
3) depart

f. The suggested spelling list contains the prefixes **dis-**, **con**, and **de-**. Refer to your list of prefixes for the meaning of each. Use the correct prefix to complete each of the following words.

1) The members of the club _____verged on the small town for the annual meeting. (*together*, *with*)
2) I am afraid Mary has become ______couraged after she did poorly on the test. (*take away*)
3) The team will ____part at 2:00 P.M. in order to be on time for the track meet. (*down*, *from*)

g. The crow used what he had on hand to meet the need of his situation effectively.

g. How does the crow in the literature passage exhibit the character quality of resourcefulness?

Day 2
a. A crow saw a pitcher.

Day 2

a. Look at the simplified sentence from the literature passage, and underline the subject once and the verb twice.

A crow saw a pitcher.

b. Now ask the question "A crow saw what?" Circle the noun that answers that question. The noun you circled is called the **direct object**. Direct objects receive the action from the verb and answer the questions *what* or *whom* after an action verb. A direct object must be a noun or pronoun.

Look at the following examples. Find the verb and ask the questions *what* or *whom*.

The boy threw the ball. (Threw what? *Ball* is the direct object.)
Mom baked a cake. (Baked what? *Cake* is the direct object.)
Ginger held it tightly. (Held what? *It* is the direct object.)

c. A sentence may have more than one direct object. Sometimes you have a compound direct object.

Ex: Dan chose Mike and Lisa to be on his team. (Chose whom? *Mike* and *Lisa* are the direct objects.)

d. A direct object is never part of a prepositional phrase.

Ex: David lifted the rock over his head. (Rock is the direct object. *Over his head* is a prepositional phrase. *Head* is the object of the preposition *over*.)

e. Underline the action verbs in the last sentence of the literature passage.

f. Read the action verbs you have underlined and ask the question "What?" If there is a noun or pronoun that answers the question, circle it. Not all action verbs have a direct object.

Ex: collected what?

Day 2
b. pitcher

e. collected, could carry, dropped, brought, saved

f. collected - no direct object
could carry - no direct object
dropped - *them* is the direct object
brought - *water* is the direct object
saved - *life* is the direct object

Day 2
g. 1) flew - plane
2) jumped - fence
3) baked - cookies, candies
4) signed - Mayflower Compact
5) developed - telescope

Day 3
a. Possible answers: Little by little does the trick. OR Necessity is the mother of invention.

b. It climbs higher.

c. ex:
One good turn deserves another.
A bird in the hand is worth two in the bush.
Pride goes before destruction.

g. Underline the action verbs and circle the direct objects in the following sentences.

1) The pilot flew his plane into enemy territory.
2) The horse jumped the fence.
3) Jenny baked chocolate chip cookies and peanut butter candies for the party.
4) The Pilgrims signed the Mayflower Compact before leaving the ship.
5) Galileo developed a working telescope.

h. Review your spelling words.

Day 3

a. *Aesop's Fables* were written to teach lessons or morals. What do you think is the moral of this fable?

b. Try an experiment filling a cup half full of water. Drop pebbles or marbles into the cup. What happens to the water level?

c. Read the following two morals which Aesop wrote about.

Whatever you do, do with all your might.

Those who seek to please everybody please nobody.

List three other morals that could be written as a fable.

d. Review your spelling words.

e. Optional: Enrichment (SAB)

Day 4

a. Choose one of the morals you listed in **3c** and write a fable about it. Fables usually use animals that talk and act like human beings. They are simply written, usually involving only two or three characters. One character faces a problem or situation and tries to overcome it. The ending will always teach us a lesson, or moral.

b. Take an oral or written spelling pretest. Review any words you found difficult to spell.

c. Optional: Enrichment (SAB)

Day 5

a. Rewrite the literature passage from dictation.

b. Read about the history of *Aesop's Fables* in a reference book or read two or three fables and explain their morals.

c. Take an oral or written spelling test.

d. Choose skills from the *Review Activities*.

Review Activities

Choose skills your student needs to review.

1. *Direct Objects*
   Underline the action verbs and circle the direct objects in the following sentences.

   a. At night many bats eat insects which they locate with their high-pitched radar.
   b. Spiders capture moths and flies in their intricate webs.
   c. In early hours of dusk dragonflies chase mosquitoes throughout the sky.
   d. Birds devour many insects during the daytime hours.
   e. Insects encounter many enemies everyday.

2. *Fable*
   Write a fable that depicts a moral message.

1.

a. eat - insects
b. capture - moths, flies
c. chase - mosquitoes
d. devour - insects
e. encounter - enemies

2. Examples of moral lessons: you can't judge a book by its cover, slow and steady wins the race, you reap what you sow

"I'm afraid you'll have to make up your mind to it, Meg. That child is a born actress. We never did anything so well, not even the Witch's Curse," said Mrs. Jo, casting a bouquet of many-coloured socks at the feet of her flushed and panting niece, when she fell gracefully upon the doormat.

"It is a sort of judgement upon me for my passion for the stage when a girl. Now I know how dear Marmee felt when I begged to be an actress. I never can consent, and yet I may be obliged to give up my wishes, hopes, and plans again."

Little Women by Louisa May Alcott

Day 1

a. Read the literature passage. Note that it is dialogue. Review the quotation rules in Lesson 7.

b. Write the passage from dictation and compare your copy with the original. Correct any errors.

c. The words *coloured* and *judgement* may look misspelled to you. Although Louisa May Alcott was an American author, she used the British spelling rather than the American spelling of these two words. Another illustration of this difference is the word *gray* (grey). Can you find any other examples?

Day 1
Possible answers:
c. labor / labour
center / centre

d. Make your own spelling list from any misspelled words or use the following list of suggested words:

actress	witch	passion
obliged	bouquet	niece

Day 2

a. Some words like *judgment* are spelled with **dg** to make the /**j**/ sound. The letters **dg** are used only after a short vowel when making the /**j**/ sound.

Spelling Tip

Words are often spelled with *dg* or *dge* following a single short vowel to make the */j/* sound.

b. Copy these words and underline **dg**. Say the words aloud as you write them.

bridge	fudge
midget	edge
badger	hedge
lodge	

c. Add these words to your spelling list.

d. Review the definition of **simile** found in Lesson 3 **2a**. Similar to similes, another literary device used by authors is metaphor. **Metaphor** is the use of a term or phrase in a different way than usual in order to suggest a likeness to another idea or item. Similes always use the word *like* or *as*. Metaphors do not.

Ex: This situation is like a thorn in my side. (simile)
This situation is a thorn in my side. (metaphor)

Day 2
e. socks / flowers
a bouquet of many-coloured socks

e. Find the metaphor in the first paragraph. What two things are being compared?

f. Write two metaphors. Be sure not to use *like* or *as* in your comparison.

g. Review your spelling words.

Day 3

a. Find the words *to make* in the first sentence. *To make* is an infinitive. An **infinitive** is the form of a verb but is not a verb. Infinitives act as a noun, an adjective, or an adverb in a sentence. An infinitive will almost always begin with the word *to*.

b. Identifying the verb of a sentence can be a little confusing when the sentence has infinitives. Circle the verbs in the following sentences and underline the infinitives.
1. The cook has arrived to make the soup.
2. The children laughed to see a lamb in school.
3. Drivers need to learn safety rules.
4. We have to have quiet!
5. My brother had to make a call.

c. Find the infinitives in this passage from *Little Women*:

Some studied how to watch the tender buds, when to spread them to the sunlight, and when to shelter them from rain; how to guard the ripening seeds, and when to lay them in the warm earth or send them on the summer wind to far off hills and valleys, where other Fairy hands would tend and cherish them, till a sisterhood of happy flowers sprang up to beautify and gladden the lonely spot where they had fallen.

d. The suffix –**fy** appears in the word *beautify* in the above literature passage. This suffix means *make*. Add it to your list of suffixes. Can you think of any other words that have this suffix? How was the spelling of the root word *beauty* changed before this suffix was added?

e. Read the last sentence: "I never can consent, and yet I may be obliged to give up my wishes, hopes, and plans again." You have learned that synonyms are words that have the same or similar meanings. The words *wishes* and *hopes* are synonyms. Words that have opposite meanings are called **antonyms**.

f. Choose the word from the word group that is the best antonym for each word.

1) tall	little, small, short
2) slow	fast, accelerate, sluggish
3) sunny	windy, hot, cloudy
4) loud	shrill, quiet, peaceful
5) near	beside, removed, far

g. Review your spelling words.

Day 3

b. 1. The cook (has arrived) <u>to make</u> the soup.
2. The children (laughed) <u>to see</u> a lamb in school.
3. Drivers (need) <u>to learn</u> safety rules.
4. We (have) <u>to have</u> quiet!
5. My brother (had) <u>to make</u> a call.

c. to watch, to spread, to shelter, to guard, to lay, to beautify

d. fy - verb
ex: rectify, intensify

the *y* was changed to *i* before adding *ful*.

f. 1) tall	**short**
2) slow	**fast**
3) sunny	**cloudy**
4) loud	**quiet**
5) near	**far**

Day 4

a. Verbs change their form in order to show the time of action. These forms of verbs are called tenses. A verb may be written in present, past, or future tense.

Ex: I stand here now. (present tense)
I stood here yesterday. (past tense)
I will stand here tomorrow. (future tense)

b. Find examples of verbs in the present tense and in the past tense in the literature passage.

c. Most verbs are changed to past tense by adding the suffix –**ed** to the verb. These are called **regular verbs**. If a verb changes in some other way or makes no change to form the past tense, then the verb is called an **irregular verb**.

Regular verb:
She *arrives* on time every day. (present tense)
She *arrived* on time today. (past tense)

Irregular verb:
I *swim* often at the pool. (present tense)
I *swam* at the pool. (past tense)

d. Optional: Enrichment (SAB)

e. Find an example of an irregular verb in the literature passage. Underline it.

f. It is important to select one tense and use that tense consistently throughout your writing and not switch to another tense.

Ex: Mary jumped up and hits the ball over the net.
(*Jumped* is past tense; *hits* is present tense.)

Mary jumps up and hits the ball over the net.
(Both *jumps* and *hits* are in the present tense.)

Day 4
b. Some examples:
Present -
am, make, is, know, can consent, give

Past -
did, fell, felt, begged, obliged

e. make, did, know, fell, felt, can, may, give

g. Read the following paragraph. Change any necessary verbs so that the text reads consistently in the past tense.

It was a beautiful morning, and Echo gallops for joy across the pasture. She stretches her long neck over the fence so she had a better view of the farmyard activities. The chickens clucked loudly from the henhouse as they lay their morning eggs. Bessie, the cow, moos from her barn stall as she waited to be milked. The barnyard cat chased a mouse around the corner and soon returns with it dangling by its tail. With his usual air of importance the proud rooster strutted into his position on the rickety fence post and crows as a signal to all that the day has begun.

h. Take an oral or written spelling pretest. Review any words you found difficult to spell.

Day 5

a. Take an oral or written spelling test.

b. Write the literature passage from dictation again.

c. Choose skills from the *Review Activities.*

Day 4

g. It was a beautiful morning, and Echo galloped for joy across the pasture. She stretched her long neck over the fence so she had a better view of the farmyard activities. The chickens clucked loudly from the henhouse as they laid their morning eggs. Bessie, the cow, mooed from her barn stall as she waited to be milked. The barnyard cat chased a mouse around the corner and soon returned with it dangling by its tail. With his usual air of importance, the proud rooster strutted into his position on the rickety fence post and crowed as a signal to all that the day had begun.

Review Activities

Choose only the skills your student needs to review.

1. *Antonyms*
   Write an antonym for the following:

   blustery ________________________
   prickly ________________________
   noisy ________________________

2. *Metaphor*
   Write the following similes as metaphors:

   When we blew on the dandelions, they exploded like fireworks.
   Dad floated down the river like a tugboat.

3. *Infinitives*
   Underline the infinities in the following sentences:

   a. Mother said it is time to turn out the lights.
   b. You are going to laugh when I tell you what happened!
   c. Adele plans to read her book in the car tomorrow.
   d. Are you going to eat all your dessert?

4. *Verb Tense*
   Write a sentence using the verb *watch* in past, present, and future tense.

5. *Regular/Irregular Verbs*
   a. Fill in the missing verb tenses:

Present	Past	Future
run	__________	__________
__________	reached	__________
talk	__________	__________
__________	__________	will drink

   b. Which of these verbs are irregular?

1. Example:
calm
smooth
quiet

2. Example:
When we blew on the dandelions, they became exploding fireworks.

Dad was a tugboat floating down the river.

3.
a. to turn
b. to laugh
c. to read
d. to eat

4. Example:
(past) I watched that movie last night.
(present) I am watching that movie right now.
(future) I will watch that movie tomorrow.

5.
a. Present:
run
reach
talk
drink

Past:
ran
reached
talked
drank

Future:
will run
will reach
will talk
will drink

b. run, drink

Notes

Laurie had vanished round the bend, Jo was just at the turn, and Amy, far behind, striking out toward the smoother ice in the middle of the river. For a minute Jo stood still with a strange feeling at her heart; then she resolved to go on, but something held and turned her round, just in time to see Amy throw up her hands and go down, with the sudden crash of rotten ice, the splash of water, and a cry that made Jo's heart stand still with fear.

Little Women by Louisa May Alcott.

Day 1

a. Read the literature passage. Write it from dictation. Compare your copy to the passage. Did you place the commas in the right places? How about the semicolon?

Day 1
b. They are divided between the double consonants.

b. Make a spelling list from any misspelled words from your dictation or use the following suggested list.

vanished	smoother	strange
resolved	sudden	rotten

Divide the words into syllables. Use your dictionary if you are unsure. This will help you remember the spelling. What do you notice about the division of syllables in the words *sudden* and *rotten*?

c. Divide the following words into syllables.

Ex: supper - sup/per
1) butter
2) master
3) fiddle
4) invite
5) cotton

c. 1) but/ter
2) mas/ter
3) fid/dle
4) in/vite
5) cot/ton

d. To form the plural of words ending in **o**, first look at the word. If the **o** is preceded by a consonant, add **es**; otherwise, just add **s**. Music related words are exceptions; just add **s** regardless of how the word ends.

Ex: hero - heroes (**o** preceded by a consonant)
banjo - banjos (music related word)
studio - studios (**o** preceded by a vowel)

Spelling Tip

To form the plural of words ending in *o* preceded by a consonant, add *es*; otherwise, just add *s*.
***Exception:* Music related words - just add *s*.**

e. Write the following words in plural form.

1) piano
2) tomato
3) video
4) alto
5) potato

Day 1
e. 1) pianos
2) tomatoes
3) videos
4) altos
5) potatoes

Day 2

a. Find the adjective *smoother* in the literature passage. Is *smoother* a positive, comparative, or superlative adjective? If you are not sure, refer to Lesson 7. What things are being compared?

b. Find the possessive noun in the literature passage. What punctuation identifies the word as a possessive noun? What object does the possessive noun own?

c. Possessive pronouns such as *her, his, my, our*, and *their* show ownership without the use of an apostrophe and **s**. Circle the possessive pronouns in the literature passage. Substitute a possessive noun for each of the possessive pronouns. Read the literature passage with the substitutions.

Day 2
a. comparative: The ice in the middle of the river is compared to the ice on the edges of the river.

b. Jo's; an apostrophe; heart

c. her heart - Jo's heart; her hands - Amy's hands

Laurie had vanished round the bend, Jo was just at the turn, and Amy, far behind, striking out toward the smoother ice in the middle of the river. For a minute Jo stood still with a strange feeling at Jo's heart; then Jo resolved to go on, but something held and turned Jo around, just in time to see Amy throw up Amy's hands and go down, with the sudden crash of rotten ice, the splash of water, and a cry that made Jo's heart stand still with fear.

Which version sounds better?

d. Who are the characters in the passage? Imagine Amy is your sister and you are at the scene depicted in the literature passage. Write a few sentences explaining what you think may have happened next in the story. Choose descriptive adjectives to express how you feel.

d. Amy, Jo, and Laurie

e. Review your spelling words.

Day 3

a. A **semicolon** separates two independent clauses that are joined together without a conjunction. Circle the semicolon (;) and underline the two independent clauses in the following simplified sentence.

For a minute Jo stood still with a strange feeling at her heart; then she resolved to go on.

Day 3

a. For a minute Jo stood still with a strange feeling at her heart (;) then she resolved to go on.

b. Look at this simplified sentence from the literature passage.

She resolved to go on, but something held and turned her round.

A comma is used before the conjunction because it joins two complete sentences. This is called a **compound sentence**.

Rewrite the following sentences as compound sentences by using the conjunctions *and, but*, or *or*. Remember the comma.

1) Jason plays baseball. Lynn plays basketball.
2) Sue likes ice cream. I like frozen yogurt.
3) We tried to be on time. We were late.

c. Review your spelling words. Be sure to sound them out by syllables as you write them.

d. Optional: Enrichment (SAB)

Day 4

a. Find and circle the action verbs in the paragraph. You learned in Lesson 29 that verbs change their form in order to show the time of an action. These forms of verbs are called **tenses**. A verb may be written in present, past, or future tense (time). In what tense is this paragraph written?

b. The literature passage was written by the author in past tense. Rewrite the literature passage as if you were Jo telling it as it is happening. (first person, present tense). The first two sentences are done for you.

Ex: Laurie vanishes round the bend. I am just at the turn, and Amy, far behind, is striking out toward the smoother ice in the middle of the river...

c. Take an oral or written spelling pretest. Review any words you found difficult to spell.

Day 5

a. Write the literature passage once again from dictation. Pay close attention to your punctuation and spelling.

b. Write a short story describing an exciting event in your life.

c. Take an oral or written spelling test.

d. Choose skills from the *Review Activities*.

b. Possible answers:
1) Jason plays baseball, and Lynn plays basketball.
2) Sue likes ice cream, but I like frozen yogurt.
3) We tried to be on time, but we were late.

Day 4
a. had vanished, was, striking, stood, resolved, held, turned, see, throw, go, stand

past tense

Review Activities

Choose skills your student needs to review.

1. *Syllables*
Divide the following words into syllables:

a. riddle
b. tablet
c. confess
d. blanket
e. bottom
f. hobby

1. a. rid-dle
b. tab-let
c. con-fess
d. blan-ket
e. bot-tom
f. hob-by

2. *Spelling*
Circle the correct spelling of the following words.

a. echos, echoes
b. tornados, tornadoes
c. sopranos, sopranoes
d. cellos, celloes
e. stereos, stereoes
f. potatos, potatoes

2. a. echoes
b. tornadoes
c. sopranos
d. cellos
e. stereos
f. potatoes

3. *Possessive Pronouns*
Underline the possessive nouns in the following sentences and change them to possessive pronouns.

Ex: Please turn down the volume on <u>Mike's</u> radio. __his__

a. We will be attending Laurie's graduation ceremony. ________
b. Lane's fishing spot is the best one on the lake. ________
c. Will the youth group's skit be done soon? ________
d. Did you know the Smith family's vacation was canceled? ________
e. Anne's horse completed all the jumps. ________

3. a. <u>Laurie's</u> - his
b. <u>Lane's</u> - His
c. <u>group's</u> - their
d. <u>family's</u> - their
e. <u>Anne's</u> - Her

4. *Regular and Irregular Verbs*
Write the past tense form of the following verbs.

a. freeze
b. spring
c. splash
d. catch
e. twirl
f. weep

4. a. froze
b. sprang
c. splashed
d. caught
e. twirled
f. wept

5. *Verb Tenses*
Find a paragraph in a book. Change the tense to past or present tense.

Here Louisa played on the grass, made friends with the passersby, or, plumping down to rest, would sit looking up at the tall elms with their high trunks and enormously long branches, so different from the round leafy beeches of the woods at her birthplace. The tall elderly houses of Beacon Hill looked down on her out of their many-paned windows, where the blue and purple glass was a sign of exceedingly aristocratic old age.

Invincible Louisa by Cornelia Meigs.

Day 1

a. Write the literature passage from dictation. Compare your copy to the passage and correct any errors.

b. Look up the word *aristocratic* in the dictionary. What does it mean?

c. Make a spelling list of any misspelled words from your dictation or use the following suggested list:

passersby	enormously
birthplace	elderly
aristocratic	exceedingly

d. Three of the words in the suggested spelling list have the same suffix. Identify the suffix. What part of speech are each of these words? Remember, most words ending in **-ly** are adverbs. Some are adjectives, such as *friendly* and *lovely.*

e. What two words in the suggested spelling list are compound words? What words make up each compound?

f. Find the word *different* in the literature passage. Usually words ending in **-ent** and **-ant** sound alike but are often misspelled. It is the same with words ending in **-ence** and **-ance**. When spelling a word with one of these endings, carefully enunciate each syllable.

Day 1

b. having the characteristic of nobility

d. -ly - adverb

e. passers-by birth-place

Spelling Tip

Do not confuse the spelling of words ending in *-ent* and *-ence* with words ending in *-ant* and *-ance.*

Day 1

g. -ant: defiant, instant, relevant, resistant, abundant

-ent: confident, dependent, insistent, persistent, insolent

-ance: instance, defiance, relevance, resistance, abundance

-ence: confidence, insistence, persistence, dependence, existence

g. Copy the following words under the correct heading.

defiant	defiance	confidence
confident	instant	instance
dependence	dependent	insistent
insistence	relevant	relevance
resistant	resistance	abundant
abundance	sentence	persistent
persistence	existence	insolent

-ant	-ent	-ance	-ence
Ex: defiant	confident	instance	independence

Day 2

a. beech - a type of tree

beach - a sandy place at the edge of a body of water

c. branches
long
enormously

Day 2

a. Find the word *beech* in the literature passage. What is the meaning of this word? Can you think of a homonym for the word *beech*? What is the meaning of the homonym?

b. The first word of the literature passage is *here;* it is telling us where Louisa played. Words that answer the questions *where, how, when*, or *how much* are called adverbs.

c. Adverbs modify or describe verbs, but they also can describe adjectives or another adverb. Look at the phrase *enormously long branches.* What is the noun being described? What word describes the branches? What word describes *long*?

d. Look at the last phrase of the literature passage.

of exceedingly aristocratic old age

Underline the adjective and circle the adverb.

e. A good writer uses strong verbs and descriptive adverbs and adjectives to help the reader see and feel what is happening. Sometimes, a writer will give human qualities to animals or objects to bring the story alive. This is called **personification**.

Ex: Bright yellow daisies peeked over the hillside. Daisies do not really peek, but with the use of personification, the daisies come alive.

Find an example of personification in the literature passage.

f. Write a paragraph that tells about your home or neighborhood. Be sure to use descriptive adjectives and adverbs.

g. Review your spelling words.

Day 3

a. A **biography** is a nonfiction story of a person's life written by someone else. Biographies contain information about a person's life such as when they were born, their childhood, their interests, and more. Think of someone you know that you think would be interesting to interview; perhaps a grandparent, a friend, or someone who has achieved goals you would also like to achieve. Make a list of questions you would like to ask him. Then ask permission for an interview and schedule an appointment. Be sure to take along a camera and take a picture if possible.

d. of (exceedingly) <u>aristocratic</u> <u>old</u> age

e. elderly houses of Beacon Hill looked down on her out of their many-paned windows

b. Below are some sample questions that could be used for the interview.

Sample Interview Questions

1) When and where were you born?
2) What did your parents do for a living?
3) Where did you grow up?
4) Where did you go to school?
5) What are some of your fondest childhood memories?
6) How many brothers and sisters did you have?
7) Did you belong to any sports teams or clubs when you were in high school?
8) What were your interests growing up?
9) What kind of jobs did you work as a teenager?
10) Did you go to college? If so, where?
11) Were you ever in the military?
12) What kind of job did you start with after finishing school?
13) Where did you first meet your husband/wife?
14) What attracted you to him/her?
15) When did you get married?
16) Where did you first live after getting married?
17) How many children did you have?
18) What was your family like?
19) What goals have you had in your life and have you reached them?
20) What is the most important advice you could give me?

c. Review your spelling words.

Day 4

a. Interview the person using the questions as a guideline. Ask the person if you may record the interview. Take careful notes of what they say. Complete on a separate sheet of paper.

b. Compare the recorded interview with your notes. Did you miss anything important?

c. Begin your biography by following these guidelines.

1) Read through your notes and determine the main idea.
2) Decide on your opening sentence. Try to capture your audience's attention by presenting your topic in an interesting way.
3) Biographies are usually written in chronological order, so write your sentences accordingly.

d. Take an oral or written spelling pretest. Review any words you found difficult to spell.

e. Optional: Enrichment (SAB)

Day 5

a. Write the literature passage from dictation. Check your copy for spelling and punctuation.

b. Complete writing the biography. Edit carefully for mistakes and make a final copy. If possible include a picture of the person you interviewed.

c. Take an oral or written spelling test.

d. Choose skills from the *Review Activities*.

Review Activities

Choose skills your student needs to review.

1. *Adjectives and Adverbs:*
   Circle the adjectives and underline the adverbs in the following paragraph.

   The sun shone brillantly in the clear blue sky. Majestic oaks gently spread their strong limbs to shade the little creatures from the scorching sun. The babbling brook gingerly wound its way through the tiny crevices in the rocky hillside. The quiet woodlands patiently waited for the coolness of dusk.

1. Adjectives: clear, blue, majestic, strong, little, scorching, babbling, tiny, rocky, quiet

Adverbs: brillantly, gently, gingerly, patiently

2. *Personification*
   Find at least one example of personification in the paragraph above.

2. trees gently spread their strong limbs

babbling brook gingerly wound

woodlands patiently waited

3. *Biography*
   Read a short biography of a famous person. Compare the biography you wrote in Lesson 35 with the one you read. Does it contain some of the same elements? Is there anything you would like to add to your next biography?

Of all the small annoyances that weight
our mental buoyances,
No chaff or cold derision is so sad as
indecision is —
It's ruined me, it's plain it has —
through life it's been my bane, it has,
It's driven me insane, it has, as anyone
can see!
Oh my! the troubles and perplexities,
Oh dear! that mar each little plan!
Oh law! sufficient quite to vex it is,
The short uncertain temper of an
undecided man!

In bed each day a-dundering, I lie
awake a-wondering
(In sad uncertain doubt of it), by which
side to get out of it,
For all I ever knew of 'em have sides (or
feet in lieu of 'em),
They've generally two of 'em, as anyone
can see!
Oh my! the troubles and perplexities,
Oh dear! that mar each little plan!
Oh law! sufficient quite to vex it is,
The short uncertain temper of an
undecided man!

I never went a-marrying but single
stopped a-tarrying,
Though lots of girls I've known, I have;
been introduced and shown, I have,
But ne'er a one I've got of 'em-no single
girl could spot of 'em,
There's such a plaguey lot of 'em, as
anyone can see!
Oh my! the troubles and perplexities,
Oh dear! that mar each little plan!
Oh law! sufficient quite to vex it is,
The short uncertain temper of an
undecided man!

I've reached a decent time of life, and tired, nearly, I'm of life,
Whom ought I to enquire of what illness to expire of?
Most men appear to fall of 'em — the short of 'em, the tall of 'em,
I cannot die of all of 'em, as anyone can see!
Oh my! perplexed and always wondering,
Oh dear! ill-natured people say,
Oh law! I'm like in all my blundering,
A donkey hesitating 'tween two packages of hay!

The Undecided Man by W. S. Gilbert

Day 1

a. Listen to the poem.

b. Practice reading the poem as follows:

Teacher:
Of all the small annoyances that weight our mental buoyances,
No chaff or cold derision is so sad as indecision is —

Student:
It's ruined me, it's plain it has — through life it's been my bane, it has,
It's driven me insane, it has, as anyone can see!

Teacher: Oh my! The troubles and perplexities,

Student: Oh dear! That mar each little plan!

Teacher: Oh law! Sufficient quite to vex it is,

Both: The short uncertain temper of an undecided man!

This type of reading is called **choral reading**.

c. Write the first verse from dictation.

d. Make a spelling list of any misspelled words or use the following suggested list:

annoyances	derision	perplexities
bouyances	indecision	sufficient

e. This poem is from a collection of light verse by W. S. Gilbert called *Bab Ballads*. Find out some information about this collection of poems using your local library or the Internet.

f. Optional: Enrichment

Day 2

a. Find the suffix –**ness** in the literature passage. This suffix means *state of.* Add this suffix to your list along with its definition and words examples.

Spelling Tip

When adding a suffix beginning with a consonant, such as *–ness* or *–ly*, do not drop or change any letters in the root word unless the word ends in *y*. If the last letter of the root word and the first letter of the suffix are the same, double letters will result. If a word ends in *y*, change the *y* to *i* before adding any suffix except *–ing*.

Ex: final + ly = finally
happy + ness = happiness
hurry + ing = hurrying

b. Add suffixes to the following words.
Ex: subborn + ness = stubbornness

1) natural + ly
2) sudden + ness
3) date + less
4) rude + ly
5) weak + ness

Day 2
a) ness - noun
ex: righteousness, emptiness

b. 1) naturally
2) suddenness
3) dateless
4) rudely
5) weakness

c. There are internal rhymes. For example, annoyances/buoyances and derision is/ indecision is. He also relies on repeating words as *has* in the third line.

d. Three of the lines are repeated in the first three verses.

e. I'm like in all my blundering, a donkey hesitating 'tween two packages of hay!
He is comparing his indecision to that of a donkey trying to decide which bale of hay to eat.

Day 3
a. For example:
The Mikado, The Pirates of Penzance, HMS Pinafore, Patience

c. Not all poetry rhymes. The selection of the words and how they are placed in a line, or the pattern of sound and words are important. What do you notice about the rhyming words in this poem?

d. What do you notice about the end of each verse? This is a technique called **repetition**.

e. Remember that a **simile** compares two unlike things using the words **like** or **as**. Find the simile in the last verse. What two things are being compared?

f. Review your spelling words.

Day 3

a. Find out about the Gilbert and Sullivan Comic Operas using a book from the library or the Internet. Although written in the 1800s, these operas are still performed and enjoyed today. The operas were known for their absurd plots and entertaining music. What are the names of some of the operas?

b. If possible, listen to some of the music from a Gilbert and Sullivan Opera. Enjoy the rhymes and absurd verses written by W. S. Gilbert.

c. Find the word *cannot* in the last verse. The word *cannot* contains the negative word *not*. Do not use two negative words in the same sentence. Some negative words are *no, not, (n't), nothing, none, never, no one, hardly* and *scarcely*.

Ex: I *don't hardly* ever go there.
(Incorrect – contains two negative words.)

I *don't* ever go there. (Correct)
I *hardly* ever go there. (Correct)

d. Choose the correct word. Avoid double negatives.
Ex: We couldn't see (<u>anything</u>, *nothing*) in the dark.

1) I don't (*never*, *ever*) run in the hallway.
2) We couldn't see (*any*, *none*) of the boats that were crossing the river.

3) She didn't receive (*any*, *no*) donations for the charity.
4) I never found (*anything*, *nothing*) in the refrigerator to snack on.
5) We (*can*, *cannot*) scarcely do anything without someone changing the plans.

e. Try memorizing the first verse of the poem.

f. Review your spelling words.

d. 1) ever
2) any
3) any
4) anything
5) can

Day 4

a. Review types of sentences in Lesson 8. Find an example of a declarative, an exclamatory, and an interrogative sentence in the poem.

b. Take an oral or written spelling pretest. Remember, sounding out the syllables as you write them will help you spell them correctly.

c. Practice writing similes. Use the following prompts:

The puppy was as cute as
The car sounded like
He was as happy as
Opening the present felt like

d. Continue working on memorizing the first verse. If you already have it memorized, start memorizing the second verse.

Day 4
a. For example:
Declarative: In bed each day a-dundering, I lie awake a-wondering (In sad uncertain doubt of it), by which side to get out of it.

Interrogative: Whom ought I enquire of what illness to expire of?

Exclamatory: It's driven me insane, it has, as anyone can see!

Day 5

a. Write the second verse of the poem from dictation.

b. Recite what you have memorized.

c. Take an oral or written spelling test.

d. Choose skills from the *Review Activities*.

Review Activities

Choose skills your student needs to review.

1. *Suffixes*
   Add suffixes to the following words:
   happy + ly
   quick + ness
   silly + ness
   swift + ly
   love + ly
   love + ly + ness

2. *Similes*
   Finish the following similes:

   The baby's laughter sounded like
   The day was as cold as
   My stomach was growling like

3. *Double Negatives*
   Rewrite the following paragraph correcting any double negatives.

   We don't hardly ever go to the store without first making a list of the items we need to purchase. I cannot scarcely understand how anyone remembers everything they need without making a list. Mary didn't need no help in getting all the necessary items together at the store, and I didn't find nothing missing when we arrived home.

4. *Types of Sentences*
   Indicate if the following sentences are declarative, exclamatory, or interrogative. Add the correct ending punctuation:

   Do you mean to say that you don't like Gilbert and Sullivan

   We went to see a Gilbert and Sullivan play last night

   I love Gilbert and Sullivan

1. happily
quickness
silliness
swiftly
lovely
loveliness

2. Ex:
The baby's laughter sounded like tinkling glass.
The day was as cold as a scornful woman's glance.
My stomach was growling like the engine of a muscle car.

3. We hardly ever go to the store without first making a list of the items we need to purchase. I cannot understand how anyone remembers everything they need without making a list. Mary didn't need any help in getting all the necessary items together at the store, and I didn't find anything missing when we arrived home.

4. Do you mean to say that you don't like Gilbert and Sullivan? (interrogative)

We went to see a Gilbert and Sullivan play last night. (declarative)

I love Gilbert and Sullivan! (exclamatory)

Assessment 4
(Lessons 28 - 36)

1. Find and underline two helping verbs in the last paragraph of the literature passage in Lesson 26.

2. Adverbs describe verbs and tell us how, when, where, or to what extent or degree. Write sentences using adverbs illustrating each of these.

3. Underline the adverbs in the following paragraph:

   The black knight ran silently away from the cave. He could smell the pungent odor of the dragon. He looked around, hoping to find a place to hide. Suddenly, the dragon flew out of the cave. The knight quickly hid behind a tree as the beast flew overhead.

4. Write the following dialogue correctly:

   I have been asked to lead the program next week and I am a little nervous. Are you ever afraid to do something new Mark asked. Sometimes replied his father.

5. Write three sentences describing yourself. Circle the adjectives you used.

6. Adjectives describe nouns answering the questions *what kind, how much,* or *which ones.* Write three sentences using adjectives that answer each of these questions.

7. Write the title of a book you've read.

8. How are adjectives and adverbs different?

9. Circle the direct object in the following sentence.

   Sharon played the piano beautifully.

10. Circle the pronouns in the literature passage used in Lesson 34. Draw an arrow to the antecedent of each pronoun.

1. *was* **hoeing**
had been **camping**
were **leaving**

2. Example:
The car moved *quietly*. how

***Today* we went to town. when**

The bird flew *up* in the air. where

The shirt was *badly* torn. to what extent or degree

3. silently, away, around, Suddenly, out, quickly overhead

4. "I have been asked to lead the program next week, and I am a little nervous. Are you ever afraid to do something new?" Mark asked. "Sometimes," replied his father.

5. Example:
I am a (tall) person with (long) (brown) hair.

I like to wear (flowery) dresses and tops.

My (favorite) book is *A Horse and His Boy*.

6. Example:
My favorite dessert is *strawberry* pie. *what kind?*
Once I ate *three* pieces of pie. *how much?*
I want the red pieces. *which one*

7. *Physical Science for Every Kid*

(Answers continued on next page)

8. **Adjectives modify (tell about) nouns and pronouns while adverbs modify (tell about) verbs, adjectives, or other adverbs.**
9. **piano**
10. **(her)- Jo**
    (she)- Jo
    (her)- Jo
    (her)- Amy
11. **Present - come, lift, open, shake, fly**
    Past - came, lifted, opened, shook, flew
12. **Regular - lift, open**
    Irregular - come, shake, fly
13. **A nonfiction story of a person's life written by someone else.**
14. **a. Sentence**
    b. Fragment
    c. Sentence
    d. Fragment
    e. Fragment
15. **noun, verb, adjective, adverb**
16. **metaphors: The sound of her voice was a summer breeze. Her eyes were blue sapphires.**
    simile: Her laugh was like a thousand tinkling bells.
17. **a. to go**
    b. to laugh
    c. to beat
    d. to ring

11. Look at the first three sentences in the literature passage in Lesson 19. Make a list of the verbs. Write the present and past tense for each verb.

12. Looking at your list of verbs from question above, which of them are regular verbs (**R**)? Which are irregular (**IR**)?

13. What is a biography?

14. Read the following sentences and write **CS** if it is a complete sentence or **F** if it is a fragment.

    a. I was tired after running the race.
    b. Gloria's sweet face.
    c. The walls were painted blue.
    d. Very fast moving ship.
    e. Running the race.

15. What are the four principle parts of speech?

16. Underline the metaphores in the following paragraph. There is also one simile contained in the paragraph. Identify the simile.

    The sound of her voice was a summer breeze that brought warmth to everything it touched. Her eyes were blue sapphires that sparkled from under thick, long lashes and glowed with happy thoughts. Her laugh was like a thousand tinkling bells awakening the world with a cheerful sound.

17. Underline the infinitives in the following sentences:

    a. Would you like to go to the movies with me?
    b. Mary is going to laugh when she hears what you did.
    c. Our team is going to beat your team in the big game.
    d. The bells began to ring in the New Year.

APPENDIX

Enrichment Answers

Skills Index

Prefixes

Suffices

Bibliography

Enrichment Activities

The Enrichment Activities answers are listed below. Since the Enrichment Activities are not numbered, you can easily locate them by the lesson number that proceeds them in the *Student Activity Book*. Some of the Enrichment Activities do not have a specific answer. For those, please read the directions in your student's book and evaluate the activity accordingly.

Lesson 1, 3c
Possible Answers: port, ant, in, an, am, or, tan, import, etc.

Lesson 1, 4c
1. big - large
2. tiny - small
3. make - build
4. rough - bumpy
5. carve - slice
6. grin - smile

Lesson 2, 4d
Possible Answers: the lady types, the bee hums, the bear attacks, the player hustles, the top spins, the pot clatters, the child hides, the star glistens

Lesson 3, 2e - Answers will vary.

Lesson 3, 4e
1. circle, triangle, circle
2. circle, circle, triangle
3. dot, rectangle, rectangle, rectangle, dot

Lesson 4, 3e
1. a rectangle on a triangle
2. a circle on a circle
3. a circle on a square
4. a square on a circle
5. a triangle on a rectangle
6. a circle on a rectangle

Carry On, Mr. Bowditch Book Study A
1. chronometer
2. ship log
3. sextant
4. compass
5. spyglass

Lesson 5, 4g - Answers will vary.

Lesson 6, 3e
1. Q
2. C
3. S

Lesson 6, 4g
Possible Answers: Atlanta, Richmond, Ottawa, Union City, New York City, Delhi, Tokyo, Hong Kong, Eiffel Tower, Washington, Ocean City, Rock of Gibraltar, London, Dublin

Lesson 7, 3e - Answers will vary.

Lesson 8, 3g
1. table
2. cow
3. broccoli
4. shark
5. paper
6. book
7. oven

Lesson 8, 4e
Sky - clouds, moon,stars
Ground - flowers, rocks, dirt

Hot - radiator, flame, summer
Cold - freezer, snowflake, ice cream

Forest Animals - raccoon, squirrel, woodchuck
Farm Animals - cow, goat, chicken

Land Vehicles - truck, car, bus
Water Vehicles - submarine, ship, sailboat

Hot Drinks - hot chocolate, coffee, hot tea
Cold Drinks - soda, milk, orange juice

Nouns - building, car, shelf
Verbs - stand, believe, whisper

Lesson 9, 3h
1. flour, dough, bread
2. vehicle, car, race car
3. sport, baseball, Little League
4. food, vegetables, beans
5. clothes, shirt, sweatshirt
6. book, novel, "Carry On, Mr. Bowditch"

Lesson 9, 4f - Answers will vary.

Lesson 10, 3f
1. antonym
2. category
3. synonym
4. part/whole
5. characteristic
6. antonym
7. category
8. synonym
9. characterisitic
10. part/whole

Lesson 10, 4e
1. degree
2. homonym
3. function
4. sequence
5. homonym
6. degree
7. function
8. sequence

Lesson 11, 3f
1. category
2. synonym
3. sequence
4. homonym
5. antonym
6. function
7. part/whole
8. characteristic
9. degree
10. homonym
11. function
12. part/whole
13. characteristic
14. category
15. synonym

Lesson 11, 4e

1. fish
2. dull
3. cold
4. winter
5. bag
6. tired
7. jar
8. build
9. not
10. run

Lesson 12, 5b

1. hit
2. finish
3. rainbow
4. army
5. relax
6. fair
7. green
8. forget
9. soak
10. shape

Lesson 13, 5b
Possible answers:

1. ship
2. state
3. hair
4. playful/cute
5. peace
6. cut
7. hour
8. baby
9. afternoon
10. whole
11. see
12. upset/stormy
13. soft
14. sky
15. disease
16. quick
17. learn
18. tail
19. sentence/paragraph
20. young

Lesson 15, 2f

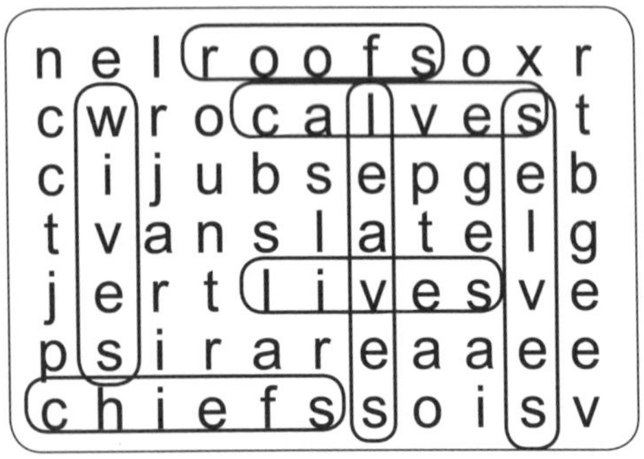

Lesson 15, 4f
Possible Answers: the girl giggles, the man shudders, the teacher instructs, the ice melts, the candy hardens, the wolf howls, the door opens, the actor entertains

Lesson 16, 2d Answers will vary.

Lesson 16, 5b
Possible Answers: *Little Women, Into the Wild, Beauty and the Beast, Railway Children, A Winkle in Time, Rip Van Winkle, You: A Novel, Big Red, Odysseus, Of Mice and Men, King of the Wind, Silver Chair*

Lesson 19, 2e

1. hot dog	hitter	peach pit	pin prick	pancake
2. hot dog	an archaeological dig	pig sty	pumpkin pie	lie down

Lesson 19, 4e

1. cat nap	car chase	chin up bar	baseball bat	bit and bridle
2. cat nap	cat nip	tip over	tin can	suntan

Lesson 22, 2i Possible Answers:

1. mean/keen
2. rain
3. toy
4. book
5. frantic
6. meek
7. frown
8. wake
9. fright

Lesson 22, 3d
I did not come to bring peace but a sword.

Big Red Book Study, Vocabulary #11

1. careening
2. ravenous
3. hypodermic
4. profoundly
5. indispensable
6. varmints
7. surreptitiously

Lesson 23, 3e
14

Lesson 23, 4e

1. a square on a square
2. a triangle on a triangle
3. a triangle on a rectangle
4. a square on a triangle
5. a circle on a circle
6. a circle on a square

Lesson 24, 4c
Possible Answers: dress, get, bug, red, add, set, etc.

Lesson 25, 2c
If at first you don't succeed, try, try again.

Lesson 25, 2d
Suzy and her friends have the most books.

Lesson 26, 3e
Possible Answers: Meatloaf, Eggplant Parmesan, Apple Pancakes, Linguini, Spaghetti, Flounder, Omelet, Red Beans and Rice, Duck, Indian Curry, Noodle Soup, Nachos, Elbow macaroni, Rib-eye

Lesson 26, 4d

1. a blue circle on a yellow square
2. a green rectangle on a red circle
3. a yellow square on a blue circle
4. a red triangle on a green triangle

Lesson 28, 4d Answers will vary.

Lesson 29, 2e
It is better to give than to receive.

Lesson 29.3d
Answers will vary

Lesson 30, 4d
John, Melissa, Elizabeth, Ryan

Lesson 31, 3d
Possible Answers: Atlanta, Cincinnati, Richmond, Orlando, San Francisco, Seattle, Anchorage, Miami, Elizabethtown, Raleigh, Independence, Charleston, Albany

Lesson 31 - 4e
1. noun
2. adverb
3. adjective
4. verb
5. adverb
6. adjective - verb
7. noun - adverb
8. adjective - noun - verb - adverb

Lesson 32, 3e Answers will vary.

Lesson 32, 4c Answers will vary.

Lesson 33, 4d Answers will vary.

Lesson 34, 3d Answers will vary.

Lesson 35, 4e
1. a red circle on a yellow square on a green triangle
2. a green square on a blue circle on a red triangle
3. a blue triangle on a green triangle on a yellow circle
4. a green rectangle on a red square on a blue circle

Lesson 36, 1f Answers will vary.

Skills Index

The numbers and letters listed after each skill refer to the Lesson number and Book Study.

Book Studies

Carry On, Mr. Bowditch - A
The Bronze Bow - B
Big Red - C
The Horse and His Boy - D

Composition

advertisement - 22
analogy - D
autobiography - 17
bibliography - 18
biography - 2, 17, 35
business letter - 27
caricature - 6
character sketch - 31
circle word picture - 6, 9
closing paragraph - 18
closing sentence - 5
creative writing - 2, 6, 7, 9, 10, 15, 19, 22, 23, 27, 32, 34, 35, B, D
dialogue - 7, 28, 29
dictation - 2, 3, 4, 5, 6, 7, 8, 9, 10, 11, 15, 19, 20, 21, 22, 23, 24, 26, 27, 28, 29, 30, 31, 32, 33, 34, 35, 36
duolog - 29
essay - 16, 17, 18, 20, B, C
expressive verbs - 23
figurative language - 3, 4
first draft - 18, 20
first person - 10
friendly letter - 5, 26
irony - 22
journal - A, 21
main idea - 17, 20
mood - 3, 10
news story - 28, 30
opening paragraph - 18
outline - 18, 20
paragraph - 5, 9, 10, 27
paraphrase - 1, 25
personification - 3, 4
plagiarism - 17
poetry - 4, 14, 29, 36
prose - 4
research - 12, 13, 16, 17, 18, 20
simile - 3, 4, 33, 36
summary - 2
supporting detail - 20
supporting sentence - 5
thesis statement - 17, 18, 20
topic - 16, 17
topic sentence - 5, 9
types of sentences - 8, 11
writing a fable - 32
writing dialogue - 7
writing instructions - 5

Grammar

adjective - 3, 7, 19, 31, 35
adverb - 5, 6, 19, 30, 31, 35
antecedent - 4
antonym - 33
apostrophe - 6, 20
articles - 19
being verb - 2
capitalization - 6, 14, 19, 27
colon - 27
comma - 9, 10, 11, 22, 23, 34
common noun - 2
comparative adjective - 7, 29
complete predicate - 8
complete sentence - 8
complete subject - 8
compound sentence - 9, 34
compound subject - 9
compound verb - 9
compound word - 5, 6
conjunction - 2, 9, 10, 34
contraction - 6, 9
dashes - 22, 28
declarative sentence - 8, 11
dependent clause - 23
direct address - 11
direct object - 32
direct quotation - 7, 11, 29
double negative - 36
exclamation mark - 8, 22
exclamatory sentence - 8
fragment - 8
helping verb - 2, 30
homonym - 10, 15, 24, 28
hyphen - 6
imperative sentence - 8, 11
independent clause - 10, 23, 34
infinitive - 33
interjection - 22,28
interrogative sentence - 8, 11
irregular noun - 15
irregular verb - 30, 33
its / it's - 19
lay / lie - 17
linking verb - 2
noun - 2, 8, 11
objective pronoun - 4
object of the preposition - 26
parenthetical expression - 22
parts of speech - 2
period - 7, 8
pore / pour / poor - 28
positive adjective - 7
possessive noun - 6, 34
possessive pronoun - 4, 20, 34
predicate adjective - 31
prefix - 1
preposition - 21, 26
prepositional phrase - 21, 26
principal parts of verb - 30
pronoun - 4, 15, 20, 34
proper noun - 2
question mark - 8
quotation marks - 7, 11, 22, 28, 29
quotation rules - 7, 11, 28
regular verb - 29, 30, 33
semicolon - 10, 21, 34
sentence types - 8
simple predicate - 9
simple subject - 9
sit / set - 15
speech tag - 7
split quotation - 11, 22
subjective pronoun - 4
subject/verb agreement - 27
suffix - 3
superlative adjective - 7
syllables - 3
synonym - 1, 24
there / they're / their - 24
titles - 16, 27
to / too / two - 15
transitional words - 5
underlining - 27
verb - 2, 5, 9, 23, 27, 32, 34
verb phrase - 2
verb tense - 30, 33, 34

Reading

alliteration - 14
antonym - 33
autobiography - 16, 17
base or root word - 3
biography - 2, 16, 17, 35
bound base - 7
character study - 31
choral reading - 36
climax - 10
comprehension - 10, A, B, C, D
conclusion - 10
conflict - B, 10, 11
context clues - 4
couplet - 29
descriptive language - 3
dialect - 14
dialogue - 7, 28, 29
Discussion - A, B, C, D
duolog - 29
elements of a plot - 10
end rhyme - 4, 14
etymology - 1
exposition - 10
fable - 33
falling action - 10
fiction - 16
first person - 10, 15, 27
foreshadowing - 26
free base - 7
historical fiction - 8
homonym - 10, 15, 24, 28
internal rhyme - 14
irony - 22
metaphor - 33
mood - 3, 10
narrator - 10, 15
news story - 28, 30
personification - 3, 4, 7, 35
plot - 10
plot line - 10
poetry - 4, 9. 14, 29, 36
point of view - 10

prefix
- **al-** 7,
- **be-** 1, 4
- **con-** 24
- **de-**
- **dis-** 27
- **en-** 24
- **ex-** 5
- **fore-** 9
- **im-** 3
- **in-** 6
- **pre-** 1
- **re-** 8
- **pro-** 15
- **under-** 19
- **sub-** 18

prose - 4
reciting poetry - 14
repetition - 14, 36
research - 13, 16, 17, 18
resolution - 10
rhyme scheme - 14
rising action - 10
root word - 9
second person - 15
simile - 3, 33, 36
speech - 24, 25
stanza - 4

suffix
- **-ally** - 30
- **-ed** - 3, 4, 9, 32
- **-er** - 7
- **-es** - 11
- **-est** - 7
- **-fy** - 33
- **-ing** - 3, 4, 9, 32
- **-ion** - 21
- **-ish** - 31
- **-less** - 27
- **-ness** - 36
- **-ous** - 21
- **-ful** - 29
- **-ly** - 5, 30, 35, 36
- **-sion / -tion** - 21, 24
- **-ious / -eous** - 21
- **-able / -ible** - 31
- **-ent / -ant** - 35
- **-ence / -ance** - 35

syllables - 3
synonym - 1, 24
third person - 10, 15, 27
topic sentence - 5, 9
triplet - 4
vocabulary - 4, A, B, C, D
word analogy - 11

Spelling

American/British - 33
-able / **-ible** - 31
-ent,-ant / **-ence,-ance** - 35
-sion/-tion /shun/ - 21, 24
adding prefix- 27
adding suffix - 4, 7, 26, 30, 32, 33, 36
c and **k** make **/k/** sound - 2
c before **a** or **u** - 2
change **f** to **v** - 15
change **y** to **i** - 9, 11, 15, 28
compound words - 5
contractions - 6
dg/dge - 33
double last consonant before adding suffix - 7, 9, 32
drop silent **e** and add suffix - 4, 9
er/ir/ur/ear - 23
i before **e** - 8
-igh - 10
-ion - 21
kn / **gn** - 20
ou /ow/ - 29
ough /o/ - 22
plural of words ending in **o** - 34
plural rules - 15
plurals - 11, 15, 28
plural of irregular words - 15
sh,ch,x,s,z - 11, 15
wor - 21
wr - 17

Study Skills

alphabetical order - 16
Caldecott Award - 16
checklist - 18
context clues - 4
Dewey Decimal System - 16
dictionary - 1, 22, 24
editing - 18, 20, 23, 30, 35
essay - 16, 17, 18, 20
etymology - 1
interview - 35, C
library - 16
map skills - A, B
memorization - 14, 24, 25, 36
moral - 32
Newbery Award - 16
news story - 28, 30
note cards - 17, 25
note-taking - 17, 21, 35
oral presentation - 25
organizing information - 13
organizing thought - 5
reference materials - 12, 13, 16, 17
research - 12, 13, 16, 17, 18, 20, B, C, D
research story - 13
sequence - 5, 23, 35
thesaurus - 1, 19
timeline - 1
word analogy - 11

Prefixes

A prefix is a letter or group of letters which come before the base or root word, changing the meaning of the word.

Commonly Used Prefixes

a, an - not, without (*anew, anonymous, apathy*)
ab - away, from (*abomination, absent, absolve*)
al - to or towards (*alarm, alcove)*
ante - before (*antecedent, antemeridian*)
anti - against (*antibiotic, anticlimactic, antifreeze*)
be - on, away (*beguile, behind, betray*)
bene - well (*benediction, benevolence, beneficiary*)
bi - both (*biathlon, biannual, bicycle*)
bio - living (*biology, biopsy, biography*)
by - near, side (*bylaw, bygone, bystander*)
circ - around (*circumstance, circumstantial, circulation*)
co, con - together, with (*cohabitant, coheir, copilot*)
contra - against (*contraband, contradict, contrary*)
de - down, from (*deprivation, depression, denounce*)
di - twice, two (*diameter, dialect, dialogue*)
dis - reverse, apart (*disarray, disappoint, disintegrate*)
dys - bad (*dyspepsia, dystrophy, dyslexia*)
en - in, into (*envelope, endow, enforce*)
ex - out, forth (*extol, excitement, exchange*)
extra - beyond (*extracurricular, extraneous, extragalactic*)
fore - before in time (*forego, foremost, forefather*)
il, im, in - into (*illumine, implant, inside)*
il, im, in, ir - not (*illegal, impartial, indivisible, irrelevant*)
im - not patient
inter - between (*intermission, interrupt, intercept*)
mal - poorly, badly (*malady, malpractice, maladjusted*)
mis - incorrect (*misspell, misinterpret, misconduct*)
mono - one (*monogamous, monotone, monocle*)
multi - many (*multiplication, multipurpose, multitude*)
neo - new (*neolithic, neonatal, neophyte*)
non - not (*nonfiction, nonsense, nonexistent*)
para - almost, beside (*paragraph, paraphrase, parachute*)
per - complete, through (*perambulate, perceptible, percolator*)
poly - many (*polygamy, polyunsaturated, polyurethane*)
post - after (*postwar, postgraduate, postglacial*)

pre - before (*preview, prevent, precursor*)
pro - in favor of, forward (*pro-life, prolific, prologue*)
pseudo - false (*pseudonym, pseudoclassic*)
quad - four (*quadruplets, quadrant, quadriplegic*)
quint - five (*quintuplets, quintet, quintile*)
re - back, again (*return, remember, revive*)
retro - backwards (*retrospect, retroactive*)
self - by oneself (*self-serve, self-indulgent, self-employed*)
sub - under (*submarine, subway, substitute*)
super - over, more (*superhuman, supernatural, supervise*)
trans - across (*transcontinental, translate, transfusion*)
tri - three (*tricycle, tripod, trimester*)
ultra - beyond (*ultraviolet, ultramodern, ultraconservative*)
un - not, release (*undress, untie, undo*)
under - beneath (*underline, underground*)
uni - one (*universe, unity, unicycle*)

Suffixes

A suffix is a letter or group of letters which come after the base or root word, changing the meaning of the word. The suffix is usually helpful in determining the part of speech (noun, verb, adjective, etc.)

Commonly Used Suffixes

able, ible - able to do (*sensible, possible, pliable*)
age - act or state of (*manage, salvage, bandage*)
al - relating to (*final, natural, remedial*)
an, ian, ese, ish - native of (*American, Japanese, Spanish*)
ance, ence - action, state of (*abstinence, reluctance, alliance*)
ant - agent, performing (*reactant, servant*)
ar, er, or - one who, that which (*operator, manager, beggar*)
ary, ery, ory - relating to, connected with, place where (*category, supervisory, infirmary, stationery*)
asis - process, condition (*hypothesis, neurosis, catharsis*)
ate - make, cause (*compassionate, suffocate, generate*)
cian - having a certain skill (*physician, musician, technician*)
cide - kill (*infanticide, suicide, homicide*)
cule - very small (*minuscule, molecule, ridicule*)
cy - action, function (*vagrancy, truancy, leniency*)
dom - quality, realm, office (*freedom, wisdom, kingdom*)
ed - no meaning
ee - one who receives the action (*emcee, employee, refugee*)
er - one who or that which *(singer, mocker)*
en - make, made of (*flatten, lighten, wooden*)
ess - female (*princess, goddess, actress*)
et, ette - group, a small one (*majorette, midget*)
ful - full of (*beautiful, joyful, plentiful*)
fy - make (*multiply, unify, amplify*)
hood - condition, order, quality (*neighborhood, brotherhood, womanhood*)
ic - nature of, like (*fantastic, poetic, heroic*)
ice - condition, state (*justice, poultice, novice*)
ile - relating to, capable of (*senile, revile, penile*)
ine - nature of (*clandestine, morphine, chlorine*)
ing - no meaning
ion, sion, tion - act of, state of, result of (*intrusion, salutation, opinion*)
ish - origin, resembling (*childish, fiendish, reddish*)
ism - system, characteristic (*Buddhism, Communism, monotheism*)
ist - one who, that which (*pianist, philanthropist, dentist*)

ite - nature or quality of (*stalagmite, infinite*)
ity, ty - state or quality of (*university, clarity, unity*)
ive - causing, making (*captive, active, submissive*)
ize - make (*victimize, scrutinize, penalize*)
less - without (*thoughtless, helpless, homeless*)
ly - like, manner of (*lovely, quickly, softly*)
ment - act or state of (*bewilderment, sentiment, advertisement*)
ness - state of (*happiness, holiness, sleeplessness*)
oid - like (*android, spheroid, steroid*)
ology - study, science (*theology, sociology, biology*)
ous, ious, eous - full of, having (*spacious, superfluous, fabulous*)
ship - office, state, quality (*fellowship, friendship*)
sis - process, condition (*hypothesis, neurosis, catharsis*)
some - like, tending to (*meddlesome, twosome, lonesome*)
tude - state or condition of (*solitude, altitude, multitude*)
ure - state of, act, rank (*seizure, rapture, culture*)
ward - in the direction of (*forward, backward, wayward*)
y - inclined to, tend to (*bumpy, silky, scary*)

Bibliography

Alcott, Louisa May. *Little Women*. 1868.

Aldrich, Thomas Bailey. *The Story of a Bad Boy*. 1870.

Brink, Carol Ryrie. *Caddie Woodlawn*. 1935.

Defoe, Daniel. *Robinson Crusoe*. 1719.

DeJong, Meindert. *The Wheel on the School*. 1954.

Henry, Marguerite. *King of the Wind.* 1948.

Kjelgaard, Jim. *Big Red.* Holiday House, 2011.

Latham, Jean Lee. *Carry On, Mr. Bowditch.* Houghton Mifflin, 1955.

Lewis, C.S. *The Horse and His Boy.* Macmillan Publishing, 1954.

Lewis, C. S. *Prince Caspian*. 1951.

Meigs, Cornelia. *Invincible Louisa.* 1988.

Milne, A. A. *The House at Pooh Corner*. 1928.

Montgomery, L. M. *Anne of Green Gables*. 1908.

Nesbit, Edith. *The Railway Children*. 1905.

Ransome, Arthur. *Swallows and Amazons.* 1930.

Rawls, Wilson. *Where the Red Fern Grows*. 1961.

Scott, Sir Walter. *Ivanhoe*. 1820.

Shakespeare, William. *The Taming of the Shrew.* First published in 1623.

Spear, Elizabeth George, *The Bronze Bow*. Houghton Mifflin, 1861.

Stevenson, Robert Louis. *Kidnapped.* 1886.

Wilder, Laura Ingalls. *Little House in the Big Woods*. 1932.

Wyss, Johann David. *Swiss Family Robinson*. 1812.